CW00383760

JACK
FINGLETON

JACK FINGLETON

THE MAN WHO STOOD UP TO BRADMAN

GREG GROWDEN

ALLEN&UNWIN

First published in 2008

Allen & Unwin
83 Alexander Street
Crows Nest NSW 2065
Australia
Phone: (61 2) 8425 0100
Fax: (61 2) 9906 2218
Email: info@allenandunwin.com
Web: www.allenandunwin.com

National Library of Australia
Cataloguing-in-Publication entry:

Growden, Greg.
    Jack Fingleton : the man who stood up to Bradman.

    ISBN 978 1 74175 548 0 (hbk.)

    Bibliography.
    Includes index.

    Fingleton, J. H. W. (John Henry Webb), 1908–1981.
    Bradman, Donald, Sir, 1908–2001
    Cricket players—Australia—Biography.
    Sportswriters—Australia—Biography.

796.3580924

Internal design by Emily O'Neill
Set in 12.5/16 pt Bembo by Midland Typesetters, Australia
Printed in Australia by McPherson's Printing Group

10 9 8 7 6 5 4 3 2 1

Contents

Acknowledgements

The idea of writing a book on Jack Fingleton first entered my mind when sitting next to Bill O'Reilly in the Sydney Cricket Ground press box, as we observed day after day of Sheffield Shield play back in the 1980s.

Before Tiger flung open his school exercise book shortly after the tea break to write his latest cricket column for the *Sydney Morning Herald*, he loved to yarn; Bradman; Fingleton; Bodyline; Ashes tours; what exactly happened all those years ago. My curiosity about the period deepened as I came into contact with Keith Miller, Leo O'Brien, Bill Brown, Lindsay Hassett and other Test players, and read *Cricket Crisis*, *Brightly Fades The Don* and *Fingleton on Cricket*.

I was side-tracked by other interests until a visit to the State Library of NSW, on the research trail of another notable Australian sportsman, brought it all back. Warwick Hirst, formerly of the State Library's Manuscripts Section, suggested that the Fingleton Collection was well worth a look. That was an understatement: it was a treasure trove of information. The Jack Fingleton Papers must rank as one of Australian sport's most important collections. In the bowels of the library there are 27 boxes, containing Fingleton's correspondence, notebooks, scrapbooks, pictures and diaries. In addition, there are several rolls of microfilm, which contain his letters to illustrious writers, cricketers, teammates, allies, enemies and even several prime ministers.

Even though it took many months—years—to go through, it was the most fruitful of exercises. I learned much about the man, and can only be grateful he was such a hoarder.

Apart from Jack, thankfully, being so fastidious about his records, I am indebted to Warwick Hirst for allowing me to go through the Collection, and making the sometimes exasperating process that much easier.

After I'd made a start, I approached the Fingleton clan. Their enthusiasm was immediate, and their support crucial, so many of the Fingleton family were willing to provide time, information, details, anecdotes and meals, as well as putting up with a pesky biographer bothering them about the most trivial detail. They handled it all with good humour, and their deep pride in their father was abundant.

They all credit their father with instilling in them strong beliefs. Not surprisingly, Jack began his cricket books with the letters that Catholic schoolchildren would put at the top of every page of their exercise books AMDG which stood for 'Ad majorem Dei gloriam', meaning 'To the greater glory of God'.

The family were eager for a warts-and-all look at Jack, and did not shy away when delicate information had to be discussed and confirmed. Each one of Jack's children—Belinda, Jim, Grey, Larry and Jacquie—played their part. I am indebted to them all, as well as their partners; in particular I must thank Mal Gemmell, the trustee of the Jack Fingleton Estate, who took an active and constructive interest in the project. Mal and Belinda were great sounding boards. Barry Flakelar and Denise Fingleton also provided crucial details about the family.

My special source was Jack's youngest brother, Father Wal. Now in his nineties, he is a biographer's dream. He remembers everything, and was able to provide me with important first-hand information on most facets of Jack's life. If I wanted to check something that happened in the 1930s, I didn't have to go to some dusty text book. I just tracked down Wal and the answer was immediate. Every conversation with Wal—and there were many—was memorable. One cannot thank Wal, and his carer Mary Connor, enough.

A visit to Brisbane in late 2007 to see Jack's long-time opening partner Bill Brown was important. Bill and his wife Barbara were marvellous hosts, and in his last interview before he died a few weeks later, he provided important information about his long-time friend and spoke about numerous contentious issues. Barbara put it all in perspective. It will always remain the most special of visits, and I am delighted that I was able to have one last drink with Bill.

As important were numerous cricketers, journalists, mentors and friends who were willing to help. They include Mike Coward, Ian Chappell, Neil Marks, Philip Derriman, Jim Maxwell, David Frith, Phil Wilkins, Don Cameron, Alan Ramsey, Rob Chalmers, Scyld Berry and Anthony (AJ) George. For anyone intrigued by the Bodyline series, I cannot recommend enough Frith's brilliant book: *Bodyline Autopsy*.

At Allen & Unwin, Richard Walsh, Patrick Gallagher and Angela Handley made the process so much easier. I can only be impressed with their professionalism.

At home, Elizabeth, Anna and Angus knew when exactly to keep their distance from the obsessed.

To all of the above, many thanks.

Unfortunately, in the many years that Fingo has been skipping around in the back of this author's mind, numerous important allies have passed on including Bill O'Reilly, Leo O'Brien, Keith Miller, Bill Brown and Ian Wooldridge. This book is dedicated to them.

My underlying hope is that this biography will convince the reader to track down Jack's many marvellous books and discover more about this incredible character. It is well worth the search.

1

A Mean Initiation

He was in agony. As he hobbled from the tram stop to the family home, he kept having to stop and wait for the pain to subside.

It came in waves, forcing him to drop his cricket bag onto the footpath.

He collected his breath, smiling stoically as locals stopped, patted him on his back, and congratulated him for what he had achieved earlier in the day. The smile was a fake, but he had to portray hardness. He couldn't let them think England had got to him.

The well-wishers had heard the dry facts on the radio or seen the scores in the afternoon papers, but they had no idea what he had just been through.

He wasn't letting on, either. This was his big moment, and he didn't want anyone to think he was anything but courageous.

At last he arrived at the light on the hill. He headed for the shower and stood under it, head bowed for what seemed an eternity. The rest of the family could hear the groans.

His younger brother Wally recalled: 'We shared the same bedroom. When he came home from that battering, I knew how much he had suffered. He was black and blue.'

Across Jack's body were nine large welts. There were two massive bruises on his left knee, one just above it, another halfway up his thigh, one on his hip where the skin had been cut, a large black bruise on his wrist, two more near his heart and one across the right hand. Here and there were smaller bruises, some still bearing stitch-mark indentations where the cricket ball had pounded into his body. And a throbbing headache made him sick to the stomach.

He was twenty-four years old. He had grown up in a tough cricketing school, playing his early games just down the road at Centennial Park on tricky wickets and against cantankerous opponents. But he had never endured anything like this.

The sporting event Australia awaited most eagerly was the Ashes cricket series. Adding to the excitement in late 1932 was that Australians were hungry for relief from the bleakness of the Depression, which had left so many in desperate straits. Avidly following their cricketing saviour gave impoverished battlers a little hope. The boy from Bowral, Don Bradman, was their white knight, Australia's national hero.

For a young, self-conscious and now struggling country, nothing mattered more than the England tour. Adding to the fervour were mutterings that England were planning aggressive tactics to nullify Australia—in particular its prized batsman.

The arrogant England captain, Douglas Jardine, was up to something. The Australians weren't exactly sure what. But they knew Jardine was obsessed with stopping Bradman, and that the other leading Australian batsmen were bound to be targets too. The England cricketing establishment had been decidedly unimpressed by the way this young upstart from the dominions had taken over their game. Jardine was seen as just the man to put Bradman and the rest of the Australian rabble back in their place.

On the previous Ashes tour to Australia, in 1928–29, Jardine had delighted in turning up his nose and sneering at the colonials. Australians did not take kindly to his imperious airs. Nor were they impressed by the way he flaunted his upper-class background by wearing the distinctive Harlequin cap of Oxford University, quartered in dark blue, maroon and buff, when he batted.

After one innings when a Sydney crowd hooted Jardine as he scored a slow, steady century, his teammate Patsy Hendren observed, 'They don't seem to like you very much over here, Mr Jardine.'

Jardine replied, 'It's fucking mutual.'

Fingleton had a taste of what was to come when he travelled to Perth as a member of a Combined Australian XI to play the second match of the tour. The England team were not in a frivolous mood. When they arrived in Perth, a stern Jardine glared at the gathered pressmen and snorted when he was asked by one, Claude Corbett, if due to pressing deadlines he could provide them with a team list for the opening match against Western Australia. Jardine stared Corbett out, then growled, 'What damned rot! We didn't come here to provide scoops for yours or any other bally paper.' Corbett did an about-turn, strode back to his hotel room, and cabled a story describing Jardine as rude and uncooperative.

Fingleton, in a team that included Bradman, Stan McCabe and Victor Richardson, went to Perth by train—a trip that took five days. He was invigorated, elated by the long-awaited chance to play against England. 'It was all very thrilling to play against the South Africans and West Indies,' he recalled. 'But—due respect to the others—the Englishmen were of the real cricketing blood. They were cricket itself, for they represented Lord's and Canterbury and Bramall Lane; Grace, Hobbs, Fry, MacLaren, Spooner and Tyldesley. They represented years of tradition and it seemed unreal that I was travelling westwards to play against such giants as Hammond, Larwood, Sutcliffe, Leyland, Jardine, Allen and the rest.'

As the train crept across the Nullarbor, the Australians occupied themselves with card games. All along the way, they were reminded of Bradman's stature. He was Australia's most recognisable figure, idolised by his countrymen. 'At lonely outposts on the long, straight railway line children clustered and called "Bradman, Bradman" as the train rushed through the night,' Fingleton later wrote.

In Perth, the station was barricaded and the players needed a police escort to get them through the thousands who mobbed the terminus and lined the streets to the Palace Hotel.

Perth was in the grip of Bradmania. The papers were cluttered with photographs of his every move through the city. In each photo, Bradman's demeanour was noticeably grim.

In Melbourne, cricket administrators had taken him, Fingleton and McCabe out to lunch. Fingleton was astonished when the Australian Cricket Board of Control's chairman, Dr Allen Robertson, proclaimed, 'Cricket is doomed in Australia.'

Bradman was wondering whether he, too, was doomed. At the time he was in conflict with the Board of Control, which was demanding that he no longer write for newspapers, and had fined him £50 for permitting extracts from a book he'd written to be serialised in a newspaper. Like so many hurt by the Depression, Bradman was a frugal man. Even more worrying, he was keenly aware that England were after him.

For some time, Jardine and other England players had noticed a potential weakness in Bradman's ability to handle express pace bowling. Sure, he was the most majestic of stroke players, the most ruthless accumulator of runs. But when short-rising deliveries were aimed at him, he appeared to flinch. This was clearly a vulnerability worth exploiting. If England could nullify Bradman, they were well on their way to winning the series. Jardine had first got an inkling of how to do it during the Fifth Test of the 1930 series in England. When deliveries on a lively Oval wicket from England's Harold Larwood leapt from a good length and careered towards Bradman's upper body, Australia's most dangerous batsman began to step back. Jardine later watched film of Bradman's Oval innings. The star batsman had indeed been decidedly twitchy about certain Larwood deliveries. 'I've got it,' Jardine announced. 'That's it, he's yellow.'

Before the Perth match, Fingleton and Bradman had a game of golf. Bradman said he was anxious to score runs, because the England players believed he would be 'daunted by pace'.

When they were at the wicket together, Bradman reminded Fingleton of his concerns. Against Western Australia, England had opted against showing off their key speedsters, resting the fearsome Larwood and Bill Voce. Their attack was hardly frightening. It revolved around their other key paceman, Gubby Allen, a classically pure pace bowler with a rhythmic bouncing action who was renowned for fair play, and masterful Yorkshire spinner Hedley Verity. But Bradman was clearly unsettled. 'I think they are going to have a pop at me,' he said, in Fingleton's account. 'These blighters are after me. They intend to bowl at my head. Will you keep Allen for a while?'

Fingleton was surprised by such nervousness. 'The request staggered me but I was very much a "new boy" in those days,' he recalled. He agreed to the Don's request. Allen was his.

In Perth, Fingleton hung around at the crease. Bradman didn't. To the despair of the capacity crowd, Bradman came and went twice on the same day—the only time in his first-class career. The spectators moaned when, caught wide at first slip, Bradman scored just three runs.

Then, after the Combined XI had to follow on, he was caught at short leg for ten. His premature departure prompted a good part of the crowd to leave. They were there for only one man—Bradman. When the star went, so did they.

Amidst silence, Fingleton was far more successful than Bradman. In the first innings he was the second highest scorer, with 29, and in the second he enjoyed an unbeaten half-century as the game petered out to a draw. Fingleton also had some flashy moments. He and Richardson scored 15 runs off the first over, then tantalised the crowd with numerous adventurous shots in their 61-run opening partnership. Bradman's failures were soon common knowledge around Perth, but a partial collapse of the telegraph line left Perth cut off from the rest of the country for several hours, so scant details of the match got through.

When England appeared in Sydney for the match against New South Wales, Jardine was as haughty as ever. While the team trained at the SCG's No. 2 ground, he refused to give autographs or talk to the locals, even those who had been called on to be net bowlers. When several of the New South Wales players, including Fingleton, headed to their dressing room to drop off their gear before their net session, they were met with stony looks from their opponents. Now, as he headed through the SCG members' gates, Fingleton could not help thinking about England's aggressive stares and Bradman's anxieties.

As he headed out of Porter Street, in the tough Sydney suburb of Bondi Junction, Jack could easily have walked to the end of the road to catch the tram to the Sydney Cricket Ground.

But no, not even the dead weight of a large, bulky cricket bag under his arm or his status as a member of the New South Wales team would let him opt for that luxury. Money was scarce in the Fingleton household, and to save a penny on the fare Jack walked the first two stops and caught the tram near the Bondi Junction terminus.

Lugging a heavy bag was probably not the best way to prepare for a first-class cricket match, because eventually your arms, which were required to be stylish one minute and stubborn the next, went numb. But a penny was a penny. By the end of the week, it all added up—and meant more food on the family dinner table.

By the time he reached the terminus, he had a group of well-wishers following him, all urging him to 'give it to the Poms.' And when the tram arrived, he was given preferential treatment. Usually he made the trip along Oxford Street on the outside of the tram, desperately hanging on. This time several passengers stood up, offering him their seats.

When Fingleton hopped off near Paddington Town Hall, the passengers gave him a cheer. He responded with a wave and a wide grin, then walked down the hill from Oatley Road towards the SCG, where he could see a large crowd milling around the members' gate.

Many of those dressed in suits and hats nodded; some whispered, 'Good luck.' Others were more raucous. That's when the nerves began to hit. He could no longer ignore the momentousness of the occasion. His body started tingling, his stomach churning. He tried to retain a semblance of calm, telling himself there was no need to get all worked up and trying to ignore the hubbub around him.

Jack Fingleton was about to encounter the best of England on his home turf. England versus New South Wales. There was only one cricket match more important: England versus Australia—and today he had the chance to impress enough in the first one to be selected for the second. As he approached

Driver Avenue, he mumbled to himself, 'Stay calm. Stay calm.' But it was next to impossible. This match would be an enormous step up from any he had been involved in before. The warning signs were all around.

When he reached the dressing room, however, there was some consoling news. Larwood was in the twelve-man squad, but the word was that Jardine would rest his most dangerous bowler. Suddenly, grim-faced NSW players started laughing and skylarking.

The sharp end of the England attack was to be Bill Voce, a tall, impressively built left-arm paceman, who could generate extraordinary bounce and movement off any type of pitch. Voce wasn't as fast as Larwood but would endlessly irritate batsmen with balls that leapt and darted at their body. Every one seemed to be headed for the batsman's rib-heart region, cramping him and restricting his stroke play, as well as hurting like hell if he missed.

At least Fingleton did not have to wait too long to find out exactly what England were up to. NSW captain Alan Kippax won the toss and decided to bat on what appeared a fairly predictable pitch. As Fingleton headed to the wicket with his opening batting partner Wendell Bill, they reminded each other to keep their wits about them. Even though Larwood wasn't playing, the England attack was sure to be lively and varied. Apart from Voce, there were Allen and the wily Maurice Tate to keep them honest.

At high noon, with the crowd rapidly building towards the 26,000 mark, Fingleton faced the first ball from Allen. He let it go, prompting a barracker on the SCG Hill to chant: 'You'll never get them out. You'll never get them out.' England were not getting them out, but Fingleton was soon tested. He had only scored a single before Voce had him weaving. Voce's second delivery was aimed at Fingleton's left shoulder, forcing the batsman to fend off the ball with a dead bat. It lobbed towards short square leg, just out of reach of a sprawling Jardine.

It was grim. Fingleton eked out a run here and there, often having to rely on cramped leg-side glides to keep the score moving. Voce was smacking him all over the body with balls that deviated crazily off the wicket. As he found his rhythm and length, it started getting painful. Soon Fingleton was gasping for air, bent over trying to catch his breath after being hit in the ribs. The game was regularly stopped as yet one more short leg-side offering missed the bat and had nowhere to go but straight into the body. Once Fingleton angrily threw down his glove and walked in a large circle waiting for the pain to stop. Other times he refused to let on that he was hurt or numbed after a Voce delivery smashed into his fingers, arms or legs. Every so often he wandered down the wicket, looking for dents or bumps to bang down with his bat. There was nothing wrong with the wicket, but the meander gave him time to regain his composure.

His partners began to change rapidly. Wendell Bill left and that was no relief for Fingleton, because out came Bradman— giving Jardine the excuse to bring on more of a barrage from pacemen Voce and Allen.

The deliveries from Voce became shorter and shorter. One smashed Fingleton near the heart. His eyes rolled back, his bat dropped, and a worried Bradman sprinted down the pitch. Bradman grabbed his partner and said a few consoling words, rubbing the spot where Fingleton had been hit.

When Tate eventually returned, Bradman was clearly relieved. Yet he still appeared unsettled, almost playing a Tate delivery onto his stumps. The next over, Bradman was trapped in front of the stumps when struck on his knee and limped off, a forlorn figure. That night he was confined to bed with a sore throat and a chill.

When Fingleton was joined by Stan McCabe, each inspired the other. McCabe, the most classic and accomplished of stroke players, was soon at ease, toying with Jardine. When he surrounded the batsman with five close-in leg-side fieldsmen, McCabe repeatedly flicked the ball over their heads. Fingleton also opened up but waited for the right time to attack the boundary, repeatedly cover-driving spinner Freddie Brown.

At last Fingleton found his stride, and the pair contributed 118 for the fourth wicket, before McCabe succumbed to the leg-side trap and was caught at short-leg. Without a pacemaker, Fingleton found himself getting bogged down. He tried to push the pace, but cramp set in. He went to swing one wild delivery past square leg, and his left leg locked.

Jardine came to the rescue. Standing over Fingleton, who had collapsed in agony on the wicket, the England skipper grabbed Fingleton's leg and pushed his toes back while others massaged his calf and thigh. Fingleton was able to get up but had to beckon for a teammate to run for him. The most gruelling of centuries was eventually achieved shortly after tea, and just before stumps Fingleton was last man standing, unbeaten on 119.

As he slowly led the teams back to the pavilion, he was elated he had stood up to the challenge and humbled by the applause of the large and sympathetic crowd. But there was also a sense of unease. Something had gone horribly awry.

Not that this was unexpected. The challenge of nullifying Australia's hero had clearly become an obsession for England. And it would only get worse, because the main man, Larwood, wasn't even playing yet.

Next morning, a large photograph of a smiling Fingleton was spread across the front page of the Sydney *Sun*. Oversized cricket balls had been drawn on it to mark where each delivery had hit him. 'Balls indicate where bruises marked his body at the end of his outstanding innings,' the caption read. There were a lot of cricket balls. Fingleton's journalistic friend Claude Corbett, under the headline: 'Bruised, Stiff, But Still Unbeaten', had written:

> Hit eight times by the ball, and half-disabled, Jack Fingleton, hero of yesterday's big cricket, said last night: 'It's all in the game.'
>
> Opening for New South Wales, he played right through the innings, gave his first chance at 105, carried his bat for 119, took all the thumps, and showed not a sign of flinching.
>
> His score included thirteen fours. Yet he got a terrific lacing from English bowlers Voce, Tate and Allen. He was so knocked about that he did not leave the ground for an hour after play had ended. Before he went he was massaged under hot water. Fingleton made his 119—14⅞ runs per bruise.

Cartoonist Jack Quayle had drawn Fingleton getting pounded with deliveries, over the caption: 'They say that after the innings, the only part of Jack that wasn't bruised was the soles of his shoes.'

Obviously those sitting high up in the heavens in the SCG press box were enthused that someone had stood up to England's aggressive tactics. For most of the day they had been an agitated mob. When they had arrived before the start of play, the large crowd had spilled into the press area—with the general public taking prime seats. Threats of physical violence were required to get many of these to move, and plenty of pushing and shoving was needed, so that the big names of the press could take their place.

When settled, former Australian captain Monty Noble wrote that Fingleton had proven he had 'the proper temperament for big occasions, so essential in international contests, and his performance has accentuated his claim for a place in the Test'.

Arthur Mailey, writer, cartoonist and one-time Test spinner, agreed, describing the innings as 'a meritorious one'. The weekly *Referee*'s cricket writer, 'Not Out', said Fingleton's courage 'was that of an Anzac'. In the *Sydney Mail*, Dr Eric Barbour judged the innings 'of the highest importance not only to New South Wales but to Australia'.

Stephen Harold 'Yabba' Gascoigne, Australia's best-known barracker and king of the Sydney Cricket Ground Hill, had attempted to get under Jardine's skin by booming out: 'Leave those flies alone, they are your only friends here.' On Fingleton, he wrote in the Sydney *Sun*: 'Brilliant. The way he batted, getting belted like he was, was wonderful. He's one of my first selections for the Tests. He's a brilliant field from any possy, and another innings like that from him and they will have the crowd waiting to get in.'

Australia had found an opening batsman who would stand up to England's intimidation. But Fingleton was still uneasy.

> I should have been deliriously happy as I returned to the pavilion, for was this not a complete realisation of a youthful dream? Could one have wished for a better answer to one's prayers, with Test selection against England also in the offing?
>
> There was, on the contrary, no wild thrill about it. I was conscious of a hurt, and it was not because of the physical pummelling I had taken from Voce. It was the consciousness of a crashed ideal.
>
> Playing against England in actuality had proved vastly different from what boyish dreams and adventure had imagined it to be. The game was not the thing, but almost seemed to be the last thing.

No gentlemanly etiquette here. 'A blow on the ribs would, of a certainty, be followed the very next ball by a delivery of similar length, elevation and direction.' For a while, he added, 'several members of the English leg-side trap either offered apologies when a batsman was hit or gave a rubbing palm in solace; but a continuation of such courtesies would, in the circumstances, have been hypocritical and embarrassing to the giver and receiver alike. The batsman was later left to do his own rubbing in the privacy of his imprecations.'

In bed that night, as Jack and his brother stared at the ceiling in the darkness, Wally asked him how he felt. 'He didn't say much. He just said, "It's unfair cricket."'

Their mother wasn't so diplomatic. Mrs Fingleton had arrived at the SCG just before the toss and found a seat at the back of the lower deck of the Ladies' Stand.

She was horrified by the England tactics. In protest, she refused to witness another match, even shunning her son's first Test against England, the following week in Sydney.

2

A Game of Chicken

The Sydney–Melbourne train line was once a pathway of progress. But the towns that sprang up along it are quiet now. The highway has taken away the people and the trade. The railways towns have dwindled or grown derelict, or just disappeared.

But in some, the memories linger.

Cullerin lies amid dry paddocks and wooded hills south of Goulburn, in New South Wales. As a boy, Jack Fingleton would visit here with his father, who had grown up near this small farming town. He loved those trips. He could ride horses for hours, exploring the tracks that wound through the ranges. He could go on rabbit hunts. He could imagine he was an explorer, a gold prospector. He could dream of ruffians, because this had been bushranger territory.

At night there would be card games, gramophone music, gossip, sometimes a dance in the shearing shed. Then, after prayers and the Rosary, he'd drift off to sleep to the ticking of the old grandfather clock.

Cullerin just after the First World War had a general store, a school, a tennis court and a post office. Behind the post office,

Jack would sleep in the back room. Most evenings, he'd sneak out for a midnight jaunt to see the Melbourne Express train fly past.

Jack would head to a small water tank beside the railway line. Getting hold of it, he would place his arms through a stanchion and wait for the train to come. The aim was to see how close he could get to the train without getting hit. He would lean out in front of the Express for as long as he could before jumping back at the last second. He had plenty of warning.

Across the Breadalbane plain towards Goulburn, you could see the headlights of the train beaming across paddocks from miles away. Then you'd start hearing the clickety-clack of a steaming engine. The light would come and go as the train line wound its way through the hills. Suddenly, it would be bright and close—heading directly towards Jack as he tightened his grip on the stanchion. There'd be a confusion of blinding light, wild rocking noises, screeching steam and flying sparks. And then, just inches away, one big whoosh as the train careered past—in a flash of steel and glass and a shot of steam. That and the train's momentum would push Jack back onto the water tank, forcing him to swing under the stanchion, perilously close to the side of the train. A few seconds of raw danger, and then the train was gone, the red light at the back of the last carriage flickering into nothingness.

Jack would sneak back to the room behind the post office exhilarated. Playing chicken with trains, he later said, gave him the courage to confront hostile bowlers attacking him from just twenty-two yards away.

The Fingletons were of Irish stock, from Portlaoise, County Leix. Around 1870, James Fingleton, a baker, and his wife Mary Nolan migrated to Melbourne with their baby son Jack in hopes of a better life than Ireland could offer them. There they had a second son, James, and a daughter Kitty. James would become Jack the cricketer's father.

One night James Snr fell asleep smoking and burned the house down. He died in the blaze, and Mary died not long afterwards. Their children were sent to an orphanage. The St Vincent de Paul Society found two brothers named Hannan who each agreed to take one of the boys; Kitty went to the convent of the Sisters of Mercy in Yass. James, aged three, went to live with Frank Hannan and his wife Theresa at their property near Cullerin. Jack went to the other Hannan family—Myles and Catherine—at Sweetwoodlea, a few miles down the road from Cullerin.

James, soon known as Jim, became Theresa's 'pet', and received a rudimentary but thorough education at the small public school near the Hannan property. Growing up at Cullerin instilled in Jim a lifelong love of the bush, and a deep sympathy for the common man, the battler. The Hannans taught him the importance of hard work and family. He also developed a strong ethic of public service. He had been saved by others; it was only right that he in turn should help others. As a teenager, Jim joined a group of mates from Cullerin to go shearing in far northern NSW. Like many in that trade, they joined the newly formed Australasian Shearers' Union. Graziers were hostile. Some drove union members out of their sheds with pick axes and even rifles, or demanded that they sign the pastoralists' 'contract of free labour' before they started working. Jim grew to admire the way the shearers banded together and stuck to their demands for better wages and conditions.

The shearing work didn't last, but the experience made him a firm believer in the union movement. At 17 he joined the Australian Labor Party.

Back in Cullerin, though, there was not enough work to keep him on the farm. Once again, his sights shifted elsewhere.

The Boer War, and the prospect of heroic adventure in South Africa, had prompted thousands of Australian youths to enlist. Jim decided to join them. Armed with a reference from a local Justice of the Peace who said he was an exemplary horseman and bushman, James clambered onto the Sydney train, all set to join the Light Horse and become a cavalryman. But by the time he went to sign up, the Boer War was virtually over. No more Australian soldiers were required.

Instead of riding horses Jim soon got a job as a tram conductor, and instead of heading to war, fell in love. Belinda May Webb was a country girl from Glen Innes who had moved with her family to Sydney. When a friend took Jim around to meet the Webbs, he was so taken with Belinda that he purposely left his umbrella behind. A few hours later he returned to get it—and asked her out for dinner.

The romance flourished, and in 1902 Jim and Belinda were married. They settled in Bondi Junction, near the main tram depot and within sight of the vast Centennial Park.

The trams were rackety contraptions. Passengers jostled for space on rudimentary wooden seats inside, or stood on running boards, clinging to the outside bars. The conductor often stayed outside, issuing tickets and, under constant threat of being hit by passing vehicles or spun off when the tram turned a sharp corner, and subject to every change in the weather. After a few years of that, Jim moved up to driver. He needed the extra money.

Jim and Belinda were both Catholics and wanted a big family. First they had Les, then Kitty and on 28 April 1908 John Henry Webb (Jack) was born. Three more children followed: Glen, Wally and Linda.

3
Glimmer of Light

He was only five. But he would remember that night for the rest of his life.

His mother shook them all awake and gathered them on the balcony that jutted out above the footpath. Away to the right, up on Oxford Street, they could hear the boom, boom of drums. It came closer, getting louder. Soon they could make out whistles, claps and cheers. Then, in the light of the gas lamps, they saw a group of men—laughing, elated—bearing another man high on their shoulders. He had his hat tipped back and a huge grin on his face. He was their father.

This working-class enclave in the posh Eastern Suburbs had just had one of its own—tram driver Jim Fingleton—elected to the NSW Parliament. His supporters—many of them tram workers themselves—were so ecstatic they'd carried him several miles, all the way from the council chambers on Oxford Street where the result had been announced.

When they put him down at the door, he came in and climbed the stairs to join Belinda and the children. Standing there on the balcony, he addressed the small crowd below. It was their fervent support, their tireless efforts—and 4,000 shilling coins collected by their union—that had helped push him over the line. He'd beaten lawyer Harold Jacques by a margin as thin as a tram ticket: just sixty-nine votes.

When Jack's father went to parliament, in 1913, the family moved up in the world—and up the hill—into a bigger house in Porter Street that even had a name: La Rose. True, it didn't always smell like flowers. There was a soap factory nearby, and a dairy that had a whiff of manure about it. But the family loved it.

There was always something going on in the street. It was there that Jack discovered the delights of cops and robbers, rounders, and street cricket. The games were pretty vigorous, and you had to stand up for yourself. With five brothers and sisters and a gang of rowdy urchins as playmates, Jack learned to mix in and get on, but to resist bossyboots and bullies as well.

Most of all, he discovered a knack with bat and ball. Someone would round up an old bit of wood and a kerosene tin for a wicket, and within minutes every kid in the neighbourhood would be caught up in a long and noisy game. Fathers would join in on their way home from work. Even Fingleton MP would occasionally roll up his sleeves and throw a few down. A decent medium pace bowler, he also enjoyed the odd social game at Centennial Park.

The beach wasn't far away, either. Having learned to swim at nearby Bronte Baths, the Fingleton kids would celebrate the end of summer schooldays with a mad scurry to the beach—Bondi, Bronte, Tamarama, Maroubra.

It wasn't all games. There were classroom lessons, too, and Jack was soon a diligent student. He could be naughty, and at St Charles's Christian Brothers School he had his share of canings. But the man who administered them, headmaster Denis

Foran, gave Jack more than the transient sting of reproach. He gave him gifts that would become part of him and help steer the course of his life.

A thick-set man with a gammy leg, Brother Foran was a devout man with a genius for teaching. He had an Irishman's love of poetry and storytelling, a lively sense of humour, and a keen appreciation of originality and eccentricity. Jack was already fond of books. Under Brother Foran's guidance, he plunged into literature as he did into the waves at Bondi.

'Right from an early age, Jack would read and read and read,' his brother Wally said. 'He saved up enough money to buy a set of Balzac.'

Brother Foran may have been lame, but it didn't stop him from being an enthusiastic sports coach. At rugby league games he would hobble along the sideline, calling out advice to his youngsters. Jack, a prolific and long drop-kicker, did a fair bit of shouting himself. After seeing him in one school game at the Sydney Cricket Ground, his Uncle Wally, later a noted league official, told the family: 'He talks too much. He wants to shut up and play more football instead of yelling.'

For the children, the First World War was only an occasional diversion. But when Jack was nine years old it pushed right into their house. Prime Minister Billy Hughes called a national referendum, asking Australian voters to let the government introduce compulsory military service. The trade unions, the Labor Party and the Catholic community raised their voices against conscription. One of those voices was Jim Fingleton's. In 1917, with voters increasingly divided over the war and conscription, he paid for it at the polls, becoming one of seventeen NSW parliamentarians to lose their seats.

A few days later, Jack's father was a tram driver again. And once again, money was tight. A strike of railway and tram workers a few months later didn't help. Nor did the end of the war, in November 1918. By then—as the so-called Spanish influenza epidemic swept the world and devastated national economies—Jim Fingleton had tuberculosis.

He began to look pale, lose weight, gasp for breath and cough blood. Trips to Cullerin were organised—those trips Jack would remember so vividly—in the hope the dry country air would improve his health. But he didn't improve. Despite being bedridden for days at a time, he stood again for state parliament, and in March 1920 was re-elected.

But he was an MP in little more than name. He attended the opening of Parliament, but never entered the House again.

'I remember him pacing up and down the hall,' Jack wrote later, 'thinking no doubt, not of his approaching death, but of leaving his widow with six young children; this was long before the days of widows' pensions.

'My last memory of him was coming up our street, almost bent double in the final stages of consumption.' In October 1920, Jim died.

On the morning of his death, the Legislative Assembly was adjourned as a mark of respect. The following day, he was buried at Waverley Cemetery.

A long procession of politicians, labour organisers, and tramway workers, led by the Tramways Band, followed the hearse from the church to the burial site.

Eighty-six years later, Wally Fingleton recalled: 'We went to the church, and a bloke said to me: "See that box up there . . . your dad's in that." That really clobbered me.'

Sad as twelve-year-old Jack was, his father's passing brought a glimmer of light. When the funeral director came to the door, Jack immediately recognised the short, lean man with the faint Yorkshire accent. It was Hanson 'Sammy' Carter—the Australian, NSW and Waverley wicketkeeper. The first player to squat on his haunches behind the wicket, he was known for arriving at big matches in a hearse.

Years later, Carter's presence would seem to Jack a kind of sign.

4

Jack of All Trades

'It was very tough when Dad died,' Wally Fingleton said. 'We had to struggle for everything. There was no widow's pension. No child endowment. And Mum, worried stiff about being left with six kids, basically had to bring us up by herself.'

Belinda opened a seafood shop in Bondi Junction, hoping to sell to the local Catholics, who ate fish on Fridays. But inexperience and lack of refrigeration defeated her. Les, the eldest, who had been taken out of Waverley College to help, 'would go to the fish market each morning,' Wally recalled. But with only a slab of ice to chill it, the fish would soon spoil. 'Mum struggled to sell anything, and lost a lot of money,' most of it borrowed. With food short and the family home at risk, twelve-year-old Jack had to leave school and get a job. He did everything going—sold peanuts, chocolates and lollies at Bondi Junction's Star Picture Theatre, washed bottles at the King George distillery, swept floors and made lunches at a boot makers, ran errands for a drug company, even touted Sargeants meat pies to punters at the racecourse. It was a time when Australia's Catholics and Protestants were divided by a social and political gulf, and telling a prospective employer you were Catholic could get the door slammed in your face.

Family connections helped. One day, soon after Jack turned fifteen, his cousin Jack O'Brien opened a door he'd never thought to knock at. O'Brien was a linotype compositor at the new Sydney *Daily Guardian* newspaper. How would young Fingleton like to work there, he asked. Jack had no idea what the job involved, but it had to be better than slaving in a boot factory.

He was hired as a copy boy, running the stories—a few sentences at a time, as they were typed on separate slips of paper by the journalists—down the stairs to the typesetters who turned them into lines of metal type.

Jack Fingleton was on the threshold of a new world. The copy boy's job was the first step on the stairway to journalism, the rite of passage into a priesthood that, however lairish or eccentric, was devoted to the written word. With so little schooling, could Jack ever measure up? He was nervous.

He went to see Brother Foran. Did he have what it took, he wanted to know. The headmaster reassured him. Jack had all the prerequisites of a good newspaperman, he said: he was a passionate reader, wrote well, was bright and inquisitive. Keep reading, Brother Foran said. 'Observe the rules of syntax and your flair for words will see you through.' He gave Jack a list of books to read. No. 1 was Charles Dickens's *Pickwick Papers*.

Jack suddenly relaxed. He'd read the book already—hunkered down near the railway line on one of those trips to Cullerin. He loved Dickens's characters, his vivid descriptions and wild sense of humour. Now Dickens would be his role model.

Armed with a reference from Brother Foran that ended with the words, 'The worthy son of a worthy father,' Jack went to work.

He soon fell in love with the newspaper life. He revelled in the noise and bustle, the rush as reporters grabbed their hats and dashed out after police cars and fire engines; the yelling into telephones, the urgent clatter as they banged away at typewriters, frantic to beat the latest deadline.

And when it came to daily papers, the tabloid *Daily Guardian* was the loudest and cheekiest of them all. It was the in-your-face young brother to *Smith's Weekly*, a hugely popular paper founded in 1919 by Sir James Joynton Smith, the son of a London gas-fitter who had made a fortune in Sydney with a string of hotels, but never quite fitted in with the city's toffs. Instead, he mixed with hoi polloi at the races and trots, joined the Labor Party and in 1917 became Lord Mayor. He looked for a way to get his views across to the masses, and, joining forces with an aggressive journalist named Robert Clyde (RC) Packer, started *Smith's Weekly*, a lively weekly described as 'a poor man's paper founded by a rich man'.

Its jaunty, irreverent tone won such a following that Joynton Smith decided to launch a daily. From its first issue in 1923, *The Guardian* thrived on sensationalism, focusing on wild crime stories, lurid court yarns, government scandals and revealing personal dramas to suck the punters in.

One of Jack's first assignments after joining the paper was hunting down evidence in a murder case in which the victim's body was rumoured to have been stuffed into a luggage trunk. Reporters were sent all over the city in search of the elusive trunk. One reporter got distracted and instead grabbed a front-page scoop when he succeeded in buying cocaine from a Pitt Street chemist. The reporter was RC's son, Frank Packer.

Fingleton thrived in this atmosphere. Every day was an adventure.

He soon moved from the turf section to the general sport department, where he was guided by the respected sports editor A.R.B. 'Pedlar' Palmer. A master of many sports and a marvellous wordsmith, Palmer had excellent connections, and had previously been the secretary of the NSW Rugby Union. He showed Jack the tools of the trade, how a newspaper was produced, taking him to the machine room, where the pages were set in hot metal. Jack learned how to 'sub-edit on the stone', moving body type around to fit, devising page layouts, and becoming adept at checking page proofs.

As importantly, Palmer provided Jack with a messenger's ticket for the Sydney Cricket Ground, which enabled him to wander around the ground as if he owned it. Any time the newsroom got quiet, he would sneak away to observe Australia's best cricketers at close range.

However, Jack's journalistic career almost came to an end before it began. Packer was hot-headed, often having screaming fits and sacking employees for virtually no reason. A regular call to his editor was, 'Sack all the Catholics!' The editor would nod and ignore the request, knowing Packer would have forgotten that direction within minutes.

One morning Jack was fooling around in the copy boys' room and threw a paste pot at one of his colleagues. The pot smashed outside RC's office. The copy boys fled in all directions, leaving Jack to face RC alone.

'Who did this?' Robert Clyde demanded.

Jack owned up.

'Go in to Vol Molesworth immediately and tell him I said to sack you straight away.'

A shattered Fingleton went to the editor's office and said, 'Mr Packer has sent me in to you to be sacked.'

'All right,' Molesworth said nonchalantly. 'I'll ring upstairs. You buzz up and get your money.'

Jack left the building with his pay in lieu of notice and headed to Bondi Beach, crushed.

A few days later, the phone at home rang.

'Vol Molesworth here. Where have you been?'

'You sacked me.'

'Don't be a bloody fool, Fingleton. Nobody takes any notice of the sack at *The Guardian*. You come in here immediately.'

Fingleton was on the next city tram. For the rest of his days at *The Guardian*, if he saw RC he would run.

Back in Pedlar Palmer's sports section, he immersed himself happily in work, making sure the starting prices for the horses at Randwick were correct so he didn't have SP bookies chasing him, and checking that the cricket scores added up, so some pedant didn't upset his Monday morning with a long whinge on the phone. One of his favourite places was *The Guardian's* file room, where newspapers from around the world were kept in large stacks. He would head for the *Manchester Guardian*, fossicking through until he found the sports pages and the lush cricket copy of Neville Cardus. So intoxicated was Fingleton by Cardus's descriptions that he risked the sack by ignoring the warning sign on the wall: 'Anybody found cutting these files will be instantly dismissed.' When no one was looking Jack would pull out a switch-blade, hastily slice out a Cardus piece, fold it and hide it in his coat pocket, take it home and place it in a scrapbook. That book, which he kept for the rest of his life, became his writing bible.

Palmer believed reporters should be versatile, and he insisted that Jack do stints on the general news and crime beats. There he got to know—and drink with—some of Australia's best newspaper writers, including Brian Penton, Hugh Buggy, Eric Baume and Cyril Pearl—and RC's journalist son, Frank.

It paid to have a nose for a story, of whatever sort. Hearing that *The Guardian's* daily gossip column was offering contributors threepence a line, Jack worked out that if he could contribute two items a week, he would have enough money for a slap-up dinner at Sydney's most reputable seafood restaurant.

The lure of a dozen fresh oysters made Jack one of the column's most reliable contributors.

When the scent of a big news story faded, Jack would always wander back to the sports section, knowing that the ever sympathetic Palmer would let the eager cadet disappear after he had turned in his day's copy, so he could pursue his other interests— in particular, cricket.

The hours of a morning newspaperman also helped. Starting at 2 p.m. and working until the last edition went to press at midnight, Jack had the mornings to himself. That gave him time not only to play in *The Guardian*'s midweek cricket team, but also to tangle with the best cricketers in Sydney in the major grade competition.

It involved sacrifices. Jack and Wally would head at dawn to nearby Waverley Oval, where they would do laps and endless fielding drills before running down the hill to Bondi for beach sprints and a surf.

He may not have had much to show for himself, but Jack was blessed by his surroundings. The Eastern Suburbs thrived on sporting pursuits—and was where many of Australia's most prominent athletes lived. Football and cricket dominated, and those who excelled soon became local identities, hailed by all.

Having Waverley, one of the most illustrious cricketing clubs in Australia—home to a long line of crusty and cultivated Internationals, including the Gregory family, Hanson Carter, Alan Kippax, Arthur Mailey and Stork Hendry—just down the street made it impossible for Jack not to avoid the summer bug. This was rich cricket territory, where he would often bump into past or present Test cricketers, and where the conversation often revolved around who scored what in which grade. Waverley was a proud club that thrived on success.

It demanded excellence from its players. Waverley Oval, with a centre wicket renowned for being unpredictable, uneven and a nightmare for any batsman, was the focal point, and where one went to learn exactly how to play the game.

Jack would join a large group of youngsters and, standing behind the boundary fence during practice, watch in awe as Australia's best performed in front of them. It was better than what any cricketing textbook could offer. Each Friday, he would sprint from school to the ground so that he could be an outfield fielder to his heroes.

He was immediately enraptured by such artists as Kippax, who made everything look so graceful, so effortless, especially when he went back onto his right foot and glided one through the gully with a majestic late cut. Jack was captivated by the shot, and one day asked the great man the correct way of playing it. 'Forget all about it, son,' Kippax said, patting the youngster on the back. Jack did.

And down the other end of Jack's street, Centennial Park— the haven for tough park cricket—beckoned. Here he learned gamesmanship and got streetwise tips required to turn a fancy cricketer into a hardened competitor.

He also had his family to keep him honest.

His uncle, Wally Webb, always kept a close eye on him. Wally was a hard man who played sport with contempt for the niceties. Apart from his passion for cricket, Wally was instrumental in the formation of the Eastern Suburbs rugby league team. His league affiliations saw him appointed the manager of the 1933 Australian Kangaroos team. Webb made a mark on that UK tour when he got involved in a brawl with England official Harry Hornby and felled him with a right hook. Irked that Hornby had bumped him aside on the way into the team's hotel, Webb knocked him out with one punch. Late in his life, angered by the foul language of a taxi driver who was taking him to a funeral, Wally forced the driver to stop the cab near Centennial Park and gave him a thrashing.

Uncle Wal, as the kids called him, hated losing, and he hated upstarts getting under his guard—including his young nephew. Wal was a Centennial Park cricketing identity, being the captain and stalwart of the Glammis club. One time when Jack and his father were playing against the Glammis team for the Waverley Guild, Wal demonstrated his scorn for his brother-in-law's bowling. For overs on end, he tried to slam the Labor MP's deliveries into the Oxford Street tram shed . . . until he miscued one and it skied towards Jack. Immediately Wal tried to unnerve Jack by yelling at the top of his voice, 'Come two, he'll miss it.' Jack didn't, much to Wal's disgust.

But his uncle soon got Jack back. Batting on an ant-bed wicket covered with coir matting, which turned any average medium-paced trundler into a frightening speedster of the Larwood ilk, Wal got one through Jack's defence, thudding the back pad. No point in a gentle appeal. Instead Wal screamed at the top of his lungs, and the umpire was so fearful for his own safety that he sent Jack to the pavilion, dismissed lbw.

'Uncle Wally resented anyone who wanted to take over his crown as the champion cricketer of Centennial Park,' Jack's brother Wally recalled. 'I was in primary school and would go with Jack to the games, where we saw Uncle Wally in his prime. And he wouldn't take pity on a young bloke like Jack. Uncle Wally was a real tiger and was always trying to get Jack out. He would be appealing for lbws all the time.'

Jack had to learn fast, because the Waverley scouts had taken notice of him. They told him to steer clear of Centennial Park, saying playing on matting would ruin his technique. Turf wickets, even that dodgy track at Waverley where you always had to be prepared for the shooter that would go under your bat and shatter your stumps, were, the officials said, the only route to success.

But the Fingleton family could not afford the fees. Luckily

for Jack, one of the patrons of the club agreed to pay them for him. Jack's park cricket days were over.

The club soon got value from the subscription when Jack, aged just sixteen, was beckoned to Manly Oval for his initial first-grade game. Herbie Collins, the Australian captain at the time, was supposed to be opening for Waverley against Manly, but his other pursuit as a bookmaker had lured him to Randwick races on the Saturday afternoon.

Waverley was suddenly without an opening batsman, and in desperation Jack was moved from second to first grade. Hanson Carter, the same man who had organised his father's funeral, was the Waverley captain that day, and he thought it too risky for Jack to face the Manly opening attack. Instead he batted at No. 11, finishing unbeaten on 11.

As Waverley had to follow on, Carter told Jack to keep the pads on, and in the second innings he was again unbeaten on 52. It was enough for Jack to retain his first-grade spot for the rest of the season.

Within a year he was starting to get noticed. The *Daily Telegraph* reporter who was at Chatswood Oval for a Waverley–Gordon match the following year wrote: 'Fingleton, a 17-year-old lad, played a great innings for his side. He does not yet possess a large range of strokes, but his sound defence is the asset which will enable him to hit up more big scores this season.'

Jack's contacts in both the media and cricketing circles also saw him invited to special midweek games at Sydney Cricket Ground No. 2 between a Colts team and Junior association sides. The Colts line-up, which comprised the most promising young grade cricketers, such as Fingleton, was boosted by an assortment of retired former Test cricketers, such as Charlie Macartney.

Macartney, known by all as the Governor General, enjoyed being an entertainer, and whenever possible was audacious when batting. Macartney once accompanied Fingleton as the Colts opening batting pair. As they walked to the crease, Macartney told an awestruck Fingleton: 'I'll take strike, son. And keep your eyes open for the first ball.' Fingleton assumed this meant Macartney was eager to go for a quick single. But as Fingleton discovered, it meant exactly the opposite. 'The first ball came hurtling back like a meteorite and was crashing against the fence while the umpire, the bowler and I were still prone to the grass as if in an air raid,' Jack recalled. 'I picked myself up and met Charlie in the middle.'

'It's always a good idea,' he confided, 'to aim the first ball right at the bowler's head. They don't like it. It rattles them. Then you can do as you like!'

Macartney turned to the bowler, who was scrambling to his feet, and said: 'Isn't that right, mate?'

Fingleton's newspaper life also took a dramatic turn. His mentor Pedlar Palmer had been lured to the *Sydney Morning Herald*, and life at *The Guardian* had lost its charm. Luckily for Jack, the newspaper world is a hive of gossip. Everyone always seems to know what everyone else is up to. Johnny Moyes, a cricketer of note who was the sporting editor of the *Telegraph Pictorial*, had heard that Jack wasn't happy, and contacted him. Was he interested in changing papers—and a raise?

The *Telegraph Pictorial* had just been merged with the *Daily Telegraph*. In Jack's first week at his new job, an executive walked into the newsroom and said: 'Gentlemen, we now have two staffs but only one newspaper. Soon we will need only one staff. Gentlemen, go to it and I wish you the best of luck.'

The reporters scurried in all directions, chasing stories in the hope of impressing the bosses and remaining on staff. Jack was taken off the main staff but kept on in a freelance capacity as the Redfern–Newtown correspondent.

The role was as unglamorous as the rough, inner-city suburb. But Jack knew the area would be a hive of stories, and he put in the leg work to get them, hanging around the law courts, council offices and police stations, and sending in a steady flow of items at twopence a line.

Within time he was making more than many of the senior writers, and the ever-frugal *Telegraph* realised it would be smarter to put Jack back on staff. His new desk was near that of the newspaper's chief columnist, Lennie Lower. Observing Lower reminded Jack that good writing did not come easily. It took hard work, much thought and plenty of angst. Readers would laugh their way through Lower's daily column, but Jack knew what it had cost him to produce. Lower, author of the immensely popular *Here's Luck*, would sit for hours at his desk, glaring into space or painstakingly typing and retyping, every so often ripping the sheet from his typewriter, screwing it into a ball, and hurling it to the floor. When he was stuck he'd go to the pub and eventually stagger back drunk to finish the column.

Jack took note: Drink before, he told himself. Drink after. But never drink while you're writing. And never do a daily column. Too harmful to your health.

5
They Meet

Right from the start, the relationship between Jack Fingleton and Don Bradman was prickly. They first crossed paths in 1929 at the *Daily Guardian*. Bradman, who was travelling from Bowral each week to play grade cricket in Sydney, was being shown over the paper's offices and printing plant after being invited by one of the newspaper executives.

When introduced to Bradman, Fingleton told him about a friend of his who had the makings of a champion cricketer until the day he ran a nail into his foot. 'He was left with a stiff right knee; he had tee-tanus,' Jack said.

It was tetanus, Bradman said with what Jack took to be scorn.

Fingleton took a mental note: this bloke was clearly a bit different.

Bradman, who was four months younger than Jack, had an air of self-assurance unusual in a teenager. But he was already attracting the interest—and envy—of players almost twice his age. As the youngest member of the Bowral Town team, he'd been almost impossible to get out. His astounding ability to score runs caught the attention of officials at the New South Wales Cricket Association, and in October 1926 the eighteen-year-old was invited to a practice session at the Sydney Cricket Ground. Just over a year later, he was in the New South Wales Sheffield Shield team.

Fingleton's ascent to first-class cricket was considerably slower. But from early on he had his eye firmly fixed on the highest levels of the game. He wasn't a stylist like Bradman, but the doggedness of his defence made him one of Sydney's standout opening batsmen.

Having Waverley Oval as his home ground, taught him to take no delivery for granted. On this devilishly tricky wicket, deliveries would be at your throat one minute, skidding towards your ankles the next. The natural response was caution. Fingleton's batting style was based on a fierce survival instinct.

There was no flourish in his back lift. Instead it was restricted, taking the bat back only marginally and relying on strong wrists and forearms to push the ball away from the centre square. The back lift had to be short to ensure one was never a victim of the dreaded mullygrubber. Jack could square cut, drive and glide as well as anyone, but the hallmark of his game was his excellent defence: he was fearless, focused and determined to wear down any bowler he faced.

Playing at Waverley bred some bad habits, though. To ensure he was ever ready for the shooters, Jack allowed his bottom hand to slip down the handle of the bat. The resulting separation of his hands restricted his stroke play. Still, Jack looked upon himself as a fighter, the backbone of an innings. To toughen himself up he took boxing lessons. He believed this built upper-body and arm strength and improved his footwork and balance. He loved showing off his latest moves to brother Wally.

'He clouted me one time. And I immediately complained to our mother. He defended himself by saying he thought I needed hardening up,' Wally said.

Jack became so redoubtable a batsman that in January 1929, three months short of his twenty-first birthday, he was picked for the New South Wales team. He joined an extraordinarily youthful side. Alec Marks, just eighteen, was also making his first-class debut. Stan McCabe was eighteen, Archie Jackson and twelfth man Mick Hogg were nineteen, Bradman—who'd made his first-class debut two seasons earlier—was twenty, and Hugh Davidson was twenty-one.

Jack was in fine form. Just a few days before the team was announced, he'd been the sole century maker in the Sydney grade round, scoring an unbeaten 108 against Petersham. The *Daily Telegraph Pictorial* ran a front-page story on the opening day's play of the Victoria game, with a photo of SCG workers painting Fingleton's name for the scoreboard.

Fingleton quickly discovered where he stood in the cricketing pecking order: deep in the shadow of Bradman, who'd marked his opening season with NSW with a century on debut.

New South Wales captain Tommy Andrews won the toss and elected to bat. The team then settled in to watch Bradman. For eight hours, No. 8 Fingleton waited and waited and waited while Bradman toyed with the Victorian bowling attack. Bradman was unbeaten on 340 when Andrews finally decided to declare the NSW first innings closed after it had passed the 700 mark.

At least Fingleton got to the crease. He let Bradman control the strike and played several reasonable drives during his unbeaten innings of 25. But he learned that when Bradman dominated, 'the batsman at the other end felt like an ineffectual goon'. Bradman 'judged himself and everybody else by runs,' Fingleton later wrote. 'He didn't care a fig for so-called grace or beauty. He was a realist.'

Fingleton's initial scoring shot in first-class cricket was a leg glance for four, but his rhythm was then affected by Bradman's hogging of the strike. Fingleton felt like a mere observer. They

were together for 87 minutes—enjoying an unbeaten partnership of 111 runs. Bradman scored 80 of those.

Even when Fingleton was on strike, Bradman seemed desperate to take his place. Bradman almost ran himself out when he
charged down the wicket after Jack had turned one to fine leg
straight to a Victorian fieldsman. Fingleton didn't move, and
Bradman had to scurry back to avoid being run out. After the
glance came the glare.

One of Jack's most vivid memories of that first partnership
was of Victorian wicketkeeper and skipper Jack Ellis endlessly
abusing the Don: 'Haven't you had enough yet, you little c—?'

Bradman ignored him.

His aloofness and self-possession irritated players on his own
side, as well.

On Bradman's first away tour with the NSW team, the
veterans decided the wonder boy from Bowral needed to be put
in his place. At Sydney's Central Station, they crowded around
him, asking him what he did apart from playing cricket.

Bradman made the fatal mistake of admitting he played the
piano.

That must be why he was so good at cricket, someone said.
Piano playing toned your wrist and back muscles. A lively debate
sprang up. Some said they wouldn't believe that till they saw
Bradman's back muscles with their own eyes. Bets were made,
and Bradman was talked into taking off his shirt. That wasn't
good enough for some. No, they said, he would have to play an
air piano so they could see his muscles in action. While the shirt-
less Bradman mimed, the other players choked back guffaws as
they solemnly inspected his back muscles.

Eventually it was decided that nothing short of seeing
Bradman at a real piano would settle the bet. So at the team's
Adelaide hotel Bradman was sat down at a piano and the joke-
sters began again, debating how well-formed his muscles were.

The following day he was duped into travelling to Glenelg for an important team errand. When he arrived at the seaside suburb, he discovered he had been the victim of a cruel practical joke. The pranks only made Bradman more aloof—and his solitary, self-possessed air only increased the animosity.

His fastidious habits set him even further apart. During the luncheon adjournment, he would meticulously place his bat, pads and gloves on the dressing room table, take a quick shower, find a quiet corner, then, a towel wrapped around his midriff, sit and chew his way through a light lunch of stewed fruit, rice custard and milk. 'Each slow mouthful,' Fingleton recalled, 'was an essay in method, in digestion, in relaxation, in cold planning and contemplation of the real feast soon to follow in the middle of the ground'.

He was invariably the first to leave the dressing rooms after play. And he was a teetotaller—didn't see the point of drinking or smoking. While the others were sharing beer and cigarettes, Bradman would be off writing letters or listening to music.

By the early 1930s, Fingleton wrote, 'the line of demarcation on Bradman was clearly defined: One either liked him or didn't.'

For some the dislike was mingled with envy, but it also came from a sense that Bradman was in cricket first and foremost for himself—the team came second. Fingleton's Waverley captain, Alan Kippax, had no time for Bradman, and it wasn't long before a trivial argument in the dressing room made Fingleton, too, keep his distance. The ever suspicious Bradman began to believe that Fingleton was purposely trying to turn the others against him.

The fact that Jack, a more gregarious character, fitted in well with his teammates only increased Bradman's wariness. The Fingleton Irish cheek helped, as did the streetwise bravado he'd learned as a young reporter. He enjoyed the high-spirited tomfoolery sporting teams got up to, especially on tour. And he found kindred spirits in Alec Marks, Bill O'Reilly and Stan McCabe.

Fingleton spent several seasons in and out of the NSW team. Then, during the opening match of the 1931–32 Sheffield Shield season against Queensland in Brisbane, Fingleton was twelfth man. However on the morning of the game, Fingleton was suddenly in the team, because the side's illustrious batsman Archie Jackson had been taken to hospital, coughing up blood.

Jackson was a batting maestro, but suffered a dreadful life, afflicted by regular bouts of bad health that eventually developed into pulmonary tuberculosis. When picked for the Queensland match, Jackson was recovering from a bout of influenza.

Just before the start of play, Jackson was sitting in a corner of the NSW dressing room, when he slumped to the floor. Within fifteen months he would be dead.

But his tragedy meant that twelfth man Fingleton would now have to open the batting with Wendell Bill. Mercifully for the shaken Jack—Jackson was a good friend—there was a rain delay, then Queensland won the toss and opted to bat. Several hours on the field soothed the nerves. After the home team struggled to make 109, Fingleton stepped up to face the most controversial bowler in Australian cricket, Eddie Gilbert.

Gilbert, who learned to play cricket at the Barambah (now Cherbourg) Aboriginal settlement, would take just four or five steps before bringing his arm over in a huge arc that took his hand almost to ground level and catapulted the ball forward at tremendous speed. His whiplike wrist action, however, had some claiming he bent his arm and thus technically threw the ball rather than bowling it. Now the crowd was agog to see what Gilbert would do to Bradman.

Fingleton played out the first over from Queensland paceman Hugh 'Pud' Thurlow. Then in skipped Gilbert, to begin an opening over that is still regarded as one of the momentous in Australian cricket history. His first delivery bucked from a good length and almost took Wendell Bill's head off. At the last second, Bill ducked but failed to get his bat out of the way. The top-edge was caught by wicketkeeper Len Waterman, prompting cheers that, according to the *Daily Mail*, could be heard 'blocks away'.

With NSW 1–0, in came Bradman. The first ball he faced was on a good length but stayed down, allowing him to get onto the back foot and block it away. But then Gilbert, flexing every sinew of his slender, 1.6-metre frame, pounded the ball into the wicket, about halfway along. As it reared towards Bradman's face, he tried to get under it, but it flicked off his cap. Bradman overbalanced and fell. A grinning Gilbert flung a third ball at Bradman, but the delivery ballooned high over the batsman's head.

Ball five was short, but Bradman would say in years to come that it was the fastest he ever faced. This time he took aggressive action, trying to hook it as it sped past. The frantic attempt to get bat on ball saw him again lose his balance. Worse, the bat was knocked from his hands, prompting wolf whistles from the crowd, who thrilled to the sight of this quiet, unassuming Aborigine making a fool of the world's best batsman.

Bradman brushed himself down and took his stance. Again Gilbert was waiting for him. There was another tiny run-up, another hop, a mad dip of the shoulders, a whip of the forearm, and the delivery was flying at the bewildered Bradman. Trying to hook it, he misjudged the shot, edging the ball to the wicket-keeper for the third duck of his first-class career. The reaction was near pandemonium. The *Brisbane Courier* said Queensland's 'amazing start sent the crowd delirious with delight. They rose en masse and cheered themselves hoarse.'

Fingleton watched it all closely. It was the first time he had seen Bradman visibly shaken.

Now it was his turn to take strike. He too later said Gilbert's bowling was 'as fast as anything I have seen'. But he handled it with more aplomb than Bradman had done.

The ground is not big behind the stumps, but the slips were almost three-quarters of the way to the fence. I was down the other end once during that hectic late-afternoon, with Stan McCabe taking strike, and I remarked to Gilbert: 'You are pretty fast today, Eddie?'

Gilbert, a slim little man of possibly no more than eight stone, looked shyly at me and said: 'I bowled a plurry lot faster if they let me take my boots off.' Gilbert didn't run. He walked in five paces and then slung, which was the best way to describe it, with a boomerang-throwing action.

In the end, Fingleton was dismissed seven short of his century, while Stan McCabe finished on 229 not out. The way his friend McCabe fended off the bowling attack filled Fingleton with awe for his batting mastery. He would always feel that McCabe was unjustly consigned to Bradman's shadow. Despite the Gilbert power attack, New South Wales cruised to an innings and 238 runs victory.

Gilbert's career failed to live up to the expectations raised that day. Other cricketers, and cricketing officials, persistently alleged that he was throwing the ball. Bradman was one of those who questioned his technique. He later recalled the Shield over as 'the fastest "bowling" I can remember,' adding, 'I say "bowling" because, without wishing to castigate the umpires, the players all thought the action decidedly suspect.' Some observers thought this was just a case of Bradman being afraid of intimidating bowlers. But in another Shield match not long after, Gilbert was no-balled eleven times. His delivery was later filmed in slow motion so his arm action could be scrutinised, but the results were inconclusive. He played his last match in 1936 and returned to Cherbourg. Thirteen years later, he was admitted to a mental home, where he remained until his death in 1978. An interesting Gilbert postscript involves Wally Fingleton. In January 1936, Wally, who had followed Jack into journalism, covered a Queensland–NSW Sheffield Shield match in which Eddie Gilbert took part, and wrote an article analysing Gilbert's strengths—and weaknesses: 'Watching this small ebony parcel of elasticity displaying a peculiar mixture of galvanic energy and absolute lethargy, one wondered if his heart is in big cricket,' Wally wrote. He thought Gilbert appeared disinterested when he started to get hit around the field by NSW batsman Ray Robinson. When Robinson was hooking and driving Gilbert's best deliveries to the boundary, 'Eddie's spirits were not high.'

> It would not only be wrong to say that Gilbert 'drops his bundle' when hit: it would be doing him an injustice. The apparent explanation is that he is not suited for big cricket.
>
> It must be very difficult for him to travel with men whose interests, outside of cricket, are vastly different from his own, and appear in what is undoubtedly for him an uncomfortable dress, before thousands of people.
>
> Gilbert, as a freak cricketer, has raised intense interest among the Australian public; but it is time for him to be regarded as just an ordinary human.

The article caused a furore. The *Brisbane Truth* newspaper said 'all cricket followers were disgusted with the [Sydney] paper'. The *Sydney Truth* was as scathing, believing it was wrong to bring up the subject of Gilbert's racial background. Queensland team manager F.J. Bardwell wrote to the *Telegraph* arguing that 'to suggest that he is not suited for big cricket is absurd.'

When Jack heard about the furore, Wally recalled, 'He was a bit sour about it. He just said that I was "just writing and getting out on my name". He certainly knew how to cut me down to size.'

That went double for his opponents in Test cricket.

6

Making the Grade

In late 1931, the second South African team to visit Australia arrived for an extensive five-Test tour. When they played NSW, Fingleton used the moment to put himself in contention for a Test opening spot. In the second innings, he scored a century, passing three figures in less than four hours, showing that he had the subbornness, skill and determination to thwart the South African attack. Also recommending Jack to the selectors was the fact that again he and Bradman enjoyed a long partnership. They appeared to bring out the best in each other.

By the time of the Second Test, in Sydney, Fingleton had been elevated to twelfth man in the national team. There, and in two more Tests in Melbourne and Adelaide, Fingleton served as general dogsbody to his teammates. It was part of the initiation into Test cricket. He used the time to explore the inner workings of the Australian team. He observed the star players closely, noting their quirks, their superstitions, their relationships to each other. Fingleton quickly saw that Bradman was the dominant force. Everyone else was a prop, a moth to his flame.

Test after Test, Fingleton sat in the Australian dressing room watching one man maul the visiting side. Bradman was merciless. 'On and on and on he seemed to go, batting into cricket eternity,' Fingleton wrote later.

The South Africans had been warned. Their first game had been against Western Australia in Perth. As they travelled east by train, children at every railway siding kept up the chant, 'You'll never get Braddles out. You'll never get Braddles out.' And through November, December, January and February it haunted them like a prophecy. No matter what they tried, they could not get him out.

Bradman used the first NSW match against South Africa as his rehearsal. He calmly dissected all their bowlers and finished with 135.

In the First Test in Brisbane, he went up a gear and finished with 226. Another NSW match involved yet another Bradman double century. Then came 112 in the Sydney Test, 167 in the Melbourne Test, and 299 not out in the Adelaide Test.

This was sheer brutality, and the South Africans did not take kindly to such treatment. They were soon sick of the sight of Bradman, cringing at the sound of his squeaky, nasal voice. Probably the most enraged was their paceman Sandy Bell. In the Brisbane Test, Bell was reputed to have lost six pounds in weight in a day of aimless bowling at Bradman, where every delivery was dispatched with disdain. Late in the tour, Bell was in the office of cricketer turned influential sports editor A.G. Moyes when Bradman made a brief appearance. As Bradman left, Bell said to Moyes: 'That's the first time on this tour that I've seen his back.'

During the Adelaide Test, Bell's exasperation got the better of him. A stout man who looked as if he spent his winters on South African rugby fields locking scrums, Bell was irritated when the docile Adelaide wicket took the sting out of his deliveries, which Bradman then treated like wayward ping pong balls. Close to exhaustion, Bell summoned enough energy to have one last dig at Bradman.

He pounded in, and pounded one down. It rose towards Bradman's upper body, hitting him in the ribs. Bradman shot an angry look down the wicket. As he furiously rubbed at the sore spot, the South Africans looked at each other. Had they finally discovered his weakness? Was Bradman unusually averse to punishment and pain? Suddenly there was lightness in the tourists' step. The next Test, in Melbourne, would be played on a far more receptive wicket, where they could easily work away at destabilising Bradman with some short ones.

But it wasn't to be.

Minutes before the start of the Fifth Test, Bradman slipped in the dressing room and twisted his ankle. Within seconds, he was a Test spectator.

Fingleton wasn't so sure Bradman's injury was real. 'The accident to Bradman was a mystery,' he later wrote. 'Nobody saw it happen and the first time we knew about it was when he was seen on the dressing room floor. He had evidently caught his sprigs on one of the coir mats that covered the rooms in those days.

'In no time our room, as was always the case if the slightest thing happened to Bradman, was chockful of medicos whose greatest thrill, which they could pass on to their mates, was getting a hand on the Great Man.'

What further raised Fingleton's eyebrows was that even though Bradman was evidently nowhere near fit enough to bat, later in the game he was able to field, and 'ran yards and yards at his top speed to catch Herbie Taylor on the boundary off [Bert] Ironmonger . . . That made us all wonder, and nobody more than the South Africans.'

While the Fifth Test sidelined Bradman, it brought Fingleton into the team. When batsman Bill Ponsford came down with the flu, Fingleton became captain Bill Woodfull's opening partner. His inclusion originally in the middle order at the expense of Victorian Keith Rigg caused some consternation, especially as the Test was being played on the omitted player's home ground.

The weekly *Referee*'s cricket writer 'Not Out' called Fingleton's selection ahead of Rigg 'a surprise, and to my mind unjustified'.

'They are different in type, and for the position in which he should go to the wickets in this match Rigg looks quite the better batsman for the side. Fingleton, being of the [Herbert] Sutcliffe type, mainly defence and patience, with patted singles to the on-side varied with an occasional off drive to the pickets, gets his runs too slowly for number six on the list.'

The Age was also sceptical, arguing that Fingleton was a 'slow scoring bat, rather difficult to dislodge. He hasn't quite the ability of the first five batsmen, and slow or fast bowling might get him.'

Fingleton wasn't surprised that the Melbourne media bridled at the addition of another Sydneyite to the Test team. The rivalry between NSW and Victoria was already legendary.

His elevation to the Test elite was intoxicating. Fingleton was so excited that on the eve of the match he went to a Melbourne studio to have his photograph taken in the team jumper and blazer so he could send it to his mother.

As he walked onto the ground to field, he went wobbly at the knees. He was in such a daze that he missed the first ball hit to him when he was fielding at point. It went between his legs. His stint in the field was short, with South Africa caught on a wet, sticky wicket, dismissed for a paltry 36.

When he settled himself for his first Test innings, he was clearly worried that Australia would struggle to make any more on the treacherous wicket than the South Africans had. His composure was hardly helped when Woodfull had his stumps shattered by the first delivery from Bell, which Fingleton described as 'absolutely unplayable'. Fingleton feared his Test career would be over as quickly as it had begun. The embarrassment of a duck in your first Test innings would last forever. But in an act of great sportsmanship, Neville Quinn made his first delivery to the newcomer a rank full toss, enabling Jack to get off the mark.

Fingleton was grateful for Quinn's generosity, and thus begun a friendship between him and Quinn, who would soon be joined by many other South Africans.

Fingleton's first Test opportunity wasn't wasted. He soon found his footing, finishing as second top scorer, with 40 in seventy-seven minutes, as Australia struggled to 153. It was the type of tenacious opener's innings that enthused selectors and teammates.

Fingleton also impressed onlookers with his ability to hold his own against better-known players. His resilient defence, cultivated on that dreadful Waverley wicket, also worked in his favour. After Fingleton joined the recalled Rigg in a 51-run second-wicket partnership, former first-class player and now cricket writer R.S. Whitington some years later wrote that 'for courage and skill mixed with some blessings from providence, [it] was worth quadruple that number'. The *Sydney Morning Herald* described Fingleton's innings as 'artistic and sound'. *The Age* said it was a 'neat display'. The *Daily Telegraph* pumped up its man by calling him 'an admirable opening batsman'. The *Sydney Mail*, explaining that Fingleton had always been a fine player on wet wickets, predicted that the newcomer would 'someday be a great success in England'.

His restrictive batting style saw him survive through a difficult patch, enabling Australia to go well ahead of the South African score, and then giving them ample time to dismiss the visitors for another low score of 45 for an innings and 72 runs victory.

At the end of the game, Fingleton was approached by Alan Kippax, his club and NSW captain, who had been the top scorer in Australia's only innings. 'You have done yourself a good turn today,' Kippax said. 'Woody [Woodfull] will never forget anybody who gets runs when the going is tough.' The following summer, however, Woodfull was among those who voted against Jack's selection for the 1934 England tour. As Fingleton said with more than a little bitterness: 'It didn't take Woody long to forget.'

Another who didn't forget was South African batsman Herbie Taylor, who spent the tour scrutinising Bradman's every move. He was particularly taken by Bradman's reaction to that short delivery in Adelaide. After the tour, Taylor headed to England, where according to Fingleton he spoke with players and cricket authorities about the best way to counter the Australian batting phenomenon. They were receptive listeners. The 1932–33 England tour of Australia was looming.

7

Bodyline Hell

For the England Test team, the 1932–33 Australian tour focused on getting Bradman. Captain Douglas Jardine believed in knowing his enemy. He had watched film of Bradman, read all he could about him, debriefed English players who'd faced him. And, having concluded that the sharp, rising delivery and the threat of a body hit made the champion 'yellow', he had come up with a plan.

With county (Nottinghamshire) captain Arthur Carr, the brilliant Larwood, and fellow star bowler Bill Voce, Jardine sat at a table in the grill room of London's Piccadilly Hotel and, using cutlery and salt shakers, showed them how bowlers and fielders were to be deployed. The aim was clear. As Larwood later wrote: 'Bodyline was devised to stifle Bradman's batting genius.'

But as the English team sailed towards Perth, a fracas in Australia was threatening to push their arch foe out of the game. The Australian Board of Control was determined to stop players writing for newspapers.

The only latitude was given to those 'whose sole occupation is professional journalism'. Fingleton fell into that category, but it required him to get written permission from the Board chairman before he wrote anything about cricket. Bradman also applied for the role. He had a contract with Associated Newspapers, as well as radio station 2UE. He had also received lucrative offers from several English newspapers to write on the series. He was disenchanted that Fingleton was granted permission to write yet he was rejected. If he was not allowed to write, he said, he would not play.

The issue raged for weeks, until public opinion grew so strong that Bradman's newspaper employers gave in, telling him they would prefer him to play than write. A reluctant Bradman was persuaded into accepting a release from his contract. The Board, meanwhile, agreed to a compromise. It allowed Bradman to talk about the Tests on radio—for which he was paid handsomely. He would soon use this vehicle to rail against Bodyline. As the First Test loomed, the England attack was clearly heavily on his mind.

When he had returned from Perth, he'd told his NSW teammates that the Test series was going to be a shooting gallery, especially when it was his turn to bat. Bradman told opening batsman Bill Brown: 'You cannot believe how big the problem is unless you've been out there. You fellas have no idea what sort of summer this is going to be!'

Australia was scheduled to open with Woodfull and Ponsford in the First Test. Fingleton—after his doughty showing with the Combined XI in Perth and with NSW in Sydney—was being looked at as a potential No. 3. The Australian selectors believed that they could nullify the England bowling attack with resilient top-of-the-order batting. If Woodfull or Ponsford could not take control, then Fingleton would be able to grind away after the loss of the first wicket.

Fingleton's role became even more crucial when Bradman abruptly fell ill. The nature of his ailment was uncertain.

Speculation was rife. Bradman had looked decidedly off-colour during the NSW–England game. Some in the England team thought he might have had a nervous breakdown fretting about their attack. Larwood said he was obviously a worried man. The official reason for Bradman's withdrawal was that he was 'run down'.

The public reaction was one of shock. As one cable reporter wrote: 'It might have been the fall of an Empire. Bulletins were posted in the shop windows, and no one could talk, think or speak of anything else.'

Bradman's absence did not soften Jardine's approach, however. The plan was to aim the bulk of deliveries above the waist, near the rib region, in hopes of scaring batsmen or, if they did hit the ball, ensuring it was quickly caught by fieldsmen stacked on the leg side. In Larwood's first over, one short delivery shot past Woodfull's head, and in the next Bill Voce bowled to a Bodyline leg-side field. The early part of the day's play saw endless bobbing and weaving from the Australian opening batsmen, until Woodfull departed after just 22 runs had been scored when he messed up a hook shot at a Voce rising delivery.

Before a crowd of well over 40,000, out came Fingleton, who looked unnecessarily bulky. He hadn't suddenly put on weight. He was armoured for another belting. He was still sporting the heavy bruises of the NSW–England encounter, and had put on extra padding.

What exactly Fingleton had on under his flannels became a lively issue two days later, when the *Sunday Sun* newspaper displayed on its front page, under the headline 'All Padded Up', a studio photograph of a copy boy with padding all over his body, including an elbow protector, chest and side padding, and a special thigh pad.

According to the caption, Fingleton had loaned his breast pad for the photograph. This photo has since been republished in numerous books, usually with a caption claiming that it showed Fingleton himself. Fingleton eventually grew tired of explaining that it didn't. It was someone with a decidedly poor defensive stroke, who didn't even know how to buckle up his pads properly or how to hold a bat. Fingleton said Arthur Mailey had thought up the idea of the photograph, and he agreed to lend the gear believing 'the picture would never appear again'.

But the picture did appear over and over again, exasperating Fingleton. Even some of Fingleton's teammates asked him if he'd really gone this far with his padding. Bill O'Reilly could not recall any batsman, including Fingleton, having 'ribbed' gear covering his body. Players, including Woodfull and Ponsford, instead wore sheets of rubber, which hung down from their necks. Some even placed rolled socks in their pockets to act as rudimentary thigh guards.

Fingleton did not resort to that, but probably wished he had, especially in the opening overs. He may have been slow-footed and cumbersome at times, but nothing got through his defence. Yet he was hit repeatedly. Like Ponsford, he was prepared to take the ball on the body instead of hitting it to leg, which could have got him dismissed.

Jardine and Larwood admired his approach.

'I was always glad to see Fingleton walking back to the dressing room,' Larwood remarked.

Jardine said that while Fingleton was 'rather foot-tied and slow,' he 'seemed more likely to make runs off leg theory than any other sort of bowling'.

It all revolved around patience. Fingleton had plenty of that. It was nonetheless stodgy viewing for the spectator. Fingleton later realised his technique was affected by a poor batting grip, and that although he had all the strokes, he was afraid 'to let himself go'. As he put it: 'I had a depressed, "safety first" mentality.'

But against England that summer it was justified. Early on, luck also went Fingleton's way. He was bowled by a Voce no-ball, and many thought he should have been given run-out during one mad scurry down the wicket. Larwood kept bashing him in the hip, but Fingleton refused to flinch. He had been there for well over an hour when he eventually succumbed on 26 after mistiming a rising delivery from Larwood and popping it up to Gubby Allen at forward short leg.

It was hardly a classic innings, but Fingleton had done what was required of him, taking the shine off the new ball and keeping the team's stroke makers—Alan Kippax and Stan McCabe—out of the firing line until the second session of play.

Fingleton was also able to get back to the dressing room in time to witness one of the most admired innings ever played by an Australian at Test level.

With Australia 3 for 82, it was Stan McCabe's turn at the crease. Just before the self-effacing country boy walked out, he told his father, 'If I get hit out there, make sure you stop Mum from jumping the fence.'

His mother didn't need to. Stan was in full control. The first delivery from Larwood was hooked to the mid-wicket fence, and for the next four hours he continued playing with style and bravado. There were missed chances and missed hits, but there were also countless classic shots. Deciding that the only way to counter aggression was to be equally ferocious, he fearlessly charged at or coaxed the deliveries to all parts of the field, mixing up his finely timed hooks with leg glances, cuts, drives and lofted shots over mid off and mid on.

He ended up unbeaten on 187, a feat that had the cricket writers running out of superlatives. Fingleton said that those who saw McCabe's innings would never forget it.

I have seen the dignified gentry of the members' pavilion grin like truant schoolboys as Bradman passed through them after one of his devastating batting whirlwinds; but never, before or since, have I seen respectable gentlemen give vent to such exuberant feelings as that day when McCabe returned to the pavilion. They roared, cheered and clapped all at once until they were red in the face; they threw their hats, sticks and luncheons away in their ecstasies, and, if space had permitted, they would have turned catherine wheels to give expression to the feelings which McCabe's innings sent surging through them.

In the dressing room, Fingleton, now with his *Sunday Sun* journalist hat on, approached an exhausted McCabe, who was sitting quietly in a corner. He embraced him, produced a notebook, and soon after filed this story:

'You know, I'm frightfully glad I got that score. My mother and father travelled down from Grenfell specially for this match. It is the first time they had seen me play in Sydney' was Stan McCabe's smiling comment as he returned to the dressing room after his grand stand of 187 not out in the Test match yesterday.

'It is my first Test match in Sydney—and it's theirs too.'

The most unemotional place in the whole of a cricket ground in a Test such as this is, perhaps, the dressing room, but even the most phlegmatic players let their feelings get the better of them when McCabe returned after that magnificent innings.

Stan took things very quietly. 'Thanks, very much,' said he calmly, but with a happy smile, as each player congratulated him.

Having phoned in the piece, he bounded out of the Australian dressing room, sidestepped the many well-wishers in the main bar, and caught the tram to the Mary Immaculate Church in

Waverley. Jack was best man at his elder brother Les's wedding, which was delayed for over an hour so he could get to the church in time. Jack still arrived ahead of the bride, Edna Carter. After the reception, at the Bondi School of Arts, he went home and had his best sleep in weeks. It had been a heady day.

Despite McCabe's heroism, the Test gradually turned England's way. Although Australia had two excellent spinners—the angular, aggressive Bill O'Reilly and the wily New Zealander Clarrie Grimmett—they lacked the pace array to finish off the England batsmen. With Herbert Sutcliffe, Wally Hammond and the Nawab of Pataudi all scoring centuries, the Australian tally of 360 was soon passed, with plenty to spare.

Australia's second-innings effort was nowhere near as illustrious as the McCabe dominated first innings. The only batsmen to show any resistance to Larwood's mighty arm were Fingleton and McCabe.

Fingleton was again cautious, constantly toying with the Englishmen by cheekily sneaking down the wicket every time he hit the ball in the hope of snaring a quick run. Partners came and went, but Fingleton, sporting eight new bruises, held out for almost two and a half hours, finishing as Australia's top scorer with a meticulous 40. It was not entirely stodgy, as half his runs came from boundaries.

But that still could not stop England enjoying a ten-wicket First Test victory.

As one of the few Australians to show any form of resistance to the England attack, Fingleton was a certainty for the Second Test at the Melbourne Cricket Ground at the end of December.

With Bradman again available, even though that remained in doubt until shortly before the start of play as he was still fighting with the Board of Control over his media duties, Fingleton was elevated to opening the batting with Woodfull. He'd been preferred to the long-time prolific run scorer Bill Ponsford, while Alan Kippax was dropped.

Again Fingleton was up to it, and before a world record crowd of 63,993 rewarded the selectors with a fastidious four-hour stint at the wicket, top scoring the second-innings running with 83. The *Sydney Morning Herald* next morning described it as a 'magnificent fighting innings'.

Fingleton was again bombarded with wild deliveries aimed at his head and upper body. But that wasn't going to inhibit his gamesmanship. After several short deliveries from Larwood, he cheekily wandered up the pitch and patted down a divot, which was usually in the bowler's half of the wicket. That only made Larwood try even harder to knock his head off. Fingleton didn't mind, because he knew how to weave out of the way of those balls. More difficult were the deliveries aimed slightly further up the wicket, which were tricky to negotiate off your ribs and away from the endless waiting hands in the leg trap.

When Leo O'Brien fell victim to a run-out prompted by Fingleton's zeal to get to the other end, Bradman came to the wicket amid deafening applause. On the way he passed England fielder Herbert Sutcliffe.

'A wonderful ovation, Don,' Sutcliffe said, as he watched the crowd noisily welcome back their king.

'Yes, but will it be so good when I come back?'

Bradman was far from composed as he walked to the middle. At the start of the Melbourne Test, he had insisted to Board of Control member Frank Cush that official action had to be taken over England's dangerous bowling.

As revealed in Gideon Haigh and David Frith's *Inside Story*, Bradman was disappointed by Cush's response:

And Frank said to me, 'Well, I've got to admit that from where I sit I didn't see anything to take exception to.' And I

said, 'Do you know why you didn't take exception to it?' And
he said, 'Why?' And I said, 'Because you're in no bloody danger
sitting up in your padded seat in the pavilion, that's why!'
Bradman added: 'I'm afraid that was the situation with the rest
of the Board. They didn't understand the problem.'

Obviously the spectators at the MCG that day didn't understand
it either. They refused to be silent when Bradman took guard,
twice prompting England bowler Bill Bowes to stop when
running in and wait for some sort of decorum to return.

Whether Bradman was unsettled by this is uncertain, but the
stroke he played to Bowes's first delivery was inexplicable.

Bradman was expecting a bouncer. As Bowes, the big,
lumbering medium pacer ran in, he shuffled across his crease.

At the non-striker's end, Fingleton looked on in amazement.

'To my surprise I saw Bradman leave his guard and move
across the wicket before Bowes had bowled the ball,' he later
wrote. 'Bradman was outside his off stump when the ball reached
him. He swung at it and hit it into the base of the leg stump. A
hush fell on the ground, an unbelievable hush of calamity, for
men refused to believe what their eyes had seen. Bradman left the
wickets in silence,' out for a duck.

The crowd was stunned. Jardine danced a celebratory jig,
while a clearly befuddled Bowes walked over to Fingleton and
said, 'Well I'll be foocked.'

The next day's headlines focused not on Fingleton's fight but
on Bradman's blunder. 'Bradman Fails', they screamed.

It was a calamity.

Fingleton hung around a lot longer, until fatigue set in.
After hours of flicking deliveries mainly behind the wicket
with dabs and prods, he played all over an Allen delivery and
was bowled.

His hand had been jarred so hard from the endless grenades

hitting his bat that the area between his right thumb and fore-finger ached for well over a week. Jardine recalled that 'the spirit of Woodfull, with an added dourness of his own, seemed to have descended upon Fingleton'.

Bradman redeemed himself in the second innings by scoring an unbeaten century, which set up an Australian victory—taking the series to one all.

Fingleton came and went, facing just nine deliveries before being caught behind off Allen. But with the tour now heading to Adelaide, he had merited a fourth successive Test appearance. Dr Eric Barbour, wrote in his *Sydney Mail* column, 'I have no doubt that a really great athlete, whether at cricket, tennis or field games, becomes a super-man when the great contest is on. Only recently I have seen one of our own players displaying against England a degree of skill and a class of batsmanship that he has never previously shown, either at the nets or against weak club sides. I refer to Jack Fingleton.'

And so enthused were the partners of a Sydney legal firm—Rowley, Roseby and Co.—that at the end of the Test they sent a letter to Fingleton offering him free legal advice and services for the next three years.

'Your plucky effort against the barrage of England's shock bowlers for four days has filled all of us with a feeling of deep admiration,' the letter said.

Fingleton filed it away, just in case.

If the first two Tests had been purgatory for the Australians, the third was sheer hell. In tranquil Adelaide, city of churches, the demons of Bodyline burst into the open. Australians had been upset about the English attack from the start. But their anger had been moderated by the response of skipper Bill Woodfull. Stern and dignified, stoical under pressure, he had kept his distaste for the England team's tactics to himself.

What happened in Adelaide, both on and off the pitch, shattered that silence. The result was a wave of outrage that almost caused a diplomatic crisis and deeply disturbed the Australian team as well. Near the centre of that storm was Jack Fingleton.

On a searing hot Saturday, Woodfull and Fingleton opened the batting for Australia. Fingleton did not last long, out for a duck after he was caught behind during an early over. At least, however, he had not been maimed by the England bowling attack.

Woodfull wasn't so lucky.

The captain was no stylist. He was cautious, disciplined. Jardine knew that such a solid boulder could be dislodged only with explosive action. Larwood was in charge of the darts.

The aim was not just to intimidate Woodfull but to show the batsman standing at the non-striker's end—Bradman—what lay in store for him. Hurt one, and in the process scare the other.

In his second over, Larwood bowled one short to Woodfull, which passed his face by just a few inches. This was followed by a perfectly pitched delivery on middle stump. It was relatively short and rising quickly. Woodfull appeared to have it covered with a defensive bat in front of his chest. But the ball suddenly deviated, smashing just above his heart.

The thump could be heard around the ground. The 50,000 spectators hooted and yelled as Woodfull dropped the bat and careered away from the pitch in agony. Gasping for air, both hands clutching his chest, he doubled over several metres from the pitch, close to collapse. But Woodfull refused to show the Englishmen any sign of weakness. Though he seemed to slump for an instant, he recovered himself and stayed on his feet.

As the English players surrounded Woodfull, the crowd's hostility intensified. So high was the tension that the mounted police situated behind the main pavilion readied themselves for an on-field charge. Even the England players were nervous, preparing to grab stumps to defend themselves if someone should leap the fence.

As Woodfull staggered, Jardine bellowed to Larwood, 'Well bowled, Harold!'

After several minutes' break, the Australian skipper picked up his bat and headed back towards the crease.

It was the end of the over, so Bradman faced the next from Gubby Allen.

Then came the moment when the Test series exploded into war. As Woodfull prepared for the next Larwood over, there was a dramatic change to the field placing. According to Larwood, Jardine suddenly stopped his bowler by clapping his hands, and began moving players across to strategic positions.

According to Jardine, Larwood indicated that he wanted a leg-side field. Nonetheless, the captain either agreed or made a dramatic change in the field. Jardine, who had told Woodfull he had the option of retiring hurt, sensed this was the moment to go all-out against the rattled Australians. He motioned to several of his fielders to move across the leg side of the wicket, basically to create a leg trap. Then Larwood proceeded to bowl a succession of bouncers at Woodfull.

The crowd were incensed. Future Prime Minister Robert Menzies, who was in the stands that day, told Fingleton that before the start of play he had been 'chatting to the man next to me, whom I didn't know . . . He was quietly spoken, cultured and most interesting. We spoke of many things before the game started. That was the day Woodfull was struck by Larwood. [After it happened] I looked at that man again and he was a changed person. He was on his feet and his face was choleric. He shouted, he raved, and he flung imprecations at Larwood and Jardine because of what his eyes had seen.'

He wasn't alone.

Fingleton observed that Jardine's action was 'a terrible error of judgement'.

Woodfull somehow survived the over, but after ninety minutes, during which he was hit on the body several more times, he mistimed a low delivery from Allen that uprooted his middle stump. Bradman did not last long, popping up an easy leg-side catch. The over so unsettled him that he became disoriented on the way back to the dressing room and headed towards the wrong exit before being pointed in the right direction.

When Woodfull got to the dressing room he headed straight for the showers and for several minutes stood under the steaming water, hoping a proper soaking would lessen the pain of the bruises that covered most of his upper body. Wrapping himself in a towel, he went and lay on the massage table. At that moment, the captain was informed he had visitors.

At the dressing room door were England manager Pelham (Plum) Warner, resplendent in his team blazer and Panama hat, and his assistant, Dick Palairet. Warner was the personification of English cricket—a man who had devoted his life to the game. After long stints as a player, Test captain and writer, he had become the leading light of the Marylebone Cricket Club.

Warner had a fractious relationship with Jardine, whom he disliked. The captain's response was to cold-shoulder the manager. Warner said of Jardine, 'He is a queer fellow. When he sees a cricket ground with an Australian on it, he goes mad.'

Warner and Palairet had come to ask how Woodfull was.

But Woodfull, like many other Australians, thought Warner was a fence sitter, trying to appeal to both sides without actually taking a stand. Even though he publicly criticised leg-theory tactics before the team left for Australia, Warner never spoke out against Bodyline during the tour. That, to many in the Australian side, smacked of hypocrisy.

What happened next became one of the most explosive issues of the series—and perhaps its greatest mystery.

8

The Leak

Later that night, an Australian Test cricketer telephoned journalist Claude Corbett in his hotel room and said he had some important information to pass on. The cricketer stressed that this must be totally confidential. Corbett must keep his identity a secret.

The cricketer knew Corbett abhorred Jardine. After Jardine had refused to give Corbett his team list in Perth, Corbett had had another run-in with Jardine in Adelaide during which he had told the Englishman, 'You can go and fuck yourself.' Corbett would be an ideal vehicle for what the cricketer had to say.

Corbett and his caller met in the cricketer's car, which was parked several kilometres from Adelaide Oval. The cricketer, knowing he would be immediately detected if any fans wandered past his car, had driven to a secluded spot near the Adelaide Parklands. There, the cricketer told the journalist what had happened when Pelham Warner came to see Bill Woodfull.

'How are you, Bill?' Warner said.

'I don't want to speak to you, Mr Warner. I don't want to discuss it,' Woodfull replied.

'Why?'

'There are two teams out there,' Woodfull continued. 'One is trying to play cricket and the other is not. It is making no effort to play the game. Cricket is too great a game to be spoilt by the tactics which your team is adopting. I don't approve of them, and never will. It's time some people got out of it. If these tactics are persevered with, it may be better if I do not play the game. The matter is in your hands, Mr Warner, and I have nothing further to say to you. Good afternoon.'

Warner said he hoped Woodfull was not hurt, but the captain brushed his sympathies aside. A chastened Warner had no alternative but to leave.

Following the rest day, every newspaper reader in Australia was a vicarious witness to the dressing room incident. 'Woodfull Protests,' the headlines read. A furious Warner demanded an apology. Woodfull refused. By Monday, the contretemps was the only news in Australia. Corbett, writing for *The Sun* and its stable mate the *Daily Telegraph*, had the most extensive report. In a story that led the *Telegraph*'s front page he wrote: 'Fires which have been smouldering in the ranks of the Australian Test cricketers regarding the English shock attack suddenly burst into flames yesterday when "Bill" Woodfull, Australian captain, spoke his mind to Mr P.F. Warner, English manager.'

Corbett wrote that Warner had learned from Australia's twelfth man Leo O'Brien that Woodfull was in a bad way in the dressing room. When he went in to see him, Woodfull was resting on the masseur's table, 'awaiting the verdict of the doctor who had examined him'.

After outlining the conversation, Corbett said there were 'several members of the Australian team and others present while

Woodfull was speaking, but Mr Warner did not reply. He seemed staggered, and walked from the dressing room.'

Corbett noted that Warner was in 'an unenviable position' because 'in his journalistic capacity in England he had expressed decided objections to the bowling of leg theory'.

Several months earlier, Warner had written in the London *Morning Post* that when Bowes bowled short-pitched deliveries for Yorkshire with five men on the on side, it was 'not cricket'. Bowes was 'not doing justice to himself, to his ability, or to the game of cricket by his present methods'.

Corbett's insinuation was that Warner was a hypocrite, complaining about Bowes one day but then refusing to stand up to Jardine.

Corbett—believing the leak was too hot to keep to himself— had shared it with other reporters. The rest of the Australian press had headed to the Barossa Valley on the Sunday rest day for a function at Seppelts Winery. Corbett remained in Adelaide, worked on his story and sent it, before informing the rest of the journalists when they returned that evening. The *Sydney Morning Herald* said it was known 'that the Australian players bitterly resent this bowling by the Englishmen, and Woodfull's protest was the sequel to a number of incidents'.

The *Adelaide Advertiser* said the dressing-room story was being repeated 'by several members of the Australian team'.

The reports galvanised the nation. Woodfull had been dignified in the face of the Bodyline attack. Now all of Australia knew exactly what he thought of it—and that at least some in the England camp were uneasy about Bodyline.

The protests grew louder—so loud they were finally heard in England. When Bert Oldfield was struck on the skull by a Larwood delivery on Monday, the third day of play, the Board of Control was forced into action.

Oldfield, who was batting comfortably at the time, prompting

Larwood to say, 'Good shot, Bert' when he caressed one of his deliveries through the covers, seemed bamboozled by his next ball. He first appeared to want to cut it, then decided to pull it through mid-wicket, only to have it rebound into his temple. Oldfield careered off the pitch, hands to his head, and fell to his knees.

As the England team rushed to Oldfield's aid, a riot appeared inevitable. It just needed one of the infuriated crowd to jump the fence. Fortunately, none did.

Woodfull, in his business suit—he had just been a guest with Bradman in the Governor of South Australia's private viewing box—strode out, took Oldfield's arm, and walked him back to the dressing room. Oldfield was taken to hospital, where a steel plate was placed in his fractured skull.

At the close of play, Warner again made a visit to the Australian dressing room. This time, Vic Richardson answered the door. Warner wanted to see Woodfull.

Richardson asked why. Warner said: 'Because I want an apology from the Australian player who called Larwood a bastard.'

Richardson turned and loudly asked his teammates: 'Which one of you blokes mistook Larwood for that bastard Jardine?'

Two days later, as England completed a 338-run victory to go 2–1 ahead in the series, the Board sent a cable of complaint to the MCC, protesting that England's Bodyline bowling was a 'menace' and 'unsportsmanlike'.

'Unless stopped at once likely to upset friendly relations existing between Australia and England,' the cable concluded.

In the following days and weeks, the issue was argued over by Australian and British cricket officials, diplomats and government ministers.

Almost as venomous—and in Fingleton's case just as harmful—was the debate over who had leaked the dressing-room conversation. Fingleton was convinced that Bradman was the leaker. In later years, he repeatedly wrote this as fact, including the account of the North Terrace rendezvous with Corbett. Bradman, rather than suing Fingleton for these claims, preferred merely to insinuate that Fingleton was the culprit.

The issue fatally poisoned their already strained relationship.

Plum Warner, meanwhile, believed it was Fingleton, the only full-time journalist in the Australian team. A furious Warner told Larwood he would give him one pound if he could bowl Fingleton out in the second innings. And he did. A classic delivery from Larwood pitched on middle and leg stump, then cut across Fingleton, taking his off stump. He was dismissed. As Fingleton headed to the dressing room, the future Prime Minister Menzies turned in his seat to talk to the former Australian captain Warwick Armstrong. 'That's a terrible thing to happen to a young cricketer, Warwick,' Menzies said. 'How can you account for it?'

Armstrong took his pipe out of his mouth, and drawled: 'Can't bat.'

That duck, added to his previous one, threatened to torpedo his chances of selection for the final two Tests.

His only chance now was the second NSW–MCC match in Sydney, a week after Adelaide.

As he headed to the ground, he knew at least one sizable score was required if he was to hold on to his spot for the Brisbane or Sydney Tests.

At the same time his new opening partner, Bill Brown, was catching another tram at Marrickville. As he got on, with his cricket bat slung onto the side of an old kit bag, the conductor looked him up and down before asking: 'Where ya going, son?'

'I'm going to Moore Park for the cricket,' Brown replied. The conductor laughed, looked at the youngster's bat, and said: 'You won't get a game there, son . . . There's a big match on. England is playing.'

Brown, the young pup of the NSW team, kept quiet for the rest of the trip.

Fingleton followed Brown to the dressing rooms. Seventy-five years later, Brown recalled that just inside the door was NSW skipper Alan Kippax, who looked surprisingly relaxed.

Brown asked Kippax: 'Who's playing?'

Kippax said it was more a matter of who wasn't playing. Several England players were going to be rested—including Larwood, Voce, Allen and even Jardine.

Recalled Brown: 'When we heard Larwood and Voce weren't playing, suddenly the sun was shining, the grass was greener, and the birds were singing.'

For Fingleton, it was gloomier. Brown took to the England B attack, combining with another youngster, Ray Rowe, in scoring the bulk of NSW's flimsy first-innings score of 180. Fingleton even had to play the minor role to Brown, scoring 19 of their 58 runs in partnership before he misjudged spinner Tommy Mitchell and was bowled around his legs.

It wasn't much better in the second innings. He was caught plumb in front of the stumps by Maurice Tate for seven, and Brown, who finished with 69 in the first innings, again outscored him with 25. Even if the match proved that Fingleton was versatile—he took over the wicket-keeping gloves from the injured Hammy Love to stump Les Ames in the second innings—he knew he was doomed. A two-innings tally of 26 runs was not going to stop the Test selectors looking for someone else to accompany Bill Woodfull in Brisbane.

Vic Richardson was handed that role for the rest of the Bodyline series, and Fingleton was left to brood. When he had top-scored in Melbourne, a notable Australian businessman sought him out, wined and dined him. Then came the two ducks. The following day, the same distinguished gentleman was sighted on an Adelaide street walking straight towards Fingleton. When the businessman saw the luckless batsman he quickly crossed to the other side of the street to avoid a meeting.

9

The Aftermath

That infamous afternoon in Adelaide hung over him like a black fog.

During the series, after explaining that Woodfull did not use a chest pad until the second innings of the Adelaide Test, Fingleton noted his response to claims that the Australian batsmen were fearful: 'Despite what some critics would have us think, Australian players have not squealed, and will not squeal—no matter what their gruel may be—but it is like rubbing salt into an open wound to hear talk about "fear complex" and having the "wind up".'

Fingleton explained how disturbed he had been by the Oldfield incident. 'It has come at last,' he wrote from Adelaide. 'As we players looked down at Bertie Oldfield as he lay, white as a sheet on the dressing room floor this afternoon, one could not help thinking that all along we had expected something like this. It was a frightening experience for Oldfield, and nauseating for those who witnessed it.'

At the end of the summer *Smith's Weekly* quoted him: 'I do not know of one batsman who has ever played fast Bodyline bowling who is not of the opinion that it will kill cricket if allowed to continue.'

The first inkling of the high price Fingleton would pay for being the alleged dressing-room leaker came a year or so later when he was overlooked for the 1934 England team. He remained suspicious of Woodfull and Bradman's involvement in the selection of that team.

Woodfull, one of the selectors, had made it well known that he was disgusted with whoever had leaked the story. Bradman, who was consulted by the selectors before the 1934 touring squad was picked, may have been covering his own back. Fingleton feared he had been made a scapegoat.

In 1942, Warner published a memoir titled *Cricket Between Two Wars*, in which he recalled the Adelaide incident: 'Unfortunately, our remarks were overheard by a member of the Australian XI who was connected with the Press, and next day, Sunday, they were blazoned all over the newspapers.'

Fingleton immediately assumed Warner was referring to him, and wrote to him, explaining that he was wrong. Warner said he was prepared to make a correction if the facts were provided. In his celebrated first book *Cricket Crisis*, published in 1946, Fingleton chastised Warner for targeting him, stating that he 'did not give the story out, and it is regrettable, from my viewpoint, that Sir Pelham did not check his facts before he made such an ill-founded statement. I know, as do others, who gave the story out, and unlike Sir Pelham, I can give facts . . .'

By then he had those facts straight from Corbett's mouth. Corbett and Fingleton were close friends. There was also a family link with the Fingletons, with Jack's younger brother Wally going to school with Corbett's son Mac. Corbett—according to Fingleton—felt he had been the victim of a slur campaign and told him the leaker was Bradman. For many years, however, Fingleton kept this to himself.

Two years later during the 1948 Ashes tour, Fingleton, accompanied by Bill O'Reilly, bumped into Warner in Hastings, England.

O'Reilly recalled the conversation in his autobiography, *Tiger*:

> 'Good morning, Sir Pelham,' Fingo began. 'Top of the morning to you. I have been waiting a long time for an opportunity to ask whether you still think that I was the culprit who leaked the story about your famous conference with Woodfull in Adelaide.'
>
> These forthright words were typical of Fingleton's approach. Warner replied immediately: 'Indeed no, Jack. I have reason to believe now that in my first hasty reaction when I wrote that you were the prime candidate for the disclosure I was wrong. I am sorry and I apologize.'

Shortly after Fingleton received his copy of Warner's book he wrote to Bill Woodfull, asking whether Warner's accusation had anything to do with him missing out on the 1934 tour. Woodfull wrote back: 'I can assure you that I did not connect your name with "the passing on" of that conversation. Indeed I seem to recall that you told me on the day it was published that you had nothing to do with it.'

Woodfull said he did not know who was responsible for the leak, as 'I have always expected cricketers to do the right thing by their teammates. Certainly the question was never raised when the 1934 team for England was under discussion and I think that was the only selection committee I sat on which concerned you.'

Fingleton wasn't convinced.

Several decades later, when Fingleton told Woodfull that Bradman was the culprit, Woodfull replied: 'A pity. That cost you a trip to England.'

At the same time as the Woodfull letter, Fingleton wrote to Board of Control official Bill Jeanes asking what he recalled of the incident and seeking his opinion of Warner. In particular, he wanted to know if Jeanes thought Warner had done enough to stop Bodyline taking shape. Jeanes conveniently sidestepped the dressing-room incident, but in the letter, which he stressed was confidential, he was quick to defend Warner.

'Don't be too hard on Plum,' Jeanes wrote. 'He was terribly distressed about the business and I really believe did all he could to stop it.'

Jeanes said Warner 'could make no impression on Jardine and was a most unhappy man. He loathed the whole business, but was in a most difficult position in that he had no control over field tactics.

'I have seldom seen anyone more distressed than Warner was in Adelaide.'

Jeanes said the main problem had been that the MCC 'did not believe things were as bad as they were'.

Fingleton doggedly refused to let the matter drop.

He finally decided to name names when writing a biography on Victor Trumper in 1978. He was advised by several journalists and friends, including O'Reilly, to forget about the issue. However Fingleton was adamant. He had been hurt too much by this slur. The truth had to be told.

As a journalist and writer, he was well versed in the libel laws. He knew he had to be sure of his facts, because if Bradman was not the culprit, he could sue.

Fingleton wrote that Corbett, 'then writing for *The Sun* and a colleague of mine,' had given him this account of the fateful evening: 'I got a ring on the phone that night at our hotel. It was from Don Bradman, who told me he wanted to tell me some-thing. Don was also working in a third-sense for *The Sun*, being associated with a broadcasting firm and a sports store. We arranged a rendezvous on North Terrace and, while we sat in his car, he told me all about the Warner–Woodfull incident. It was too hot a story to run on my own, and I gave it to all the Press.'

Fingleton wrote that he had 'always held it against the Don that he did not own up and clear me'.

Fingleton repeated the story in 1981, in his final book, *Batting from Memory*. 'For years I was given the blame,' he wrote.

> 'Plum' very much pointed the bone at me. Bradman would have saved me a lot of backlash in the game had he admitted that he had given the leak. Part of his job was writing for the Sydney *Sun* and he had every right to leak such a vital story.
>
> Warner was being more than naïve, in the tumult and tenseness of those times, if he thought a story like that wouldn't surface from the Australian room. One other of our team had a strong press affiliation.

Bradman used other writers to get back at Fingleton. Shelves full of Bradman biographies were published. The hagiographic tone of several of them exasperated Test teammates of Bradman, who knew that Australia's greatest cricketer was no more flawless than any other man. In 1983, two years after Fingleton's death, a biography by Michael Page that relied on 'the private possessions of Sir Donald Bradman' and was vetted by the Don, stated that Fingleton was the 'man who snapped up this tit-bit'.

'Fingleton soon realised he had stirred up a whirlwind and he always denied responsibility for this breach of confidence. In later years he attempted to shift the blame onto Bradman, against whom he carried a grudge for an incident that had nothing to do with bodyline.'

The biographer added that Fingleton 'shortly before he died
. . . circulated an absurd fabrication' about Bradman having a
meeting with Corbett and leaking Woodfull's comments. Noting
that Fingleton had not made his allegation until after Corbett's
death, Page wrote that Bradman had 'always resented this slur on
his reputation and integrity'.

Bradman maintained that he did not hear Woodfull's remark,
that Fingleton's story was a lie, and that he had no part in leaking
the incident to the press. Fingleton's story, Page wrote, was 'yet
another of the smears invented by lesser men'.

Fingleton's mate Bill O'Reilly was not prepared to let this
slur pass.

In *Tiger*, O'Reilly wrote that 'had he [Fingleton] lived long
enough to find himself branded a liar one can imagine the spon-
taneity of his vigorous reaction. From my first-hand experience
of Fingleton, formed over fifty years of sport, business and social
friendship, never did I get the slightest impression that he was
a liar. He was not.'

In numerous conversations with the author over many
years, O'Reilly repeatedly stated that he was convinced Bradman
was the Bodyline leaker, and that he wanted the dressing-room
exchange made public in order to counter England's tactics,
which he fervently believed were aimed at physically injuring
him. Personal safety, according to O'Reilly, was the Don's prime
motive.

'The Knight [Bradman] was a master of diverting blame. Jack
did not leak the Bodyline story. I know Jack. I know the Don.
I know who to trust,' O'Reilly told me.

If the culprit was Bradman, however, he had a busy night.
As well as meeting Corbett in North Terrace, he also visited
the studios of Radio 5AD, where he vented his disdain for the
England tactics.

'To my mind,' Bradman told his Adelaide listeners, 'it is

practically impossible for even our leading batsmen to make runs against the present type of English attack without getting at least one or two severe cracks. Bowlers cannot afford to get hit, especially on the fingers, and if recognised batsmen cannot prevent their fingers being hit, how much more dangerous is it for the bowlers.'

The renowned British journalist and broadcaster Michael Parkinson, who developed an intense friendship with Fingleton, found Page's allegations less than credible. In an article in Australia's *National Times* newspaper, he wrote:

> Unlike Page, I knew Jack Fingleton well. He was not a liar.
>
> He was an honourable and scrupulous man who believed Bradman to be the greatest player who ever lived. He was also intelligent and perceptive enough to realise that the superstar he grew up with was a complex and enigmatic figure.
>
> Fingleton, being a proper journalist, wanted to define the mystery, seek the truth behind the legend. Had Page ever spent more than a couple of hours in Fingleton's company, he might have written a better book and one more worthy of sport's greatest figure and most profound mystery.

Roland Perry, who wrote several books about Bradman, pushed the Don's case.

In his 1995 biography, also written with Bradman's close involvement, Perry claimed that Warner had confronted Corbett and asked who gave him the information. Corbett purportedly replied: 'Jack Fingleton.'

This account has been laughed off by many informed observers, including one of cricket's most authoritative analysts, David Frith.

Frith enjoyed a long, fruitful, but sometimes rocky relationship with Fingleton, but as a young writer during the 1968 Ashes tour of England, he sat beside Fingleton in cricket press boxes and revelled in the retired cricketer's wisdom.

During that series Fingleton told Frith that Bradman was to blame for the leak. Then he gave one of his famous 'if looks could kill' glares, before adding: 'But don't you breathe a word of this while I'm alive!'

Frith didn't.

While researching *Bodyline Autopsy*, his outstanding book on the 1932–33 series, Frith spent considerable time looking into the dressing-room incident, and uncovered information that backed Fingleton. One key source was Australian journalist Gilbert Mant, who covered the Bodyline tour for the Reuters news service. When Mant died, in 1997, his widow sent Frith a parcel that included a letter written by Mant containing details on the leak. The letter explained that while researching his 1992 book, *A Cuckoo in the Bodyline Nest*, he had been in contact with Bradman. Bradman had told Mant that as he was the only journalist alive who was part of the Bodyline media contingent, he could 'put the record straight'. Bradman had continued to claim that Fingleton was the 'culprit' and said he refused to forgive him for the 'dastardly lie he concocted about me'.

Bradman told Mant there were numerous reasons for Fingleton's animosity towards him. These included religious differences and the fact that Bradman preferred Bill Brown as a batsman.

Mant decided to investigate further. He contacted Claude Corbett's son Mac, who told him his father had never mentioned the dressing-room incident to him. Mant then questioned Corbett's daughter Helen. She had told him that after Corbett's death in 1944, her mother had confided to her that her father had explained 'Bradman had been the culprit, confirming the secret of the after-dark meeting as alleged by Fingleton'.

Mant was in a quandary. 'Now where does that leave us?'

Mant wrote in his letter to Frith. 'I believe implicitly in Bradman's denial and have no reason to doubt [Helen's] story. Claude Corbett was a down-to-earth, hard-drinking and convivial character, fond of a practical joke. Perhaps he had perpetrated a gigantic leg-pull on Fingleton, but it was scarcely conceivable that he would do the same thing to his wife.'

Frith also telephoned Corbett's daughter, who confirmed the story.

The Fingleton family have always vehemently defended Jack on this issue, supporting his claim—made often in later years—that he had been the victim of a 'blatant injustice—blamed for something I had nothing to do with'.

His brother Wally was adamant that Jack 'would never tell an untruth'.

'Jack's integrity can never be questioned,' Wally said. 'Bradman waited until Jack had died until he came out with some comments. Bill O'Reilly was very voluble on the subject.'

In 1997, after *Sydney Morning Herald* columnist Gerard Henderson suggested that Fingleton may have been the source of the leak, Wally wrote to the paper. 'My brother, Jack, was in journalism from his teenage years,' he wrote. 'Journalists, at that time anyway, had to learn the ethics of the profession and observe them.' Wally said that in accusing Fingleton, Warner had been 'acting on a false presumption and egregious lack of logic'. 'Foremost ethical sports writer of that period, Claude Corbett, revealed the source, or one of the sources, of that Adelaide leak, and it was not Jack Fingleton. Bradman says that it was not he. Corbett says it was.'

Seven years later, Wally again responded to criticism of Fingleton in Christine Wallace's book *The Private Don*, which revolved around letters between Bradman and journalist Rohan Rivett. In an interview with *Sydney Morning Herald* journalist Philip Derriman, Wally said: 'I was close to Jack, and I know he did not tell lies. Honesty and courage were his great virtues. It was absolutely wrong to call Jack a liar.'

Another staunch defender of Fingleton's reputation has been his son-in-law Malcolm Gemmell, who married Fingleton's eldest daughter, Belinda. Gemmell, a Sydney solicitor, is trustee of the Jack Fingleton estate. Shortly after Page's biography on Bradman was published, Gemmell wrote an extensive letter to the *Australian*, which had printed extracts from the book. The paper published the letter as an article. In it, Gemmell explained in intricate detail the evidence supporting Fingleton's assertion that Bradman was to blame for the leak.

Gemmell said Fingleton had written about the meeting in three of his books and that there was 'a great deal of logic' in his father-in-law's case for numerous reasons. These included that Corbett worked for the Sydney *Sun*, to which Bradman was contracted; Bradman had prior to the Adelaide Test 'vigorously protested' against Bodyline and had urged the Board of Control 'to do likewise but the board had refused'; Bradman was engaged in a dispute with the Board over his writing and broadcasting contracts and was 'openly criticising' England's tactics; and 'the dressing-room incident presented a marvellous opportunity to press home what was already a very strong argument against Bodyline'.

Gemmell wrote: 'Jack Fingleton has never asserted that Bradman heard Woodfull's remark first hand and of course one would not have to hear the remark first hand to pass it on. For those who ever knew Fingleton to say his story was a lie, having regard to his character, is inconceivable. As indicated earlier there was ample opportunity after 1978 for the matter to be aired while Jack was still alive and it is a pity he is not here to defend himself against Page's statements.'

When Perry's book appeared, Gemmell also wrote to him, via his publisher, explaining that the Fingleton family were incensed by the claim that Jack had 'made up a story'. These comments were 'all the more galling' because 'honesty was at the forefront of Jack's personality'.

Gemmell noted that between 1978, when Fingleton named names in his Victor Trumper biography, and his death, three years elapsed, but 'during this period there was no response'. It was only after Fingleton had died 'and Jack was not alive to defend himself' that the Fingleton-is-to-blame line had once more gathered momentum. The family did not receive a reply from Perry.

Gemmell also wrote to Frith in 2002 praising his book *Bodyline Autopsy*. He said the Fingleton family were pleased that 'some verifiable corroboration' had finally been unearthed over the dressing-room leak, and that it had also been aired in an ABC documentary on the subject. 'As for Gilbert Mant's suggestion that perhaps Corbett had pulled a gigantic leg-pull on Fingleton, I think that smacks somewhat of desperation,' Gemmell wrote.

'More likely, and as I expect you would appreciate, it may well have been a disclosure made in the context of journalist to journalist or with an innate desire on the part of Corbett, the man as well as journalist, for fairness and truthfulness to ultimately prevail so the record could be set straight.'

Around the same time, the *Sydney Morning Herald*'s political correspondent, Alan Ramsey, penned a glowing tribute to Fingleton. In a letter of appreciation, Gemmell wrote: 'The growing tendency of the Australian public, encouraged by a manipulative media, to elevate its sporting heroes (warts and all) to sainthood status is a bit on the rich side. It clouds the realities of human frailties and flaws. Truth becomes lost in a sea of sentiment and emotion.'

Amid the many files of letters that Fingleton kept were two from Australian cricket writer Ray Robinson. Fingleton and Robinson were professional rivals, and in private the player at times took pot shots at Robinson. But they still respected each other immensely.

In one letter Robinson said it was to Fingleton's credit 'that you have qualms now and again about whether you are too hard on the little bloke [Bradman] in spilling the beans. But surely the essential point is to give a truthful picture that cannot be refuted and at the same time to take pains in the writing of it to avoid the faintest suggestion of any personal antagonism?'

Shortly after, Robinson wrote to Fingleton about an article he had to write on Woodfull for *People* magazine. 'Thanks for your guidance on that matter of Bill Woodfull's rebuke to Plum Warner. Bill Corbett confirmed what you said.' Bill Corbett was Claude's brother, a boxing and football journalist.

In another article, Robinson confirmed that many players believed Fingleton was not the culprit. 'This deduction by Sir Pelham ran counter to a well-founded belief in the Australian team that another batsman with quick perception, realising the full significance of his captain's reproof, thought it would be a mistake if the truth were hushed up,' he wrote. He added that the players were also aware of this batsman's rendezvous with Corbett on North Terrace, and that 'not to leave an obvious trail', Corbett had shared the story around.

Michael Davie, the former editor of the Melbourne *Age*, offered an interesting insight when he expressed regret for not posing a key question to Bill Ponsford. In the early 1980s Davie visited Ponsford, who produced his scrapbooks. The subject of Bradman came up, and as Ponsford turned a page, he said to Davie: 'Bill Woodfull never forgave him for a couple of things.'

Davie didn't press him on what those 'couple of things' were.

'What might have been the answers to the question I failed to ask?' he wondered.

Davie said that Woodfull was irritated by the dressing-room leak.

'Woodfull, I suppose, might have known that Bradman was responsible and held it against him for not coming clean,' Davie wrote.

Numerous teammates were also convinced that Woodfull was disappointed in Bradman for being so nervous about Bodyline. Some said that at one stage the captain was even deliberating over whether the Don should be dropped from the team.

The claims and counter-claims over the Adelaide Test incident will continue. And with all the actors in the drama now gone, the exact sequence of events will never be revealed to the satisfaction of everyone. However, those who back Fingleton have justifiable reasons for believing Bradman deliberately undermined him. And not just on the cricket field.

10

Standing His Ground

Jack Fingleton could be abrasive, petulant and infuriatingly forthright. He had a way of upsetting people. He spoke his mind, even when diplomacy was the smarter option. It was the cheeky, headstrong Irishman in him. Journalism, and the dogged effort of extracting the truth from evasive sometimes deceptive, sources, had given him a cynical streak.

But he never hid in the shadows or let other people do his dirty work. Nor did he fear confrontation. If he thought he had been maligned, he would immediately confront the person responsible. 'Jack had strong convictions,' said his brother Wally. 'He was not an aggressive man, but he was never backwards in coming forwards.'

When Fingleton was left out of the Australian team chosen to tour England in 1934, he blamed Bradman, and told him so.

Fingleton was incensed that on the day the team was selected, Bradman had used the pages of his own newspaper, the Sydney *Sun*, to criticise his running between the wickets.

Shortly after the members of the touring squad were

announced, Fingleton and Bradman bumped into each other in *The Sun* offices. Fingleton shook Bradman's hand and wished him well for the tour. When Bradman replied 'Bad luck'—for having been omitted—Fingleton gave him a piercing look and said, 'I think I have largely got you to thank for missing out.'

End of conversation.

Fingleton believed he deserved to go. He had been one of the top NSW batsmen that season, scoring 665 runs at 59.54. Ahead of him were Bradman, with 1192 runs at 132.44; Bill Brown, 878 at 67.53; and Alan Kippax, 863 at 71.91.

But he was certain there was a concerted campaign against him, and that Woodfull, Bradman and wicketkeeper Bert Oldfield had undermined him by talking him down to the Australian selectors. Apart from questioning Fingleton's running, when Bradman was asked to weigh Fingleton against his NSW opening partner Bill Brown, he sided with Brown, arguing that his technique would probably be better suited to English wickets. Bradman later said he thought Brown was a better opener than Fingleton.

He conceded that his opinion 'might have had some bearing on' the selectors' decision, and believed his involvement was 'why Fingleton conducted this vendetta against me'.

On that he was wrong. The England tour freeze-out was just one of many grievances Fingleton had against Bradman.

Fingleton also felt a distinct cooling in Bill Woodfull's attitude to him. And Woodfull was himself a selector. Bert Oldfield was another question mark. Fingleton thought that for several of his NSW teammates, 'the belief that I had leaked the Warner–Woodfull story . . . didn't do much for me . . . I sensed I was not liked personally by Bradman, and Oldfield would have his own special reason for not wanting me in the side . . . Though he could be most charming and was generally liked, most of us regarded him [Oldfield] with suspicion. He had a habit of asking mighty personal questions and we considered him a leaker of dressing-room gossip.'

In a crucial NSW–Victoria match at the time the Test team was being picked, in late January 1934, Fingleton had scored a century. He expected that to clinch his place. But several incidents during the match had the opposite effect.

The Victorian bowling attack was a worthy opposition against which to show his mettle. It included such notables as pacemen Ernie McCormick and Hans Ebeling, and spinners Bert Ironmonger and Les 'Chuck' Fleetwood-Smith. Fingleton and Brown handled them with aplomb. Until Jack had to retire hurt after an accidental blow to his calf when he was 78, the opening pair was near unstoppable.

The following day, Fingleton returned and completed his century, while Brown went on to score a double century. However, when Fingleton was on 86, he attempted to cut 51-year-old Ironmonger through the covers, only to edge the ball to the slips, where Ebeling dropped it. Ebeling threw the ball to wicketkeeper Ben Barnett, who, noticing that Fingleton had wandered along the wicket to pat down part of the pitch, removed the bails and appealed. Umpire George Borwick dismissed Fingleton as run out.

Fingleton gave Barnett an icy look and headed to the pavilion, but Bill Woodfull, the Victorian captain, raced after him, grabbed him by the arm, and asked him to come back. 'We don't want wickets like that,' Woodfull said sportingly.

'No, Bill, the umpire has given me out. I must go.'

Woodfull said he would ask the umpire to change his decision, and Borwick did so. Fingleton completed his century and went on to score 145.

After the innings, NSW skipper Kippax told Fingleton it was wrong to argue, or seem to be arguing, with Woodfull. Fingleton dismissed that perception as a misunderstanding, but it took hold. Popular belief was that Fingleton and Woodfull had had words. Or, as *Australian Cricketer* magazine put it: 'Fingleton rather resented being given out for taking what he considered to be a batsman's privilege.'

The brief exchange between the pair became such an issue that the NSW Cricket Association discussed the incident at its March 1934 meeting. The executive committee had been asked to inquire into the matter, and provide a report on the respective powers of the captain and the umpire to change a decision. Letters had been written to Woodfull, Fingleton and the umpires seeking their views. Fingleton did not reply.

Bill O'Reilly later said he thought the run-out incident 'might have cost Fingleton his trip'. 'His reluctance to seize Woodfull's hospitality may have been construed quite wrongly by people in executive cricket positions.'

If that didn't unsettle Fingleton, then what Bradman wrote in his *Sun* recap of the game certainly did. Recalling the run-out of NSW batsman Ray Rowe, Bradman wrote that he had driven the ball to mid-off and run, 'only to be left stranded, as Fingleton declined the run . . . Fingleton's running showed considerable improvement until the occasion when Rowe was run out,' Bradman concluded. 'Jack can run fast and can judge a run well, but he must learn to respect his partner's judgement as well as his own.'

An infuriated Fingleton avoided Bradman for the rest of the match.

More than forty years later, the slight still festered. In *Batting from Memory*, Fingleton related Bradman's 'vitriolic attack'. 'This article from Bradman at such a time was, I thought, hitting a bit low.'

Fingleton believed Bradman must already 'have known that I would not be in the team, else he wouldn't have written so critically of a teammate. Moreover I found out later that Bradman's opinion on the tour had been sought by several of the selectors and that he didn't favour me. That probably was fair enough but, occasionally seeing his capers against Bodyline from the other end, he wasn't top of the pops with me either at that particular time.'

Bradman, however, wasn't the only critic of Fingleton's running. W.M. Rutledge, in *The Referee*, wrote that his 'running between the wickets has been most unsatisfactory this season, and again in this match he showed far too much tendency to ignore his partner's call. One bad runner makes two bad runners. Thus Brown was unable to do justice to himself in running while Fingleton was his partner.'

The *Sydney Mail's* Dr Eric Barbour agreed, saying Fingleton 'still exhibits the bad fault of interfering with his partner's legitimate call. No player can achieve confidence between the wickets if he is continually sent back after calling for what appears to be an easy single.'

But he had his defenders too, including Johnny Moyes, the *Sunday Sun* sports editor, who said he would have selected Fingleton, 'who will play better cricket on the other side'. Arthur Mailey also picked Fingleton.

When the team was announced, *The Sun* headlined its story 'Fingleton Misses a Place', and said the selection of Arthur Chipperfield ahead of Fingleton was a surprise.

In a bitter letter to Woodfull, Fingleton said he felt disgraced. 'Apart from the recognition of being chosen to represent one's country and the pleasure and joys of such a trip, there is a recompense that would give me a good financial, social and educational footing in life,' he wrote. To be deprived of that 'is a sickening blow to oneself, Mother and family and immediate friends. I do think the selectors are illogical. One solitary Test failure—in a season of immeasurable Test failures—would seem to have drowned me. When I top scored for your side in Melbourne

in the only Test Australia won last season, I was sitting on top
of the cricket world. One failure and out of everything. You,
yourself, did not have a successful match against the English in
the Third Test.'

Fingleton then chronicled all his best innings, including
several important knocks against the South Africans, while
reminding his captain of the 'hidings' he had taken during the
Bodyline series after Woodfull had implored 'various batsmen to
stand up'.

'You knew what a very few of us went through last season
and how many did their darndest for you and Australia; and it
was because of that that I expected much of you this season. But
Bill, you hardly gave me your usual cheery "good day" on the
field—a fact I could not help but notice with apprehension.'

Fingleton wrote that there were those in the Australian side
'who probably do not want me as a teammate', while 'fellow
pressmen, naturally jealous, were not the only ones I had to fight
against last season'. Nonetheless, he concluded, 'I think 655 runs
at 59 was surely good enough—allied to my fielding. I'm sure you
were not only wrong, but inconsistent as you have chosen chaps
who obviously do not like fast bowling and others, I think, who
might as well remain on the *Orford* [ship], when you encounter
turning and sticky wickets. And your fielding side—well!'

Fingleton noted that several players had told him they were
surprised by his omission. Even Jardine had commiserated with
him, writing: 'Never mind, they cannot possibly leave you out of
the trip to England.'

(At the end of the Adelaide Bodyline Test Jardine had come
to the Australian dressing-room door and asked for Fingleton.
'I'm sorry,' he said, 'that you had to bag a pair. But don't worry.
Some very good men have had the same experience.' According
to Fingleton, those words 'forged a friendship' between him and
Jardine.)

Fingleton continued: 'You are probably disgusted with me for writing this but had you missed a tour such as I have, you'd know what a relief it is to get it off your chest. Finally let me again assure you that my opinion of your judgement has in no way warped my opinion of you as a man. My admiration of you will not be changing and again, I wish you good fortune.'

It is unknown whether Woodfull replied to this missile, but it is unlikely. Fingleton fastidiously kept copies of every important letter he wrote and its reply. No Woodfull reply was found in the Fingleton files.

Wally Fingleton said his brother 'always held it against Bradman for not getting picked for that tour. He thought Bradman had poisoned the well. He impugned Jack's character, especially at the time he was so far ahead of everyone else in the batting averages. There were a number of little threads to this disagreement involving Jack and the Don. The thought among many of his colleagues was that Bradman wasn't a team man. He was off making money, and was in such demand that he was not always a team bloke.'

A man who never left anything to doubt, Fingleton wrote to Bradman after the tour was over, seeking his side of the story. Bradman replied in April 1936:

In your moment of extreme disappointment at missing selection for England in 1934 you appeared rather bitter against me and expressed the opinion that my press utterances had helped keep you out of the team.

At the time you would not listen to my denial of this accusation, but I feel quite certain that a subsequent dispassionate perusal of my comments have convinced you that they were in no sense personal, but were fair comments in the ordinary course of match description.

Your own writings since that date must have led you to the

realisation that it is impossible to please every participant in every game unless the writer regards the contest as being perfect, and such happenings do not occur.

If you remember the occasion I refer to, you may recollect a statement I made to you that you were only a young man and that you sink your momentary disappointment and strive to attain greater heights in order to make the England trip in 1938. That you have already made such a vast improvement is a tribute not only to your skill, but also to your pluck and determination, which qualities makes your future success unlimited. You will undoubtedly play in next season's Tests, and if it is my privilege to be one of your teammates I hope to witness for myself many fine scores from your bat, to the credit of yourself and your country.

Bradman ended the letter by asking Fingleton to send his regards to, among others, Claude Corbett and Johnny Moyes.

Although Fingleton never completely got over that tour omission, he was eventually able to put it in perspective. After all, seven of the squad were from NSW, and if Woodfull and Charles Dolling, a Victorian and a South Australian, had added an eighth, they 'would have been slaughtered on their return home,' he wrote.

Some of Fingleton's teammates also thought the prime reason Ernie Bromley got in ahead of him was that he was playing for Victoria.

At the time, NSW and Victoria dominated cricket affairs, and there was a distinct rivalry between the two, even at the administration level. The final make-up of the squad was seven from NSW, seven from Victoria and two from South Australia.

The Board attempted to soften the blow on Fingleton by at least giving him a representative tour at the end of the season. New Zealand had been lobbying for an Australian team to visit.

Australia eventually agreed, and selected a thirteen-man side for an eight-week tour at the end of the 1933–34 season.

The team, to be skippered by Victor Richardson, was to include Fingleton, Charlie Badcock, Ernie McCormick, Lisle Nagel and Hughie Chilvers. Fingleton was named a tour selector, and after numerous withdrawals, including those of Richardson and his vice-captain Keith Rigg, who were unhappy with the poor pay on offer, was elevated to vice-captain. However, the team went nowhere. Concerned that the lack of big-name Australian cricketers in the squad would make the tour a financial flop, New Zealand called it off.

To salve his wounds Fingleton focused on his journalism, working extra shifts if he could but still keeping a close eye on the cables coming through with the latest scores and stories from England, where Australia succeeded in regaining the Ashes.

As expected, Bromley proved an uninspiring selection. Playing in just one Test, in which he contributed five runs, he had a mediocre tour, finishing with 312 runs from 20 innings. Fingleton never disputed Brown's selection, as he was a good friend, but it stung to think that the low-performing Bromley had probably pushed him out of the squad.

As Bill O'Reilly put it, Bromley's 'bowling ability was mainly in the minds of the selectors'.

Fingleton's new goal became the tour to South Africa, then just over a year away. Woodfull and Ponsford announced their retirements after the England tour, opening up two early-order spots, and Bradman's move from Sydney for Adelaide made playing for NSW more attractive. There wasn't a stream of tears from Fingleton and his friends when the Don announced that following the 1934 tour he would join the stock-broking firm run by H.W. Hodgetts, a long-standing South Australian member of the Board of Control.

Fingleton began the 1934–35 Sheffield Shield season with a flourish, combining with Bill Brown in a 249-run opening partnership and scoring an attacking 134 in 182 minutes against South Australia in Sydney.

Bradman, however, was missing from the field, a severe attack of appendicitis kept him from playing for his new home state.

Bradman was set to be a selector for the South African tour, but late in 1934 he told the authorities he was resigning because of his ill health and would not be available for the tour. A strong ally of Fingleton's—Victor Richardson—was appointed in his place. Richardson was also named captain. Fingleton & Co., who much preferred him to the taciturn, self-absorbed Bradman, were delighted.

Fingleton knew he stood a better chance of impressing Richardson than Bradman. Finishing top of the NSW batting averages with 593 runs at 59.3 helped, as did a pair of centuries against Western Australia, results that made him the country's most prolific run-getter for that domestic season.

But there were still a few hurdles to negotiate.

At work, Fingleton was urged to write a piece for the *Daily Telegraph* castigating the Board of Control for not allowing Alan Kippax and Hugh Chilvers to be part of a private tour of India headed by Frank Tarrant and Jack Ryder. The Board said the players were needed for local cricket.

Eric Baume, the vigorous, outspoken editor, bounded up to Fingleton's desk and demanded a front-page story on how these Australian players had been victimised. 'Tear strips off the Board,' Baume said.

Fingleton was in a quandary. If he wrote this piece, he could be kicked off the tour. The Board did not take kindly to criticism, especially from someone whom they had just granted a tour spot.

Fingleton reminded Baume that he had just been chosen for the Australian touring side.

'I know that, and that's the point,' Baume said. 'One of the Board's own men attacks the Board. That will make it all the better.'

Fingleton suggested writing under a pseudonym.

Baume was unswayed. 'I suppose you realise what the alternative will be,' he said.

Fingleton knew. The sack. But after being overlooked for England in 1934, he was determined not to miss this tour. He decided to take the risk. No, he said, he would not write the piece. Baume stormed off, and Fingleton waited. Luckily, the editor-in-chief overruled Baume.

Fingleton was on his way.

The intense seriousness of Woodfull's reign as captain was soon forgotten. His successor, Richardson, wanted the South African tour to be as enjoyable for the players as possible. He was a good leader and comfortable taking command, but he also believed that a relaxed team is a successful team.

As the team headed by train to Perth, and their ship to Durban, however, some got a little too relaxed for Richardson's liking. Fingleton cheekily placed a bucket of water over the door to the captain's compartment. Richardson was soaked to the skin—and furious. He immediately called the team together. 'If I catch the idiot who did this, I'm warning you he will be on the first train home. His cricket career will be over.'

No one owned up. Then O'Reilly noticed Fingleton was not in the carriage. He found him hiding out in a toilet.

O'Reilly banged on the door and yelled: 'Fingo, you'd better get yourself down there. Take your medicine, or I'll never talk to you again.'

O'Reilly knew he was probably the only one who could talk his stubborn mate around. After all, their links were deep, with two years earlier Fingleton being in Tiger's wedding party, as a groomsman.

A sheepish Fingleton owned up. The skipper eventually cooled off, and let him stay. But it was a chastened opening batsman who boarded the ship.

Fingleton and most of his teammates described South Africa as the best tour they had been on, far more enjoyable than more important Ashes tours of England and producing a wealth of amusing anecdotes.

The fun began soon after the team disembarked in Durban. At a dinner on the opening night of the tour, Western Australian Harold Rowe, the team manager, told the tale of former Australian captain Warwick Armstrong, who was as renowned for his girth as for his talent.

A bowler complained to the umpire that Armstrong's ample body completely obscured the stumps. 'Leave it to me,' the umpire replied. 'If you hit him on the pads he's out, but if you hit him on the arse it's a wide.'

When Rowe finished speaking, Richardson touched him on the arm and said: 'That peculiar little thing in front of you, Harold, is a microphone. That joke of yours should go well over the air.' It had just been broadcast across South Africa.

On the morning of one of the tour matches, one team member, a well-known hypochondriac, told Richardson he wouldn't be able to play that day. He wasn't feeling well.

'Got a sharp pain over the eyes?' Richardson asked.

'Yes,' said the ailing one.

'Nasty taste in the mouth, too, I suppose.'

'Yes.'

'And your tummy seems to be turning over.'

'Yes, indeed,' he said, stunned by Richardson's astuteness.

'I feel like that most days. You'll be right to play.'

Fingleton had been bluffed into believing that in Durban, elephants and hippopotami roamed the suburbs, but as he soon discovered, parts of the city were infested with monkeys.

Several players also indulged in a fair bit of monkeying around. South African women threw themselves at the visiting Australians—a few of whom boasted extraordinary conquests. The most notorious Casanova was Chuck Fleetwood-Smith, who would bed as many as four or five women a night. Finding time to sleep proved the hardest chore for the Australians, especially as their South African hosts threw parties for them most nights. But somehow, amidst this social whirl, Fingleton was able to get enough rest to put his name in the record books.

Playing conditions during the tour were highly diverse. Matches were even played on matting in Bulawayo and Bloemfontein, where the players were greeted with an earthquake. Seconds after the first tremors, O'Reilly was out of his second-floor hotel room and sprinting for safety down the street.

The only disagreement between the hosts and their visitors occurred in Kimberley, where local authorities forbade alcohol consumption during the match. Several hot and sweating Australian bowlers asked the twelfth man, Arthur Chipperfield, to bring them glasses of beer. A South African official refused to allow this. Richardson stopped play, walked off the field, and fronted the official. A few minutes later, to a roar of cheers from the tourists, out came the beer.

South Africa was short several players for the Test series, and Australia, relying on a devastating three-prong spin attack of O'Reilly, Clarrie Grimmett and Fleetwood-Smith, took advantage of that.

Australia's batting also had good depth, with Fingleton and Brown opening and McCabe at No. 3.

In Durban, the Test series opened with a 140 km/hour gale whipping in off the Indian Ocean. Trees near the ground were uprooted, spectators' hats ended up miles away, the bails had to be stuck down with chewing gum, and strokes played gently towards mid on and mid off did U-turns back towards the batsman. There was even the risk of a run-out when batsmen charged into the wind. Fingleton had a relatively tame First Test, scoring two and being undefeated on 36 in the second innings. Australia emerged with a nine-wicket victory. In the next Test, in Johannesburg, Fingleton top-scored in the first innings with 62, and helped Australia to a first-innings lead. In the second innings, he was a close-hand observer of yet another majestic McCabe innings.

After South Africa's middle-order batsman Dudley Nourse resurrected his country's fortunes with a classic double century —prompting Fleetwood-Smith to say the only way they would dismiss him was to 'shoot him', McCabe took strike.

Before the innings, McCabe had told Richardson, 'I won't be able to play today, Vic. The altitude's got me. I won't be able to run.'

Richardson would have none of that. McCabe was his team's chief batting hope. 'You just have to bat,' he said. 'Just hit fours, Stan.'

As Fingleton later wrote, the pitch had been 'worn cranky and irritable by 898 runs, and of all wickets, even a wet and sticky one, none is more difficult than that off which the ball shoots and bites'.

But McCabe still 'pulverized the South African attack into the dust'.

'McCabe never put a foot or his bat in a false position,' Fingleton recalled.

'To me, at the other end and fully aware of the difficulties of maintaining even a defence on such a wicket, McCabe's batting bordered on the miraculous.'

During their second-wicket partnership, McCabe scored more than 80 per cent of the 177 runs.

'In the middle afternoon,' Fingleton later wrote, 'lightning flashed with startling vividness in the mineral-laden Johannesburg air. Peals of thunder rolled over the [Old] Wanderers [Ground], but not even the wretched light of the impending storm could dim the Australian's brilliance.'

The ball was rising and darting alarmingly, yet McCabe completed his century in just ninety minutes, playing majestic strokes to all regions of the field.

Midway through the match, the light became murky. Even though it is customary for batsmen to appeal against poor light, South African captain Herbert Wade instead appealed from the field when McCabe was 189 not out and Australia still required 125 runs to win.

'Stan was batting so brilliantly he was endangering my fieldsmen,' Wade explained. The umpires agreed the fielders were at risk, and the teams went off. A few minutes a torrential downpour ended the Test.

Bill Brown shared Fingleton and O'Reilly's respect for McCabe, describing him as the 'finest stroke player I ever saw'.

'When Stan was in command, he was so magnificent to watch, and he left everyone, including Bradman, for dead. Certainly Bradman scored more runs, but Stan was the batsman you most wanted to be,' Brown said.

At the Third Test, in Cape Town, more rain meant there was no play on the opening day until tea. The unhappy crowd barracked the Australians for not taking the field. One spectator even went so far as to leap the fence, set down a wood stove and start a fire in it on the Newlands centre wicket.

When play at last began, Fingleton and Brown again took delight in dominating the South African attack. Fingleton found the speed of the Newlands wicket, and the erratic nature of the South African attack, to his liking, scoring his first Test century in just 180 minutes.

Throughout their 233-run opening partnership, Fingleton and Brown vied to outdo each other, especially in the nineties, when it appeared each might have bet the other that he'd be first to three figures.

Though Fingleton was the more aggressive, Brown won the bet by eight minutes.

The pair's perfect start enabled Richardson to declare early, before South Africa capitulated twice to give Australia an innings and 78-run victory.

Fingleton batted only once in each of the next two Tests, but made his mark each time, scoring centuries in Johannesburg and Durban to ensure two more Australian Test triumphs and an eventual 4–0 clean sweep of the series.

Being in South Africa obviously agreed with Fingleton. He cast off his reserve and showed his teammates that he could attack as well as anyone else. The *Sydney Morning Herald* correspondent was especially impressed by his Johannesburg effort, writing that the opener 'had never before been seen in such dashing mood . . . From the very outset he threw off the cloak of cautiousness which has characterised his previous Test innings, and attacked with deadly thrust.'

At Newlands, for the third time in the series, he finished as Australia's top scorer with 118. Three successive centuries was a real feat, and all the more satisfying for coming after the despair of the previous year. Fingleton would remark to teammates: 'Wonder whether the Don is closely perusing these score cards?' His pleasure in cricket was back, though the pain did not completely go.

Some years later, in a letter to Fingleton, Bill Brown recalled a conversation they'd had in South Africa.

I realise now what a blow it was to you to be left out of the 1934 side to England. Apart from the fact that you had a good year, you had been in the thick of Bodyline and apart from any other reason that alone should have earned you a tour.

> I remember you telling me once in South Africa how you went out and walked the streets after the team was announced. You must have read of Ernie Bromley's failures time and again, he never looked like making any runs, and cursed the injustice of things.

During the South African Test series, Fingleton also enjoyed the fielder's role as part of O'Reilly's deadly leg trap. As if O'Reilly's wild spitting medium-pace leg spinners weren't enough of a danger to the South African batsmen, Richardson and Fingleton perched themselves within the batsman's shadow at forward and square short leg. They described it as 'Madmen's Corner'.

It was Fingleton's idea. 'I loved fielding, but became very bored when placed in the old gentlemen's position,' he recalled.

> No captain was more approachable than Vic Richardson, a factor which contributed towards his greatness as the best Australian captain I knew, and I put it to him at Johannesburg that I would like a bigger fielding finger in the pie.
>
> 'Come up with me, then,' said Vic, and I moved up to silly square leg. It would be impossible to estimate how much sting that double 'suicide' trap took out of the Springboks. O'Reilly's peerless length and unusual pace for this type of bowling allowed us to sit on the Springboks all the season and pick their bats for catches. We took decided risks and the South Africans threw their wickets away often trying to drive us out.

The fearless Fingleton relished playing the psychological game, savouring the nervous twitching of the batsmen as they tried to avoid an edge. As the results of the Fifth Test showed, it was all but impossible, with five catches going Richardson's way in the second innings.

O'Reilly was forever indebted to Fingleton putting his body on the line. Some years later he sent him a copy of his book *Cricket Conquest*. On the inside cover he wrote: 'To John Fingleton as a token reparation for his trials and tribulations in the "leg trap"—a position he filled with great distinction for himself and immeasurable satisfaction for Bill O'Reilly.'

To cap off the tour, Australia showed their versatility by playing an exhibition baseball match against Transvaal and winning 12–3.

The local paper said: 'The Australians out-played and out-talked the home side.'

That summed up their tour. They had tamed South Africa in every respect, and enjoyed themselves to the hilt doing it. They performed hard on the field and showed incredible stamina in numerous off-field pursuits. They had out-played the locals; out-talked, out-socialised and out-wooed them.

The fun continued on the voyage back to Sydney. As the ship came through the Heads, Jack was met on deck by his brother Wally, who, as shipping reporter for the *Daily Telegraph*, had been allowed to take the launch out and mingle with the VIPs.

Wally saw Jack and Bill Brown standing together and walked up to them with right hand outstretched.

Jack looked Wally up and down and said, 'You've got my bloody tie on.'

For those on that tour, cricket would never be as much fun again. For the rest of their lives those fourteen players enjoyed a special bond—a bond that did not extend to Bradman.

11

The Divide

He was revitalised by South Africa, his self-confidence soaring. But back in Australia, Fingleton had to go on defending himself.

Three adventurous centuries failed to produce the accolades that might have been expected. In part that was the result of a lack of coverage. A tour to South Africa did not attract the same level of media attention as the local and England Test series. Fingleton's centuries got headlines in the metropolitan news-papers, but the reporting from the wire services was on the whole bland, with scanty commentary. Readers and listeners would have had to examine the statistics closely to get any idea whether Fingleton was playing with flair or just piling on the runs. If his centuries had been compiled on Australian wickets, the praise would have been far more widespread.

When *The Referee* described him as a 'stonewaller', Fingleton went to the trouble of writing to its sports editor J.C. Davis, for whom he had considerable respect. Davis, he believed, was one of the few in the cricketing press who had any idea of the game. In his letter, Fingleton explained that his bouts of highly defensive batting hadn't always been his fault. Often he had been following the captain's instructions. 'I do not deny [the accusation of stonewalling] or the fact that I played many innings at times that would make a saint swear—and me also. There have been one or two occasions, however, when things were slightly different.' These included the Fourth Test in Johannesburg, when he had scored a century at almost a run a minute. During his career he had often been forced to 'hold up an end', he said, and when hitting out at bowlers had been told by the captain 'not to do it again'.

'I do not mind these orders in the least, but the point is "acceptance of responsibility" must have a derogatory effect upon batsmanship. When you are concentrating upon doing a job in which defence is the keynote, your batting must become cramped. This is the position in which I often find myself.'

He went on, harking back to Bodyline: 'I can remember trying to stand up to the best of my ability against Larwood and Co. These experiences put my cricket back years. The nervous stress of that time, more pronounced than any since, was terrific, and I, for one, did not recover too quickly. The next year, however, it was the lads who "cut and run" [I use the term advisedly] who were the first chosen for England. This is not written vindictively, but purely from an observation viewpoint.'

'The African trip,' he said, 'was my reply to the selectors.'

That summer, England would be touring for the first time since the Bodyline series, and their new captain, Gubby Allen, was determined to restore decorum to Australian-based Ashes series. It would be a 'peacemaking' tour, aimed at healing the wounds of Bodyline.

Bradman, now fit, had the full support of the Board of Control to return to the Test selector position he'd relinquished before the South African tour. It was widely assumed that he would also serve as captain.

The Australian players were divided. In light of the enjoyable and highly successful South African tour, some wanted Richardson to remain. But Richardson, despite his vibrant captaincy, was on the wane as a batsman, having scored only 84 runs at 16.8 against the Springboks.

Richardson was also 42 years old. At the farewell before his team left for South Africa, Harry Hodgetts, Bradman's stockbroker boss and a Board of Control member, angered several when he said that Richardson was 'at the end of his career'. Former Test cricketer Clem Hill bellowed back: 'End of his career? Bunkum!'

Soon afterwards, South Australian Cricket Association officials suggested to Richardson that after the South Africa tour he should retire from first-class cricket.

Hodgetts vociferously supported Bradman as captain, and his fellow Board members Aub Oxlade and Frank Cush sided with him. Support wasn't as widespread among players. If Richardson was not to continue as Test skipper, said some, why not appoint his deputy McCabe, who, unlike Bradman, was liked by the entire side? Fingleton, O'Reilly and others believed Bradman lacked the necessary leadership qualities, the attributes that had endeared Woodfull and Richardson to the players. Woodfull and Richardson were seen as men's men, who would come to their teammates' defence if they were in trouble. Woodfull had shown that during the Bodyline series. Richardson in South Africa. Such leaders inspired players to perform and excel. The Don didn't. He was, argued his opponents, too aloof and single-minded to cater to the needs of the rest of the side. The criticisms went on: Bradman was too sensitive, too suspicious, too set in his ways, too much of a loner, obsessed with making money. His sole motivating principle was self-promotion. After the 1930 Ashes tour to England, one of his teammates told a journalist: 'He is not one of us.'

O'Reilly later said that 'in a lot of ways Bradman did a tremendous amount of damage to Australian cricket. He didn't ever come clean as a personal member of the side; he was always a far-distant relative.'

Lindsay Hassett wryly observed: 'Don got just about what he deserved to get out of cricket—a lot of runs, a lot of money and very few friends.'

Bill Brown, a staunch Bradman supporter, conceded after his death that there were good reasons why players preferred other captains to Bradman. His leadership style was not to everyone's liking, Brown said, and it suffered by comparison with Richardson's:

> Vic Richardson was a wonderful skipper, and his captaincy was crucial in making that South African tour such an enjoyable experience . . . Vic was first out at night and last in in the morning. He was the most popular of captains. He drank with the boys. He played with the boys, but he never lost his stature as captain. We liked him, especially how he always stood up for the players. You would play for him.
>
> With Don Bradman, he was captain, and you treated him as captain. I don't know if he went out of his way to mould a team. He kept on being Don Bradman, and it was up to the rest to fit in with that. Don was more for himself.
>
> Still, as an on-field captain, you couldn't go past Bradman, because tactically no one was better.

Fingleton believed one of Bradman's chief problems was that his teammates resented his 'apparent lack of effort to bridge the widening gulf between himself and the rest of the side. They rarely saw him. He was always busy with an engagement here or an appointment there, and practically the only time some of his teammates met him was when he walked with them through the pavilion gate. "Who's the stranger?" was the sarcastic quip. Bradman did not make friends easily nor did he court popularity.'

Fingleton also observed that older players, 'possibly resenting the manner in which he had turned their cricket world upside down, never went out of their way to be particularly friendly towards him. Bradman did not mind that, because he had enough to engage his attention.'

In contrast, McCabe was highly respected for his generous, modest and inclusive approach.

The anti-Bradman group also worried that the great camaraderie that had developed during their months in South Africa would be lost under Bradman. You were either for or against the Don. Nor could they forget that Bradman had returned earlier than his teammates from the 1930 Ashes tour of England, allegedly to receive all the praise. Fingleton said it was characteristic of Bradman's 'immaturity' and lack of diplomacy that 'he left the 1930 team when it reached West Australia and hurried on ahead to make public appearances as the "world's greatest batsman". A touring team should go and return together as a team.'

Also galling was that after scoring a world record of 334 runs in the Leeds Test of that series, Bradman had received a £1000 cheque from a doting expatriate Australian businessman and not even offered to buy his teammates a round of drinks. Instead, that night, when the players were expecting an impromptu party, Bradman went to his room to listen to gramophone records.

Fingleton said this exorbitant gift to Bradman 'influenced his teammates against him and gave rise to later claims against them of jealousy'.

★

Bradman never bothered to stand his teammates a pint (many would not have had one) to acknowledge their part in aiding him or to toast his good fortune. One thousand pounds was big money in those days. Bradman was then, in many ways, an immature lad; he was not quite twenty-two. Had this happened in later life, I think he would have been diplomat enough to quell any feeling against him. But he didn't help his cause with those avid to carp at him by cutting himself off from his fellows on returning to Australia, and making 'See the Conquering Hero Comes' appearances at various theatres, or by writing that he had no objection when some who had criticised him stayed late at the ground, drinking. These teammates avoided public fraternization as much as Bradman, and to suggest that they would stay behind drinking at public bars was nonsense. They would have a beer in the dressing room, and a song too, but that was their way of life and of cricket, even if it wasn't Bradman's.

Fingleton knew his subject backwards. Apart from lengthy stints with Bradman on the field, he regularly travelled with him, and not just at state and international level. In 1933 the two men, along with Alan Kippax, McCabe and Oldfield, were in a NSW Cricket Association team that toured NSW by bus, covering almost 2000 kilometres in just over a fortnight. As they played and travelled from Mudgee, Dubbo, Cowra and Holbrook to Albury, Leeton and Orange, Fingleton had time to observe Bradman closely, discovering at first hand his idiosyncrasies. While the Test team were in South Africa, the allegedly ill Bradman had apparently been healthy enough to play for his new state, South Australia, racking up a multitude of massive scores in the Sheffield Shield ranks.

Bradman, for his part, felt ill at ease with several of his prospective Ashes Test colleagues, especially the Roman Catholic clique of Fingleton, O'Reilly, Leo O'Brien, Ernie McCormick, Fleetwood-Smith and McCabe, who had become closer than ever in South Africa and who Bradman believed were conspiring against him.

Bradman had known O'Reilly for some time. They had confronted each other on the Southern Highlands cricket fields well before their first-class careers. The quiet, self-conscious introvert who was happy to be left alone was the polar opposite of the volatile, rambunctious, gregarious O'Reilly, who loved a tussle and knew how to hate.

Bradman thought O'Reilly was the greatest bowler he ever faced. O'Reilly believed Bradman was the greatest batsman. But the love-in went no further. They irritated each other.

As Bill Brown, another in a long line who rated O'Reilly a consummate bowler, explained: 'Tiger was very much his own man. He fitted in so well with the rest of the team, and was aptly nicknamed. When bowling, his delivery was preceded up the wicket by waves of hostility. His general attitude towards batsmen was: "If I had a gun, I'd shoot you, you bastard."'

Fingleton had many O'Reilly stories. Perhaps his favourite was about the time someone, obviously uneasy about the number of Catholics in the team, complained to Tiger that too many in the Australian side had 'O' before their name. The no-nonsense O'Reilly, who had learned to bowl using a gnarled banksia root as a ball, looked the enquirer up and down and growled: 'Much better in this game we play to have an "O" in front of your name and not after it.'

Bradman knew O'Reilly would work with him in the interest of team success, but would not pretend to like him. O'Reilly said that he and Bradman were as compatible as a cat and a fox terrier.

Richardson was no ally, either. He first got to know Bradman on the 1930 England tour, and soon realised he had little time for the world's cricketing idol. It was well known that he resented the fact that the Don had been chosen ahead of him as South Australian skipper. Richardson's teammates were sympathetic, privately vowing to try to put Bradman in his place during a testimonial match in Sydney at the start of the 1936–37 season.

The match, put on to hail two former Australian Test cricketers, Warren Bardsley and Jack Gregory, pitted the South African tourists, led by Richardson, against a rest-of-Australia team skippered by Bradman. The tourists' plan was to use the O'Reilly leg trap that had worked so well in South Africa to stifle Bradman.

But Bradman was fiercely determined to annihilate those who had succeeded without him in South Africa. He batted like a demon against O'Reilly, scoring a frenetic double century, the second coming in just 61 minutes.

It has often been expressed that Bradman absolutely belted O'Reilly. But according to Fingleton, there were extenuating circumstances. Commenting on the match, Fingleton wrote that as it was a benefit match, it was crucial that Bradman remain at the crease for a long time to please the crowds.

> That Australian team was pardonably proud of the unbeaten record it had in South Africa, but thoughts of its record had to be cast aside when Bradman came to bat. It was Saturday morning and just prior to lunch. O'Reilly was in magnificent bowling form and had taken several quick wickets. He was immediately taken off. He was itching to get at Bradman before he settled down, but the afternoon crowd could not be risked . . . O'Reilly did not bowl at Bradman until long after lunch. He was then settled, made a big score and Richardson's South African team suffered its only loss.

Fingleton said O'Reilly was fuming because Richardson had not bowled him early on against Bradman.

The Don relished the reprieve, boasting later that his team 'beat the tourists quite comfortably, and I don't think they were very happy about that. They thought they were a great side until we beat them.' As his biographer Charles Williams wrote: 'The truth was that Bradman had deflated the reputation of his future colleagues. Furthermore, he knew it, and seems not to have been too shy in pointing it out.' The deflation and the boast together served only to increase the hostility of those future colleagues.

In November, Bradman was endorsed as captain of a Test team that included four newcomers, Jack Badcock, Ray Robinson, Maurie Sievers and Frank Ward.

The exclusion of Clarrie Grimmett in favour of Ward led to more mutterings among the players about Bradman's skills as a selector. O'Reilly was outraged that Ward had been preferred over his long-time bowling ally, and was convinced Bradman was directly behind the injustice.

His fury increased when, at the start of the England innings, Bradman told O'Reilly he had to field in the dangerous short-leg position.

After England batsman Stan Worthington attempted to hook an Ernie McCormick bouncer, O'Reilly ducked for cover to 'stop myself from being killed'. Picking himself up, he walked over to Bradman and said, 'You better make some arrangement about that position you've got me in, Don, because I'm not going back there.'

Bradman's leadership was put to the test even before the toss. The fact that there were no grandstand tickets available for McCabe's wife had prompted some Australian players to threaten not to go onto the field until seating was found for her. Bradman came to the rescue, organising the required tickets, but the threatened 'strike' disgruntled cricket officials and made the captain decidedly edgy.

His condition did not improve during the Test, which England won by 322 runs after Australia fell apart in the second innings, scoring just 58 in seventy-one minutes on a dreadful wicket. Bradman's contribution was scanty—38 and a duck. Masked by large black sunglasses, he left the Gabba shortly after the defeat.

Many of the England players were aware of the animosity within the Australian team. Gubby Allen noted that Bradman was 'very jumpy'. While Allen had a good relationship with Bradman, he believed the Don had faults. At the end of the Bodyline tour, Allen wrote a letter home, describing how Bradman had played 'some incredible shots' but was a 'terrible little coward of fast bowling'.

The only local triumph in the Test was Fingleton's. He became the first Australian batsman to score four centuries in successive Test innings, and the first to score centuries in four consecutive Tests. It was not until 1947 that South Africa's Alan Melville matched the feat, and not until the following season that West Indian Everton Weekes went one better, notching up five centuries in consecutive innings.

Fingleton's batting, however, was far more inhibited than it had been in South Africa. Under the watchful gaze of his new captain, in Brisbane he returned to his old ways. The Australian innings, somewhat vulnerable because of all the newcomers, required a backbone, and it was up to Fingleton to provide it, especially after England applied the pressure with a solid 358-run first innings.

When Bradman joined Fingleton after the early fall of opener Badcock, Fingleton was eclipsed, a near-forgotten figure at the other end. As Neville Cardus observed from the Brisbane press box that day, 'Fingleton was always doing good by stealth, observed by the scorers, if not always by the rest of us.' The crowds were there to see Bradman, and Fingleton had to be, as

Cardus put it, a 'worthy anonymous helpmate to the darling and paragon of the crowd'.

But not even Bradman could satisfy the Gabba crowd. When he chopped a Bill Voce delivery into the slips and was caught on 38, spectators were stunned. Denzil Batchelor wrote in the *Sydney Morning Herald* that it 'seemed unthinkable, after his brilliant start, that [the Don] could fail by Bradman standards—that is, be dismissed for less than a paltry single century . . . With Bradman out, the cricket slowed to the ruthless war of attrition traditional to Test cricket. Fingleton played a lapidary innings, faultless enough, and with many fine facets of scoring strokes.'

As wickets continued to fall, Fingleton remained 'the one staunch buttress of his side'.

> He batted as he so often does, as if only the master's delicate certainty of touch could prevent utter disaster, and, in view of what happened immediately his own wicket fell, his caution was abundantly justified. When Fingleton was still there runs, if only off [Walter] Robbins, were still within the range of practical politics, but that was all over once Verity, with the air of a research scholar, discovered a way to his middle stump, which had previously seemed as hidden as the secret of the North-West Passage itself.
>
> Fingleton's innings will long be honourably remembered as a great defensive innings.

As if to counteract Batchelor's lyricism, the sub-editors had headlined his report: 'Dreary Play in Cricket Test Match. Fingleton and Voce in Major Roles'.

In his report, Neville Cardus praised Fingleton's pluck, describing the century as 'a worthy crown for hours of patient, devoted batting, all for his side, never showy or vain, but sheer steadfastness and shrewd skill; not a picture innings—an innings for the accountancy of cricket rather than for the art of the game, none the less an innings to be proud of, a conquest by character as well as by craft.'

Fingleton's former captain Bill Woodfull, now part of the press troupe, was delighted that his one-time partner had blossomed, describing the century as 'a masterpiece'.

But several days later, the Australians left Brisbane as losers, and Fingleton was one of many wondering how everything could have changed so quickly. His second innings had lasted just one delivery. He'd even lost his stumps, which went all ways to Voce.

The Sydney Test followed a similar course: Bradman struggled, Fingleton held up and England won. On paper Fingleton's second-innings score of 73 was the more impressive, but Fingleton always thought his first innings of 12 on a 'sticky wicket' was his best knock of the summer. While Leo O'Brien, Bradman and McCabe all went for ducks, 'the merit in my 12 was that I stayed there for seventy-five minutes while the pitch improved,' Fingleton said.

His pluck prompted more paeans from Cardus: 'He is a brave, patient batsman, who never plays to the gallery, and is ready to do his bit in fair or foul weather. I have little regard for those cricketers who wait for the favourable hour and for the perfect wicket. Fingleton is the kind of man I should want in my side when the odds were against us. The bowler has to get him out. He does not bend to the unfriendly wind.'

Others did, and Australia's second successive Test loss brought a wave of criticism. Most of it was directed at Bradman, whose start as Test captain had been disastrous. His dismissal in the second innings in Sydney prompted C.B. Fry to write that the 'greatest run-getter in the history of cricket has made the worst stroke in the history of cricket. A wild hook with his eye off the ball.'

The criticism brought the friction within the team to a head—and into the open. The day after the Second Test loss, the

Daily Telegraph headlined its main cricket report: 'Bradman Not Fully Supported by Team'. The story said cricket officials were 'disturbed by a suggestion that the Test team are not pulling together, and that Bradman has not had the support generally given to an Australian captain'. Although the discussions had apparently not 'reached an official stage', 'some members of the team have not been giving Bradman the co-operation that a captain is entitled to expect. There is definitely, and has been for some time, an important section of the team that has not seen eye to eye with Bradman, either on or off the field.' This had seen Bradman's captaincy 'seriously handicapped'.

> There is no doubt that the present Australian team, quite apart from the ill-luck in weather, and the unexpected failures of leading batsmen, has looked less like a team, when fielding, than any of its predecessors since the war. In cricket circles it has been suggested that Victor Richardson should be called back to heal a breach that does not go deeply, and to coordinate the team into the combination it showed in South Africa.

It was unlikely there would be a change in captaincy, the *Telegraph* opined, but 'strenuous efforts are being made behind the scenes to gain for Bradman the support that an Australian captain must have from his men.' In other words, the officials, especially those closely aligned to Bradman, wanted to weed out the agitators or frighten them off with a warning.

Despite the ructions, Australia regained its momentum in the Third Test in Melbourne, and revelled in a 365-run victory.

Key to the revival were Bradman and Fingleton. After taking a lead of 124 runs in the first innings, Bradman feared his team might quickly collapse in its second innings, as the wicket had turned into a dreaded Melbourne gluepot. Consistent rain followed by a heat wave had made the wicket nearly impossible to play on, and prompted Gubby Allen to declare England's first innings at 9–76. He clearly hoped that in the short time left on the second day they would wreak the same havoc again.

Bradman was up to that ruse, and sent out two of his batting bunnies—tail-enders O'Reilly and Fleetwood-Smith—as openers, with Frank Ward, normally No. 10, as the night watchman. The tactic worked. Fleetwood-Smith somehow hung on until an appeal against the light was upheld. The following day, conditions had improved markedly. The wicket was, as Cardus put it, 'as easy as middle age, old slippers and vintage port', and Bradman took over.

Fingleton was once again the closest and best witness to Bradman's on-field dominance—and his arrogance. In a sixth-wicket partnership lasting more than six hours, with Fingleton the anchor and Bradman the emperor, they racked up a record-breaking 346 runs. Fingleton was soon reminded by his captain what his role was. In a mid-wicket conference, Bradman told him, 'You keep your wicket up. I'll do the scoring.'

When the opener tried to hit one of the England bowlers out of the ground, he got a lecture from the Don. 'No, no, no,' he told Fingleton. 'I want you to keep your wicket up.'

Bradman was unstoppable, while Fingleton stopped everything with, in Cardus's words, 'a straight bat, seldom lifted higher than his knee'.

Still, Fingleton's dour knock—he again 'played perpendicularly, not obviously thinking of runs'—was celebrated by the crowd, who were ecstatic when he passed three figures. Cardus was astounded by 'roars of applause, the general like of which I have seldom heard at a cricket match; they were prolonged, and culminated in three crashing cheers. It was the sort of ovation the foreigners give to Toscanini after he has conducted an opera.'

It was the first and last time Fingleton was compared to Toscanini. Bradman was more accustomed to such accolades, and expected them after this innings, and his first success as Test captain, which he believed scotched 'the rumour that cares of captaincy were upsetting my play'.

The controversy over his leadership, however, soon got another boost. As the players were showering in their dressing room, the Victorian Cricket Association secretary, Harry Brereton, asked O'Reilly, McCabe, Fleetwood-Smith and Leo O'Brien to attend a meeting in its rooms at 3 p.m. They were baffled. Why had they been targeted? Bradman appeared equally at a loss. He was in the showers at the same time as Fingleton, and asked him, 'What's all this about?'

'Don't tell me you don't know,' Fingleton said. 'The Board has asked four of the lads to appear this afternoon.' Fingleton named them.

'It's news to me,' Bradman said.

Fingleton told Bradman this was his chance to prove his mettle as captain.

'Well, as the skipper, Don,' he said, 'I hope you'll go along [to the meeting] with them.'

'It's nothing to do with me,' Bradman replied. 'You know how well I get along with the Board.'

Fingleton was incredulous.

The four players were shown into a room where Board chairman Dr Allen Robertson was seated with members Harry Hodgetts, Jack Hutcheon, Aub Oxlade, Roger Hartigan and Dr Ramsey Mailer. All looked extremely ill at ease.

O'Reilly recalled:

We sat down. Dr Robertson began to read from what looked like a long typed statement, about four pages long. After a few lines it was obvious that . . . members of the Board believed that some members of the Australian side had been indulging in too much alcohol and making no effort to get into top physical condition. Lack of team spirit and insubordination was also mentioned.

There were also thinly veiled suggestions that one of the four players was not 100 percent loyal to Bradman. O'Reilly immediately assumed he was the man in question. He interrupted Robertson and asked whether the four were being held responsible for being the disloyal slackers and boozers.

The reply was 'no'.

O'Reilly then asked what they were there for and why the Board was wasting the players' time. There was also a muttering that the days of the Spanish Inquisition were over, and the players would answer the charge if they were brought face to face with their accuser or accusers. The meeting drifted into small talk, and the rest of the screed was not read out.

The meeting broke up, with the Board members imploring the players not to tell the press anything about it. McCabe said the press already knew, and had asked the Australian players about the proposed meeting as soon as they emerged from the dressing room.

The players were incensed they had been targeted, but surprised that the other Catholic in the team, Fingleton, was not among them. He was, after all, known not to be the leader of the Bradman fan club.

Fingleton had in fact been on the original list, but at the last moment the Board cried off, fearing he would leak details of the meeting to his and other newspapers. It would also have been clumsy to haul in someone who had just enjoyed a record batting partnership with skipper.

Fingleton thought Bradman should have gone to the meeting. 'A good commanding officer looks first to the interests of his men,' he wrote later. If he had attended, the captain would have 'forged a firm personal link with his players.' Instead, by failing to stand by the players, he lost their support. O'Reilly and O'Brien believed Bradman had actually instigated the meeting. They could not be convinced that the Board acted alone.

O'Brien said in 1990 that some years after the meeting Board officials told him Bradman had consulted several of them before the Third Test, expressing concern that some team members— O'Reilly and Fingleton were two names mentioned—were not supporting him because they wanted McCabe as their captain. Some officials thought O'Brien and Fleetwood-Smith might have been swayed into backing the push for McCabe. The pair were naturally surprised to be summoned: Fleetwood-Smith had not played in the first two Tests, and O'Brien was not involved in the Melbourne victory. McCabe was equally puzzled. He was seen as particularly loyal to Bradman and would never have been an active party to his overthrow.

O'Brien provided this information on condition that it not be made public while he and Bradman were alive. O'Brien died in 1997, almost four years before Bradman.

He said he admired Bradman, but 'he had an inferiority complex, except when he had a bat in his hand . . . There was a strong feeling that he wanted to take over the game himself, and he regarded McCabe as a threat at that time to his Test captaincy. Bradman was savagely intent on getting the captaincy and retaining it.'

O'Reilly was just as insistent that Bradman was behind the meeting. If not, he said, why not attend and defend his teammates? Bradman's excuse that he had a low opinion of the Board was less than convincing, since he was well known to have close relationships with several of the delegates.

A number of pressmen at the time believed Bradman had instigated the action and stated this as fact in their reports. A cable sent to England said Bradman had complained to the

Board about the off-field behaviour of the four players, who had denied doing anything wrong.

Those involved in the incident mulled over it for years. In a 1980 letter to Fingleton, O'Reilly suggested another possible reason for the Board interrogation—a social one. O'Reilly said he hoped Fingleton had in his memoirs 're-arrested the story of the threatened sit-down strike in Brisbane in 1936 when three or four of us promised to back Napper [McCabe] if he decided to protest about [his wife] Edna not being favoured for a ticket for the match'.

Jack Hutcheon [an influential Board member] refused his application which he had made belatedly on the morning of the match. Edna had rung him that morning to advise she was flying up . . . Bradman who lived away from us at The Daniel was contacted and he quickly arranged the ticket.

That was the little boy's [Bradman's] first captaincy job in Tests; it could have been a sensational start. Remember how we were crowded two to three in rooms at The Carlton, and how hot that game was. That was the time when Napper [McCabe] and I neglected to invite [Frank] Cush [the Board Treasurer and a friend of Bradman's] to an informal shindy we arranged in our room the day before the match began and thereby precipitated I have not the least doubt the Board investigation of the Micks at Melbourne two Tests later.

The controversy over that investigation gave the first public airing to the friction between Micks and Masons in the Australian team. The ramifications of this sectarian rift haunted O'Reilly, Fingleton and Bradman for many years, creating tension and suspicion and pushing Fingleton and O'Reilly further and further from Bradman.

12

Hostility

Bradman defended his claim of no involvement in the controversial Board of Control meeting as tenaciously as he defended his wicket during his long run of marathon innings. But his vehement denials did not convince many of his colleagues. They had seen him try to divert blame before.

Suspicion turned to rancour. Any time the subject was raised, Bradman would take a pot shot at Fingleton and O'Reilly, and they would hit back. Bradman made his exasperation over the affair clear in his 1950 autobiography *Farewell to Cricket*. 'I was captain of the team, but had not been consulted,' he wrote. 'I was afterwards told, unofficially, that such a procedure was designed to protect me, but in actual fact I immediately felt that I was suspect of [*sic*] having made adverse reports on these players. Nothing could have been further from the truth for I was in complete ignorance of the whole affair.'

A long line of Bradman biographers have taken up cudgels in his defence. Charles Williams calls the quarrel 'one of the most divisive rows in the history of Australian cricket'. He said Fingleton, O'Reilly, O'Brien, McCabe and Ernie McCormick had all been to South Africa and 'formed something of an alliance . . . Of course, as their names imply, they were all of Irish origin, all Roman Catholic and mostly Labor in politics because of it.'

According to Williams, Bradman said 'Fingleton was the ring leader,' and noted that on their return from South Africa, 'When they [the Catholic Test players] arrived at Melbourne Railway Station they were met by a bunch of priests in cassocks.'

That remark astounded the Fingleton family. Wally, who had become a priest, wrote to the *Sydney Morning Herald* to say it 'deserves a big laugh'. He went on: 'Met by priests—fair enough. In cassocks? Not Pygmalion likely. Was Bradman, who did not tour, on the station?'

Bradman's most authoritative biographer, Irving Rosenwater, notes that journalists at the time were certain the captain had been behind the meeting. He concludes that Bradman's denial 'certainly is consistent with his absence from the emergency meeting, but as captain the Board still might have been wiser to have had him there'.

Another biographer, Roland Perry, argues that Bill Woodfull was involved. Woodfull, he writes, reportedly told fellow teachers at Melbourne High School that 'O'Reilly and Fingleton want McCabe to be captain. With Australia 0–2 down they have decided that this is the moment to lobby against Bradman.' Woodfull had allegedly informed the Board of the internal dissension but later denied it, telling friends that 'the dissent was well known in and outside the team. Board representatives in each State knew who the dissenters were.'

A revealing insight into Bradman's side of the controversy emerged in a 1993 interview he did with the Australian Cricket Board's Bob Parish, which is quoted in Gideon Haigh and David Frith's *Inside Story*. Bradman told Parish he had complained to Frank Cush, 'one of the Board members who was a close personal friend of [Bradman's],' that they should not have called his teammates up without his knowledge, because 'obviously they are going to say that I have complained, I have reported they are not supporting me or something like that. Whereas I have done nothing of the sort, I have not complained and have got no complaint to make.' Bradman said he told Cush, 'I will never be able to live this down because they will always believe I reported them.' His fear had been correct, he said: 'Until his dying day O'Reilly believed that I was behind the calling of these fellows up before the Board.'

Bradman added that he didn't blame the players for being angry, because 'it was a dreadful thing for the Board to do, absolutely dreadful thing'.

He insisted he 'didn't care two hoots whether a man was a Catholic or a Mason or a Church of England or what he was'. But 'the public and the press took up the religious element', claiming there was a feud between the Catholics and Bradman because he was a Freemason. He knew that two of the Catholics—O'Reilly and Fingleton—wanted McCabe rather than him as captain. 'I don't think there is any doubt that that existed behind the scenes but, of course, that never got anywhere because the Board always stuck to me.'

O'Reilly neither believed Bradman's claims of innocence nor forgave him. He felt that the meeting had damaged his reputation and could have led to his being sacked from his job as a teacher at Sydney Grammar School. He was also angry because no one else ever owned up to having instigated the meeting or gave a reason for it.

Many years later, O'Reilly told an interviewer he was still furious with Bradman. The Don immediately wrote to the *Wisden Cricket Monthly* magazine, repeating that he 'knew nothing about it until the happening was reported in the press. O'Reilly impugns my integrity by refusing to believe me.'

Bradman repeatedly played down the Catholic–Protestant

divide within the team, saying he did not believe the Masons were prejudiced against the Catholics. In a television interview with Bradman in 1996, journalist Ray Martin asked the Don about O'Reilly's and Fingleton's complaints.

Bradman replied:

> It so happened that the fellers who were called up before the board were all Catholics, and one or two of them were not really very friendly towards me. But the religious thing didn't surface between us. There was never any argument between us on religion. I knew O'Reilly was an Irish Catholic. I knew Fingleton was a Catholic. That didn't bother me. It didn't bother me one iota.

'Don said he did have trouble with some of the players he was responsible for,' Martin told the *Sydney Morning Herald*'s Malcolm Knox. 'He said he had no problems with Catholics at all, but it was just that he wasn't into drinking in bars, playing cards all night and womanising. He was ostracised for that, but that was his nature.'

Cricket writer David Frith also believes the prime reason for the split was not religious but more to do with personality: 'Don was so different to the rest of them.'

Bradman was indeed a Mason, as were teammates Bill Ponsford and Bert Oldfield and officials Aubrey Oxlade and Hodgetts. He made it known that on the ship to and from England, it irked him that the Catholics would gather to celebrate Mass each Sunday. During one Sydney match, Bradman was told that Fingleton had had his bat sprinkled with holy water by a Catholic bishop. When Fingleton returned to the dressing room after a short stint at the crease, Bradman taunted him, saying as he headed to the wicket, 'Now we'll just go and see what a dry bat will do out here.'

A few hours later, another Bradman century was being celebrated.

Despite Bradman's protestations, religion was an important social identifier in the 1930s. The Irish Catholic faction pushed the notion that cricket favoured and promoted Protestants. The religious divide was even believed to influence Australian team selections.

It was an old rift. Australian Catholics maintained that Protestants were heretics who worked against them through the secret societies of Freemasonry. The Protestants thought the Catholics were anti-Establishment and anti-English, and were disproportionately represented in the public service. The Protestants were supposedly conservative, deeply loyal to the British monarchy and Empire. The Catholics were supposedly the ratbags of society, promoting socialism and republicanism. The religious divide extended into politics, with the Liberal Party having a Protestant heritage while the Labor Party relied on the support of Irish Catholics.

Cricket's roots lie deep in Protestant England, and for most of its history in Australia it revolved around a similar base, with Protestants dominating both on the field and in the back rooms. From the 1920s into the 1960s, many cricket officials at state and national level were Freemasons. Several well-known cricketers, including post–Second World War Australian captains, were encouraged to join the Masons because it would improve their chances of leading a Test team.

There was the occasional Catholic official, such as Edmund 'Chappie' Dwyer, a good friend of Fingleton and O'Reilly's, who became a Test selector. Fingleton was convinced that if Dwyer hadn't been on the selection panel he might not have played Test cricket at all. He was equally certain that McCabe would not have become one of Australian cricket's most notable batsmen without the continuous support of the same fellow

Catholic. Dwyer was a first-grade cricketer by the age of fifteen, and after captaining the Marist Brothers Darlinghurst team he played for Paddington, Gordon, Waverley and Mosman. He conceded that probably his biggest contribution to cricket was 'helping to put Stan McCabe into big cricket'.

In 1928, Dwyer saw Stan and his brother Les playing in Grenfell, immediately spotted their potential, and pushed for them to be included in the NSW Colts team. The selectors were reluctant, but Dwyer was so persuasive that they eventually included Stan. Two years later, McCabe was playing for Australia.

But Catholics like Dwyer were certainly a minority in cricket's halls of power. The NSW Cricket Association is not believed to have employed a Catholic until the 1970s, more than 110 years after it was formed. For several decades the general rule in NSW cricket administration was that big decisions were made not at official meetings but at the Masonic Lodge a short time before. Even the Test umpiring ranks were dominated by Protestants. Col Egar in the 1960s is believed to be the first Catholic umpire ever appointed for an Australian Test match.

Wally Fingleton said a lot of the friction arose from the fact that 'the Masons were running the game at that time. There was a far different attitude in those days, and there was quite a lot of enmity. This prompted a lot of stupid stuff.' That stuff included a belief among Catholics that they would always be rated second best by the Protestant administrators, especially dinosaurs like Syd Smith, the NSW Cricket Association president and Board of Control secretary, who had made his anti-Catholic beliefs known. Smith, a Mason, had notoriously said there had 'never been a good Catholic captain of Australia', though the team had not been led by a Catholic in decades. Smith ensured that the NSWCA was dominated by fellow Masons, including Oxlade, Syd Webb and Harold Heydon.

Catholic officials and players complained privately that they had little chance of advancement at the NSWCA. Dwyer overcame the hurdles, remaining an Australian selector for almost twenty years and a NSW vice-president for as long, but he was one of the few to do so in the faction-poisoned 1930s. Dwyer ran a chain of Catholic bookshops, and it was at his offices that he, O'Reilly, Fingleton and McCabe would hold regular Friday get-togethers.

So when four Catholics were singled out to front the Board of Control and their Protestant captain refused to join them, suspicions naturally rose.

But Bradman deserves praise, too. Despite the turmoil within the side and the looks of mistrust some of his teammates shot at him, he somehow banded them together to complete the Test series against England and win the Ashes. Or at any rate took the lead—so dominating proceedings that everyone else just had to follow.

Bradman's batting completely dominated the final two Tests. He followed his 270 in Melbourne with another double century in Adelaide, and finished the Fifth Test in Melbourne with 169. In the final three Tests, Bradman batted for almost nineteen hours, a marathon effort that saw Australia win the series 3–2 and become the first Test team to triumph after being down 2–0. It was such a towering effort that C.B. Fry dubbed Bradman the eighth wonder of the world.

From his conquering height, Bradman frowned upon those on the team who he saw as too frivolous. During the Adelaide Test, his deputy McCabe was in one of his cavalier moods. Heading for what appeared set to be another entertaining Test century, he was caught on the boundary playing a reckless shot. Bradman told him later it was probably not the time to play such an adventurous stroke.

'Well, Braddles,' McCabe said. 'All I can say is that if a similar ball comes along in the second innings, I will try and do the same thing with it.'

Braddles got the message.

Fingleton was nowhere near as flourishing, finishing the series with frugal scores of 10, 12 and 17 but at least satisfied that he ended up fourth in the Australian batting averages, behind Bradman, McCabe and Ross Gregory, with 398 runs at 44.2.

Surely, he thought, that was enough to warrant a berth in the 1938 team to tour England. But Fingleton had grown accustomed to disappointments. He doubted Bradman would select him, especially as the captain was convinced he did not have the full support of his opening batsman and his close colleague O'Reilly, the key leg-spin bowler in the side.

Both knew they had to keep performing.

But before another cricketing season and a tour took over everyone's attention, Fingleton had another important duty. His sporting enthusiasms weren't confined to cricket. He was an avid follower of rugby union and rugby league; indeed, as a child he had at one stage pondered a football career. Even after opting for cricket, he missed several Sheffield Shield matches because of a football injury.

So when the opportunity came for him to cover the 1937 Springbok tour of Australia for *The Sun*, he immediately volunteered. He later described it as one of the most enjoyable times in his career. He was also asked to cover the tour for the South African Argus newspaper group. For decades afterwards, he served as the Australian stringer for several South African papers.

Fingleton picked a good one as his initiation to rugby tours. The feats of one of the greatest Springbok touring teams provided an abundance of news, dramas, coaches' duels and journalistic subterfuge.

Fingleton quickly discovered that not every journalist is trustworthy when a South African pressman pulled a swiftie on him. Before the final Test, a notice was posted in the Springboks team room stating that a curfew had been enforced. The South African was the only journalist with access to the team room. To conceal his identity, he passed on the story of the curfew to Fingleton, knowing that once it appeared in the Sydney press he could bounce it back to his own papers. Fingleton got the story, but also had to cop the blame—and an interesting, albeit derogatory lecture from NSW coach Johnnie Wallace. He wasn't too concerned, because his editors were delighted with the scoop.

The series yielded an abundance of great yarns. The Second Test in Sydney, in particular, degenerated into one of the dirtiest internationals of all time. Players were king hit and kicked in back play. The Australians singled out Springbok halfback Pierre de Villiers, passing the ball to him from line outs before pummelling him. According to a Springbok teammate, 'De Villiers was in a terrible state, his eyes were rolling and his tongue was hanging out.'

Fingleton revelled in the excitement, and *The Sun* gave his rugby reports prominent play.

For all its intrigue, politicking, religious differences and interpersonal friction, cricket suddenly seemed a far more genteel game.

13

England at Last

Relief rather than excitement was Fingleton's reaction to the news that at last he had made an Australian touring team to England. He knew his inclusion was deserved but, ever suspicious, also wondered if it was a square-up by the selectors for having wronged him four years earlier.

At the *Sun* offices, a large group of journalists, with Fingleton in pride of place, crowded around the teleprinter as it sputtered out the names of the Australians who had just been chosen in Melbourne: Bradman, Badcock, Barnes, Barnett, Brown, Chipperfield, F . . . I . . . N . . . G . . .

A huge cheer went up. The whole staff rejoiced in their colleague's success. And Fingleton rejoiced with them. He was going to enjoy this tour to the hilt.

He maintained his status as Australia's premier opening batsman in the 1937–38 season, helping NSW to its first Shield win in five seasons. Bradman, as usual, led the averages, with 983 runs at 98.3 for South Australia. Fingleton was next best, with 494 at 54.88.

This time there was no excuse for leaving him off the England tour. And Bradman was smart enough to know that sometimes it is better to have your detractors beside you rather than firing from the opposing trench.

Nor was there any question who the Australian opening partners should be. Fingleton and Bill Brown, who had combined so well in South Africa, remained the best pairing in Australia, with a relationship so effective it sometimes seemed telepathic. The two would exchange hardly a word when they were at the crease, but they knew each other's mannerisms so well they could tell exactly what the next move would be. Fingleton once said that he and Brown never called for a run: 'I can tell by his attitude if he wants to come for a run; and he does the same with me.' Brown said: 'There was a certain amount of each knowing what the other one was doing, but we did call. There was still a good sense of anticipation between the two of us.'

Brown thought Fingleton might have privately blamed him for keeping him out of the 1934 tour by taking the last batting spot, but that did not affect their relationship. At one time Fingleton queried Brown's mettle, but they soon became close friends.

'Jack wasn't a graceful batsman, but he was certainly effective,' Brown said.

His main asset was that he was such a tough competitor. He had this real tough streak. He was such a fighter, as was shown during the Bodyline series when he handled what England threw at him as well as anyone. With the new ball, they tried everything to upset him, but he never shirked. I never saw him take a backward step against any bowler. He would take all the knocks, and not complain.

He was also a wonderful partner to have at the wicket. He ran extremely well, and never left you for dead in the middle of the wicket.

Their running between wickets, so critical during the tour of South Africa, was of the highest calibre, and not even Bradman found grounds for a dig in the press about Fingleton's indiscretions. His running had improved markedly since the last England tour selection, and the South Africa trip had shown he could succeed overseas.

Still, Fingleton and Brown always knew their place. They were never going to be pin-up boys, or crowd pleasers. They knew most spectators wanted them out of the way so they could watch the next man in—Bradman. The pair were barracked constantly. Brown later said he and Fingleton could hear virtually every word uttered by the off-field critics, notably Stephen 'Yabba' Gascoigne, from his vantage point on the Hill at the SCG. 'You would be batting away, and after you had played a defensive stroke, Yabba would emit this loud *yawn* which would echo around the ground,' Brown said.

In Fingleton's case, Yabba would wait until the ever-careful opener sneaked a single to bellow, 'Blimey, he's alive!'

Brown and Fingleton found it all but impossible to stifle a laugh when Yabba was in full cry.

'You would hear the crowd saying, "Why don't you give someone else a go?"' Brown said.

'When there was an appeal, not just the bowlers and the fielders would bellow, but so too would a huge percentage of the crowd, because a lot of them thought, especially if we had started well, that we were now batting in the Don's time. The crowd thought we were in the way. We understood that, and it really didn't upset us.'

But while Fingleton and Brown were thrilled to be going on their second straight overseas tour, not everyone was so lucky.

Yet again there had been a selection storm, and again Bradman got some of the blame.

The Australian players were at a loss to explain why Clarrie Grimmett had again missed out. Grimmett and O'Reilly both assigned most of the blame to Bradman. Forever after, when the 1938 tour was mentioned around Grimmett, his head would drop. His anger over the rejection never abated. He was gutted by it. O'Reilly at the time was outraged that his prime spinning partner, who had been so invaluable in England in 1934 and South Africa in 1935–36, was not on the list.

He described Grimmett's omission 'as the most biased, ill-considered piece of selection known to Australian cricket' and said he 'always suspected that Bradman himself was the guiding hand.'

Fingleton was of a similar opinion. Grimmett's reign might have been far longer, he believed, 'had it not been for a fault in Bradman's judgement in 1938'.

The issue simmered for years. Shortly before O'Reilly died, he alleged that one of the reasons Grimmett missed out on the tour was that he had upbraided Bradman for playing a loose shot late in the day during a Sheffield Shield match against Victoria. Grimmett believed Bradman did not want to face Victoria's aggressive pace bowler Ernie McCormick with the new ball again the next morning. 'They say that those ill-chosen words at an ill-chosen moment brought about the end of Clarrie Grimmett's career,' O'Reilly said.

And there it was again: the allegation that Bradman shirked it against intimidating bowling. It wasn't the first time O'Reilly had mentioned this incident: he often discussed it in the SCG press box during his time as the *Sydney Morning Herald*'s cricket columnist. O'Reilly said Grimmett had told him he was ostracised because of that dressing-room incident, because Bradman was embarrassed by again being accused in front of his cricketing colleagues of putting himself ahead of the team.

When O'Reilly's comments were made public, Bradman retorted that his story was a 'complete fabrication. The alleged incident never occurred.'

The 1950 book *Cricket Caravan*, by Keith Miller and R.S. Whitington, contains a description by Whitington, a South Australian teammate of Bradman's, of the Victorian match at which the Don 'earned the displeasure of some of the more seasoned members of his team'.

Bradman, when on 192, had played two odd lofted drives, one dropped by Ernie Bromley and the next caught by Leo O'Brien. When he returned to the dressing room, he was 'roundly castigated in front of his team' by Grimmett, Whitington wrote, adding: 'I often heard it said afterwards that Bradman, who had not relished Ernie McCormick's fastish flyers early in his knock, did not wish to face him, refreshed by a Sunday rest, on Monday morning, and therefore he deliberately threw his wicket away.' Whitington said Grimmett and Richardson both attributed the spinner's omission from the 1938 team 'to his outburst that evening at the Melbourne Cricket Ground'.

In support of this, Whitington explained that although Bradman was only one of the three Test selectors, he still 'wielded a wealth of influence'. It was well known, Whitington wrote, that those omitted from Test teams during Bradman's time as selector were often among the Don's 'most outspoken critics'. It was also clear that Bradman was far more enamoured of the other South Australian spinner, Frank Ward, than of Grimmett, who he believed was too old, a liability in the field, and a waste of time with a bat.

Grimmett had not exactly helped himself by being openly critical of the Australian selectors when they ignored him during the 1936–37 Test series. As well, he and Richardson had been critical of some of Bradman's actions during the 1930 England tour as well as during the Bodyline series. Woodfull, Ponsford and Kippax had expressed similar criticisms of Bradman. O'Reilly confirmed that Woodfull was less than delighted with Bradman's attitude, believing he should have taken greater responsibility during the Bodyline series.

Adding to the confusion was that Frank Ward was regarded by Australia's leading batsmen as anything but a threat. This toiler was even tagged 'After-Ward' by his Australian teammates, because the spin he imparted to the ball was so slow and easy to counter. Several of his 1938 tour colleagues quickly distanced themselves from the newcomer, describing him as 'a queer cove'.

Near the start of a testimonial match in Adelaide for Grimmett and Richardson in November 1937, Grimmett bowled Bradman for just 17—and was near apoplectic with joy. Sidling up to Richardson, he said, 'That will teach the little bastard I can still bowl a leg break.'

Richardson glared, knowing the impact on crowd figures of an early Bradman dismissal. 'You've just spun us out of an extra £1,000 each from this afternoon's gate,' he said.

Fingleton repeatedly tried to console Grimmett. 'It was a terrible piece of cricket thinking, and an injustice, that you were not on the 1938 tour,' he wrote to Grimmett in 1970. 'The little bloke "did you badly there".'

No guesses who the 'little bloke' was.

At Grimmett's funeral in 1980, attended by a good number of his teammates, including O'Reilly and Fingleton, disparaging private comments were made about Bradman, who was also among the mourners.

Instead of Grimmett, in England O'Reilly had to make do with Ward and Chuck Fleetwood-Smith. Soon he discovered he had become the team's bowling workhorse, forced to carry several of Bradman's mates, in particular Ward, who, while he excelled in the county games, was not up to Test standard. Touring had suddenly become a slog, and as he rose in the morning, O'Reilly would say to himself: 'Oh, God! Not another day's cricket.'

The touring squad was an eclectic mob with its fair share of mug lairs, the chief being Sid Barnes. The NSW batsman was a cunning businessman and the ultimate opportunist. No one wanted to room with him on tour because he would be on the phone day and night stitching up deals—selling anything he got his hands on, from cricket gear to typewriters to cigarettes to American clothing.

There were other merrymakers on the tour, and several took pleasure in stirring Bradman wherever possible. This group included Merv Waite, one of the Don's South Australian team-mates. Each tour, Bradman would have his favourite. In 1948 it would be Ron Hamence. In '38 it was this honest, though far from match-winning, all-rounder.

Bradman made it clear at the start of the tour that he would stand for no nonsense. With numerous troublemakers in the squad, he realised that if he did not impose his authority early on he could lose control. Bradman was stern, but it didn't stop some from having a go at him.

In the North of England, several players bought small boxes which, when toppled over, made animal noises. When some cricketing notable would start boring them silly with an over-long after-dinner speech, they would turn the boxes over and watch while everyone tried to figure out where the mooing and baa-ing were coming from.

Bradman was incensed. He warned all the players that there would be dire consequences for anyone caught in such a juvenile act. The very next night, when Bradman was in the middle of a speech, he was drowned out by laughter and what sounded like an entire flock of sheep.

Fingleton, a central figure in a strong batting squad, was among the more sober-minded members of the team. But from the moment the ship left Australia he was as determined as any of them to enjoy the tour. The luxury of first-class berths on the RMS *Orontes* was a good start. But he also delighted in the other passengers—particularly a ravishing teenager and her mother. Jack was intrigued by both. The girl was strikingly beautiful, but her mother seemed strangely familiar. Fingleton, ever curious, asked around and discovered that the mother was none other than Jessie Street, one of Australia's most influential feminists, who had devoted her life to women's rights and peace issues. He could easily have been intimidated by such a protective overseer, but she only made the chase more of a challenge.

The wife of Kenneth Street, who later became the Chief Justice of NSW, Jessie was a renowned and often feared figure. Her passion for improving the welfare of women saw her become secretary of the NSW National Council of Women, a leading light in the Australian Federation of Women Voters, the president of the United Associations of Women, and a foundation member of the Sydney branch of the League of Nations Union.

Despite her considerable wealth, one of the most imposing homes in Sydney's affluent Eastern Suburbs, and the perks of marriage to one of the city's most respected lawyers, Jessie was an avowed socialist. Tagged 'Red Jessie' and often wrongly labelled a Communist, she was seen by many as a class traitor. But that only boosted her reformist zeal.

The widely travelled Jessie was on her way to Europe, to attend the General Assembly of the League of Nations but also take her daughter Philippa on a grand tour of Italy, Great Britain, Czechoslovakia, Germany, Hungary, Russia and the United States. Believing it would be an ideal education for the 18-year-old, Jessie had let Philippa suspend her science studies at the University of Sydney, which she had begun after leaving SCEGGS, the Sydney Church of England Girls Grammar School.

Jack Fingleton's parents, Jim and Belinda, on their wedding day in 1902.

Ally Regan, a friend of the Fingleton family, with four of the children. From left, Jack's sister Kitty, brother Glen, Ally, friend Agnes Haynes and brother Les. Jack is sitting on the floor at the front of the group. The other younger siblings, Wally and Linda, are not in the photo.

A rare photograph of Don Bradman in the NSW dressing room at the Sydney Cricket Ground. Sitting (from left): Don Bradman, Gordon Amos, Syd Hird, Cyril Solomon, Jack, Bill Hunt and Wendell Bill. Standing (from left): Henry Theak, Ray Boyce (selector) and Alec Marks.

An early batting shot of Jack taken on Sydney Cricket Ground No. 2 (now replaced by the Sydney Football Stadium).

Jack, excited to be in the Australian team colours for the first time, commissioned this portrait and immediately sent it to his mother.

Jack is comforted by Don Bradman after being hit during his courageous innings for NSW against the 1932–33 England tourists at the Sydney Cricket Ground. The England captain, Douglas Jardine, is at the right of the picture.

A newspaper clipping showing exactly where Jack was hit during his century against England.

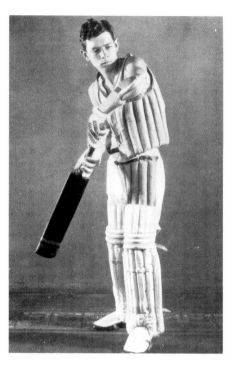

The famous photograph of a *Sun* copy boy wearing Jack's Bodyline breast padding. Jack often had to explain that it was not him in the photograph.

Harold Larwood about to deliver. Larwood sent this photograph with the message: 'To Jack . . . fond memories'.

The 1935–36 Australian team to tour South Africa. Led by Vic Richardson, Fingleton is standing in the back row (second from right) next to his close friend Bill O'Reilly.

Hitting Eric Dalton for six against Natal in Durban, during his highest first-class score of 167.

J. FINGLETON

Cricket cards, badges and postcards produced during Jack's cricket days.

J.H.FINGLETON

No.12 — J.H. Fingleton

J.H.FINGLETON

No. 8.—J. H. Fingleton

J.FINGLETON
N.S.W.

Bill Brown and Jack head onto the Sydney Cricket Ground to open the Australian innings.

To Jessie's indignation, Philippa's education was broadened in more ways than she had intended. The Streets left the ship at Naples, but not before Philippa had fallen in love and her mother had spent endless nights in her dressing gown frantically combing the decks for her elusive daughter.

Jessie did not dislike Fingleton. She found him 'a tall, slight, good-looking young man, very charming and with a good sense of humour'. Toward Philippa he 'was most attentive . . . It was not long before they were constantly in each other's company and although I found him interesting, this was something of a strain for me.'

When Jessie and Philippa disembarked, Jessie hoped they'd left 'the problem' behind. But the problem lingered.

Philippa's first impressions of the Australian cricketers were also ambivalent. She thought they were an uncouth mob, especially when she saw several of them throwing toilet rolls rather than streamers at the crowd on the wharf at Fremantle. For a while, encouraged by her protective mother, she stayed well clear of the cricketers. But they too were in the first-class section. And Jack's attentions soon swayed her.

He first summoned up the courage to confront Pip as they passed each other in the corridor one day.

'Where are you going?' he asked.

'To play the piano.'

He was impressed. Here was a woman of style and musical taste as well. What he gleaned of her family background also fascinated him.

Pip was impressed by Jack's physique, in particular his muscular legs, which she saw as he sunned himself by the pool.

Opposites so often attract, and the two, despite their eleven-and-a-half-year age difference, were soon inseparable. Jack talked to Pip of the hardships of growing up fatherless in the Depression; Pip told him of her childhood surrounded by nannies, cooks and nurses. It was a privileged lifestyle, but constricted, too. She had been forbidden to attend birthday parties or go into the kitchen. Her meals were cooked and served by nannies or helpers, and her parents kept a strict eye on her.

Jack was Catholic; Philippa Anglican. Jessie foresaw the problems they would encounter if their relationship was allowed to flourish, and fervently hoped this would be a quickly forgotten ocean romance.

But Jack was clearly smitten.

It wasn't his first time in love. Not long before, he had been attracted to a woman who, at the same time as he was courting her, was also being courted by tennis player Adrian Quist, who had just won the 1936 Australian singles title.

After stumps in a Sydney Sheffield Shield game, Fingleton told his teammates he had to rush off because of a 'hot date'. The following morning, he stormed into the rooms, clearly in a foul mood.

'She's told me she doesn't want to see me again because she's keen on Quist . . . that skinny, asthmatic, foot-faulting son of a bitch,' Fingleton fumed.

With Philippa, he was more cautious. Parting in Naples, they agreed to meet a few months later in London. Test tickets formed part of the lure. Jessie looked on disapprovingly, which only made Philippa more determined to make the rendezvous.

For Jack, the attractions of sea life, which included fancy-dress parties, à la carte dining and mixing with the hoi polloi, did not just revolve around Philippa. The sights and sounds of new countries tantalised him.

There was the intense heat of Colombo, where Bill Brown and himself 'husbanded ourselves over a century opening partnership, and then solicitously ushered ourselves back to the cool of the pavilion, content not to try or trust the majestical sun too far'.

'And may you top the day off as pleasantly as Brown and I did when, with the young lady off the ship (later to become my wife), we wheeled quietly along that night to dance at the Galle Face. The soft pit-pat of the ricksha boys' feet was the only sound on the night, a night wrapped in stars and tied with a new moon.'

There was a trip to the top of Vesuvius, where the cricketers 'looked like a procession of monks' and then 'four truants, sitting on a Nice boulevard' sipping French beer and thinking how pleasant it was not to be Bradman—who unlike them was being pestered by all.

Arriving in England, Fingleton fell in love at first sight. He later wrote:

> It is impossible to describe the effect that the mellowed English countryside with its soft lights, well-ordered hedges and fields and its countless hues of green, has for the first time upon Australian eyes long accustomed to gum trees, strong, glaring sunlight and paddocks undisturbed by fences for hundreds of acres. This soft, conserving light must surely be the reason why Englishmen still play the game when fifty.

Fingleton shared the devotion many Australians—cricketers, especially—felt to Mother England. 'The first step on London soil—station asphalt in this case—is the big moment in any Australian's life.'

Just as big was his first step onto the hallowed turf of Lord's Cricket Ground:

> It is Lord's, of all grounds, that holds most interest for the touring cricketer. I could not imagine cricket without Lord's; it is truly, as has been so often acclaimed, the mecca of the game,

and one is filled with reverence and tradition as he enters the ground itself . . . Everything that goes before in the trip through London—from Trafalgar Square, through Admiralty Arch, past Buckingham Palace with its Royal Standard and red-black attired sentries spanking it along the side railings, through Hyde Park—all this prepares one for the majestic grandeur and old-world charm of Lord's, dozing in the watery sunlight of a late April afternoon.

Thus began a 40-year love affair with England.

Fingleton made the most of his time there, using every spare minute to see the sights, from the West End theatres to the Houses of Parliament. He wasn't sure if he would ever return, and with echoes of his beloved Dickens all around him, he was not going to waste time discussing cricket in some dingy pub. He went to Wimbledon—with Bradman—took in concerts, and talked his way into the House of Commons. He took it all in as one big history and culture course.

On the cricket front, however, it was less exciting. He struggled on the slower-paced English wickets, gradually realising that his rigid batting technique, with its forceful drives and cuts, was inadequate here. It was only after he retired that he figured out exactly what was wrong. He couldn't play the pull shot. And as he later said, 'to go to England without the pull shot is like touring without a pair of pyjamas'.

So concerned was Fingleton about this weakness that during one net session at Lord's he asked a long-time ally, former Test wicketkeeper Sammy Carter, to stand behind him and analyse why he didn't play the pull shot. Carter was at a loss. But Fingleton eventually worked it out. Instead of going across the pitch with his back foot, which would open his shoulders, he was going directly back towards the stumps. This locked his shoulders and inhibited his play.

Still, his technique was good enough to guarantee an Australian opening spot for the whole series. He began the tour with a flourish, scoring a century in his second match against Oxford University, and once again showing off his wicket-keeping skills by effecting three stumpings in Oxford University's second innings. In his early days as a cricketer, in fact, Fingleton had wanted to be a wicketkeeper. But that changed fast. In one of his first matches, he lost sight of one delivery and it smashed into the middle of his forehead. He immediately gave up the gloves, deciding that being a specialist batsman would be a lot safer.

His Oxford keeping feat still didn't excite his skipper, however. And Bradman was even less impressed when he became frivolous at the end of the game. The last Oxford batsman was well out of his ground and should have been run out when Bradman's return flew right over the stumps, straight into Fingleton's gloves. But Fingleton ignored the stumps and threw the ball back to the bowler, Fleetwood-Smith.

Why, asked Bradman.

'I think I can stump this chap,' Fingleton replied. Luckily, he did so on the next ball, for his third victim, or a Bradman harangue would have been inevitable.

Fingleton scored a century in the match, but it failed to dazzle. C.L.R. James, author of the classic *Beyond a Boundary*, reported in the *Glasgow Herald* that it was 'difficult to say exactly what his quality is'. Although an accomplished batsman, James went on, he 'did not give the impression of high class which one got from McCabe, for instance'.

A run accumulator he was, though, and he followed up with 111 a week later against Cambridge University. By late May, Fingleton appeared to be on top of his game, with an unbeaten 123 against Hampshire in Southampton. But those were the high points. Against numerous county sides, his scores were minimal.

The Test series began at Trent Bridge. Fingleton showed resistance in the second innings with a pugnacious 40, but he managed to upset the local crowd with a pointed on-field protest that brought him the dubious honour of being castigated by the editor of *Wisden Cricketers' Almanac*.

Stan McCabe, however, produced a spectacular innings that Bradman himself hailed as the finest example of batting he had witnessed. During his playing career, Bradman was not exactly renowned for generous tributes. But McCabe's stroke play was so glorious that at one point the captain, standing next to Fingleton on the dressing-room balcony, called inside to the players: 'Come and see this. Don't miss a moment of it. You will never see the like of it again.'

As the innings developed, McCabe increased the tempo at an exhilarating rate. His double century was the fastest yet recorded in Test cricket, and included the highest percentage of boundaries of any double century—63 per cent, comprising 30 fours and a six. McCabe's innings ended on 232.

As he unbuckled his pads in the dressing room, Bill Brown later recalled, Bradman knelt before McCabe and said: 'Stan, if I could play an innings like that, I would be a very proud man. I would give a great deal to be able to play an innings like that.'

It was the ultimate accolade, but McCabe looked intensely embarrassed. Brown recalled: 'Stan shuffled his feet, and looked at me as if to say, "Why don't you say something?" Then again, you could never get Stan to talk about himself. He was so humble.'

McCabe's brilliance could not save Australia. Thanks to centuries from Len Hutton, Charles Barnett, Eddie Paynter and Denis Compton, England had amassed a sizable first innings lead. As the runs mounted inexorably, Fingleton spied Robert Menzies, a future Australian Prime Minister, in the crowd.

Did Menzies have any ideas as to how they could curb the England batting onslaught? Fingleton asked.

'It's not ideas you want, my boy,' Menzies said. 'It's a miracle.'

In the second innings, Fingleton and Brown tried desperately to manufacture one, or at least salvage a draw. The resulting stint of negative batting angered the Trent Bridge spectators, who began a slow hand clap.

Suddenly Waite appeared in the middle with a message from Bradman. If the slow clap continued when the bowler was running in, he wanted them to draw away from the stumps.

Fingleton said the clapping wasn't worrying him, but Waite said, 'Well, those are the skipper's orders.'

The barracking continued, and got louder still when Fingleton did as he was told and walked away from the stumps. When umpire Frank Chester asked what Fingleton was doing, he said, 'Don's sent out an order that I am to do this.' To which England captain Wally Hammond replied, 'That's all right by me.'

As the clapping intensified, Fingleton decided to be cheeky. He sat down on the wicket. 'It was only for a moment, but the crowd went into a fury,' Fingleton later wrote. 'It was sheer bedlam.'

Fingleton knew what he'd done was stupid. Just as misguided was his chat that night with *Daily Express* cricket writer William Pollock, who turned his confidences about what happened in the middle into an exclusive report. Next morning, when the story appeared, a chastened Fingleton telephoned Bradman to explain. Although the journalist had let him down, he was still expecting the captain to fine him for breach of contract, since only the captain and manager were allowed to speak to the press. But Bradman backed Fingleton and never mentioned the matter again.

The editors of *Wisden* weren't so supportive. Their report on the series in the 1939 edition described Fingleton's on-field actions as 'regrettable'. The summary of the tour noted Fingleton's sit-down with disapproval, saying he had 'appeared to lose all true sense of the situation by laying down his bat, removing his batting gloves and sitting on the turf—an extraordinary action on the part of a cricketer in a Test match.'

This, in *Wisden*'s view, showed an 'unwarranted lack of appreciation', because 'only a very small proportion of the onlookers expressed audible disapproval of the slow play'. Even cricket writer Neville Cardus agreed that Fingleton's actions were 'perhaps an unwise gesture'.

It was clear *Wisden* editor Wilfrid Brookes was no fan of Fingleton's. He rebuked Fingleton for failing to fulfil expectations on his first England tour: 'Here was a batsman who was inclined to flatter ordinary bowlers and who seldom brought into play an attacking stroke.'

In the build-up to his Second Test appearance, Fingleton seemed on track again, losing his wicket just four runs short of his century against Lancashire.

However, at Lord's, he disappointed again. While Bill Brown scored an unbeaten double century in the first innings, and Bradman kept the second innings steady by scoring 102 not out, Fingleton contributed just 31 and 4.

When the Third Test in Manchester was abandoned because of rain, Fingleton made up his mind to shine in the Fourth Test to ward off any thought that he was out of his depth. But a week before the Test, he was on his way to hospital. In a match against Warwickshire at Edgbaston, Waite bowled a long hop to Percy Santall. Fingleton, fielding close in on the leg side, didn't have time to get out of the way.

I ducked instinctively as I saw the ball coming for the middle of my forehead and it hit me a glancing blow, shooting up, I believe, tens of feet in the air. As I was lapsing into semi-unconsciousness, on the ground I could hear Bradman's piping voice from cover, mixing with bird calls, and calling out:

'Catch it; catch it!' A practical man, Bradman! My friends caught me instead and off I went to hospital. Had I not ducked, it would have been the morgue.

Fingleton had a headache for days, but recovered in time to hold his Test spot. There was joy in Leeds when Australia retained the Ashes, but Fingleton's contribution was minimal: just 30 and 9. Again Bradman was the Australian mainstay, with another century, while O'Reilly and Fleetwood-Smith amassed seventeen wickets between them. Crucial to their tactics was Fingleton hovering nearby, relishing the chance to shadow English batsmen in the close leg trap fielding position. Even *Wisden* admired that part of his game, remarking that his 'chief value to the side was in fielding, in which respect he often took the eye when placed close in on the leg side to O'Reilly'.

Fingleton was indeed best used when he was set to hover around batsmen. There was no more courageous infield fielder. As he wrote some years later to the English cricket writer Alan Gibson: 'You missed nothing by not seeing me bat—but I could field. Loved it!'

Despite low scores, Fingleton kept up his enthusiasm. But not even he could withstand the strains of the Fifth Test at the Oval, a torture session that became known as 'Hutton's match'. England opener Len Hutton spent 13 hours and 17 minutes grinding out history's biggest Test innings, in which he broke Bradman's record with a score of 364.

Not surprisingly, there were casualties. The first to go was Fingleton, followed by Bradman, both seriously hurt while fielding. And once again Fingleton discovered where he came in cricket's pecking order.

After two days in the field, Fingleton pulled a leg muscle with a snap 'like a bullet shot'. His teammates carried him to the boundary, from where he crawled up the stairs to the dressing room. Not one Oval member offered to help him.

Then Bradman fell over while bowling and fractured a bone in his ankle. He was also deposited to the boundary by his teammates. But this time, according to Fingleton, 'Innumerable Oval members rushed to lend a hand in carrying him up the steps and one could barely move in our dressing-room for all the members of the medical fraternity who wanted to be in on the act with him.'

Infuriatingly, Fingleton had organised Test tickets for Philippa and Jessie Street, yet they'd only seen him wandering around the field for two days and then being helped off. It was hardly the impressive show that Jack had hoped for.

That was it for him. His England Test series was over for a total 123 runs at 20.5. At least his overall tour record had been more respectable: 1141 runs at 38.03, including four centuries, ahead of McCabe, with 1124 at 36.25.

Still, the tour did give Fingleton a welcome chance to show his loyalty to his captain and partly repay him for not making an issue about his outburst to Pollock, the English journalist.

Bradman had asked the Board of Control if his wife Jessie might join him in England at the end of the tour. The Board refused, saying this would breach the players' tour contract. A furious Bradman fronted team manager Bill Jeanes and heatedly argued the issue. The Board's autocratic approach upset the whole team, while Bradman was so outraged that he drafted a retirement notice. At a meeting of all the players except Bradman, Fingleton played the role of shop steward, telling Jeanes 'what we thought', he later wrote. Fingleton told Jeanes the players were 'heart and soul' in favour of Bradman's request and had unanimously resolved to cable the Board and demand that it reconsider.

It was no idle threat. The players, Fingleton warned, were fully prepared to strike on behalf of Bradman, and Jeanes 'could play the final part of the tour on his own'.

The Board, terrified by the prospect of Bradman's sudden exit from cricket, backed down, and the players' wives were allowed to join their husbands at the end of the tour.

Numerous players later cited this incident as evidence that, as Fingleton put it, 'some of the Test players of his age made more gestures towards Bradman than he made towards them'.

'Had war not intervened,' Fingleton went on, 'undoubtedly some of those who figured prominently in the move to have Mrs Bradman come to England would have felt the lash of the Board's distaste; but, only just previously, Bradman had not shown the same disposition towards team solidarity'—a reference to Bradman's refusal to join his four teammates before the Board in Melbourne during the 1936–37 Ashes series.

The England Test series was one long string of frustrations for Fingleton. But the trip had its high points, like the time he and Brown gave residents of Swansea, in Wales, an exhibition of body surfing, and the pilgrimage he and McCabe made to St Andrew's to play nine holes on the celebrated old golf course.

The finale to the tour—a trek to Ireland, the land of Fingleton's forefathers, was also memorable. Over three days, the Australians played two matches against the Gentlemen of Ireland, in Belfast and Dublin. Fingleton revelled in the trip—and the blarney. The Belfast match was held up while O'Reillys 'for miles around gathered to honour their Australian cousin,' even walking to the middle of the field with him, 'chatting of this and that'. It was the only venue where O'Reilly congratulated a batsman for hitting him for four.

Before the Australian team—which included four Catholics, Fleetwood-Smith, McCabe, Fingleton and O'Reilly—took the field at the Trinity College ground in Dublin, a priest knocked on their dressing-room door.

'And who among ye is McCabe?' he demanded.

'Here, father,' answered McCabe, rising.

'As 'tis a small man ye are, I expected something better, but good things are often wrapped in small parcels. Michael Collins himself was not a big man. And where is O'Reilly?'

'Here, father,' said O'Reilly, drawing himself up to his full height.

'Ah, now, here's something like it. A fine man ye are, O'Reilly. A credit to your forefathers. And a fine head ye have, too. 'Tis good stock ye come from, O'Reilly. I've heard that you are something of a left-handed batsman, one who has been known to crack the ball and high over long on. Well there's a new and fancy Anglican Cathedral being erected in just that direction. Do you fancy that you can do something about it, O'Reilly, as a true and faithful Catholic?'

O'Reilly tried but failed, falling for a duck.

With O'Reilly in tow, Fingleton later said, how could they not have a marvellous time in Ireland?

Dublin we loved with its green trams, green telegraph posts, green telegram forms, green on everything that would take green. And the lovely, soft, rich voices! Ah, begorrah! The game at Trinity was an unqualified success and nearly every spectator there seemed to go down to the wharf to farewell the team when it left by boat. Spontaneously, as the ship pulled out, the crowd began to sing *Come Back to Erin*.

Hassett and I, who stayed on in Ireland for ten more days, sang with the crowd. It was one of the most moving scenes I have witnessed.

There was also the thrill of scoring a century at Lord's, not in a Test match, to be sure, but still, a flashy 121 against the Gentlemen of England.

His prime pursuit in that innings was to convince Cardus, the cricket writer who had inspired him as a cadet reporter and whom he had corresponded with for years, that he was a cricketer of worth. Early in the tour, Cardus had quickly picked up Fingleton's chief weakness—flicking or poking at balls outside the off stump, usually outswingers.

In that match at Lord's, however, off came the shackles and out flew the shots as Fingleton 'got a move on', majestically cover driving and flicking the bowlers to all parts of the ground. When he next saw Cardus, Fingleton told him he'd played the innings especially for him.

'I never saw it,' Cardus said. 'I went home early.'

Their friendship only grew closer. It was yet another reason Fingleton cherished his trips to England—even if they would never again be to play on the first-class arenas. Instead he would be on the other side of the fence, observing other people's foibles.

14

Bastards I Have Known

In the wake of the England tour, Fingleton's fascination with cricket began to wane. Now thirty, he knew his best playing days were past him. It was time to establish himself in his career, with which cricket had for so long competed for time and enthusiasm.

He had also been sidetracked by romance. He and Philippa resumed dating and soon began discussing marriage. But her parents were wary. There was such a difference in their ages—and their religious backgrounds. The Streets wouldn't hear of their daughter marrying before she turned twenty-one. Fingleton, for his part, insisted that the wedding ceremony must be a Catholic one.

But Jessie Street was not enamoured of the Catholic Church. As a fierce advocate of birth control, she had had run-ins with Catholic leaders. The idea of Philippa converting from Anglicanism—and at a time when sectarianism was at its height—filled Jessie with dismay.

The Fingleton family diplomatically noted that Philippa was still two years from turning twenty-one. Why not wait and see, they said. If the romance faded, the religious issue would become meaningless.

But the couple only got closer. Soon they were nearly inseparable.

Jaded after the England tour, Fingleton wasn't looking forward to the 1938–39 Sheffield Shield season, as it would entail several lengthy trips away from Sydney—and work, and Philippa.

New South Wales officials had other ideas. The needed a captain to look after a young, new-look state side. Fingleton missed the first Shield match, but when Stan McCabe was injured, he agreed reluctantly to lead the team on its southern tour.

The first stop was Adelaide, where a Bradman batting barrage loomed. On the train, Fingleton and Bill O'Reilly discussed ways to quell it. They agreed Bradman would probably make a century, but decided to do everything they could to ensure they 'closed him off from a huge score'. Their tactics hit home. Bradman did score his century, but it was among his slowest. He looked cramped and uncomfortable, and his completed innings of 143 included 91 singles. Eventually he declared South Australia's first innings closed on 600, but irked Fingleton and O'Reilly by bypassing the customary gesture of waving his batsmen in. Instead Bradman got the 1938 tour manager, Bill Jeanes, who was also South Australia's cricket association secretary, to make an announcement over the public address system. The NSW team were surprised to hear Jeanes's voice booming out over the ground: 'Announcement, Announcement, the South Australian captain has now declared his innings closed.'

Fingleton was so angered by this 'unnecessarily boorish' action that he contemplated not leaving the field. But he knew that would be pointless. One of the umpires, Jack Scott, was a close friend of Bradman's and 'considered himself very much part of the Adelaide establishment'.

Bradman's offhand attitude continued for the rest of the match. 'At the end of the game, in which we were well whacked,' Fingleton recalled, 'Bradman did not come to our room, as is the custom of home captains in Australia, to thank us for the game, to bid us farewell and wish us good luck for the summer. Bradman could be ungracious when he felt like it.'

Fingleton also had a sneaking suspicion that owing to an odd arrangement whereby the umpires shared the dressing room with the visitors, Scott might have overheard NSW players criticising Bradman and passed on their remarks.

So one of Fingleton's last encounters with the Don on the cricket field was 'an unpleasant one'.

The pain continued when the NSW team went to Victoria for a Christmas match. After being beaten in Adelaide by an innings and 55 runs, the tourists lost at the MCG by four wickets. Back in Sydney, Fingleton pulled out of the team, telling NSW officials he was needed at work (he was now the *Sydney Morning Herald*'s night police roundsman). His withdrawal halfway through the Shield season raised hackles. One of his NSW teammates, Sid Barnes, said it was a selfish move.

Barnes was originally a mate of Fingleton's. But that changed. Indeed, several of his Test teammates kept their distance, suspicious of Barnes's financial dealings. Fingleton eventually lost all faith in Barnes after he agreed to help 'bash into shape' parts of his autobiography and a tour book released soon after it but was never paid.

If Fingleton's 1938 season was lacklustre, the 1939–40 one was calamitous. The outbreak of war in Europe in September threw Australian sports into turmoil. While many were abandoned for the sake of the war effort, the government allowed the Sheffield Shield to continue in 1939–40, believing it would boost public morale. Crowds remained strong, and Fingleton agreed to play when he could. After the first three matches, poor form and a leg injury saw him overlooked. But not before suffering more humiliation at Bradman's hands. On another exasperating trip to Adelaide, again as captain, Fingleton fielded forever as the Don finished unbeaten on 251 in the first innings, followed by 90 not out in the second.

With a duck and three runs against Victoria at the MCG over Christmas 1939, Fingleton's first-class career was effectively over. He tallied 6816 first-class runs at 44.54, with 22 centuries and 31 half-centuries, and 1189 Test runs at 42.46.

And after he joined the Army in November 1941, even grade games with Waverley became a rarity.

After enlisting in the AIF Artillery, Fingleton underwent general training at Warwick Farm, on the outskirts of Sydney. He had a dreadful time there, chafing under the strict discipline. In later years, whenever he drove past Warwick Farm racecourse, he would wind down the window of the car and blow a raspberry in the training camp's general direction.

But there was a bright spot: Jessie and Kenneth Street had finally capitulated, Philippa had agreed to convert, and marriage plans were under way.

Fingleton approached Father James Freeman, who would later become Cardinal Freeman, and asked if he would instruct his future wife. When he learned who Philippa was, however, he said, 'This is too hot for me.' According to Wally Fingleton, Freeman recommended that Jack go to Father Daniel Hurley at St Patrick's Church in the city, because as a New Zealander he wouldn't know who the Streets were.

'When the word Street was mentioned, it could have been the main road as far as Father Hurley was concerned,' Wally recalled.

Eventually Jack persuaded Freeman to help.

'Cardinal Freeman later told me what a big impression Philippa made on him during instructions,' Father Fingleton said, 'while the Street family became very supportive of the marriage. I found Jessie a great lady. She was at my first Mass and came up to the altar for a blessing.'

The wedding date was set for 17 January 1942, at the Church of Mary Immaculate in Waverley. Fingleton asked his old friend Frank Conway to be best man, and told the mates he invited to be on their best behaviour. He had received a few lewd letters of congratulation from fellow Waverley and NSW players. And a well-known Test teammate, when asked one day where Fingleton was, had pointed up a staircase and said; 'Jack's up the street.' He had no desire to expose his high-class in-laws to such ratbag antics.

The ceremony took place on a bright, hot summer day. In the wedding photographs, Fingleton's new father-in-law looked stern, but Jessie Street appeared delighted. The reception attracted the Sydney social set and several politicians as well as the inevitable platoon of cricketers. Neville Cardus proposed the toast.

The Army had Fingleton back on duty in no time, and Philippa spent the first months of her marriage at Greenoaks, the Streets' palatial home in Darling Point.

Jack and Jessie Street soon became firm friends. As well as a lively, impish sense of humour, they shared many political views.

Army life, however, continued to grate. Fingleton, who was accustomed to standing up for his rights, repeatedly found himself offside with his superiors, but his gift of the gab usually got him off the hook. He even managed to avoid charges of being AWOL when he went missing in May during the Japanese midget submarine attack on Sydney Harbour. He was supposed to have been on duty at an Army post in Double Bay. Instead he was visiting his wife. He asked permission the next time. In September he took official leave to attend the birth of his and Philippa's first child, Belinda, who arrived prematurely.

But within days Jack was saying goodbye to wife and child as he headed for a new post in Townsville, Queensland. Waiting for the feared Japanese invasion was a dull grind. His legs weren't up to the strain of marches and drills, so he was transferred to the Press Relations unit, and put to work on censorship, intelligence analysis and report writing. He also accompanied some high-ranking officers on secret flying missions over New Guinea that he told Wally were so 'hush hush' he could divulge neither their purpose nor their destination.

Despite a chronic shortage of spare time in the Army, Fingleton now decided he had to find some. He wanted to get serious about his writing. He was no longer a cricket player. The only way for him to remain a force in the game was to become an analyst. And the best way to prove himself in that exclusive field was to move on from scribbling for the papers and write a book—if possible, a bestseller.

There were many factors working in his favour.

He had first-hand knowledge: he had been out in the middle at the highest level of the game. He knew and had observed at close hand all the main players, in particular Australia's most admired sportsman. If anyone was equipped to cut through the aura and reveal the real Bradman, it was Fingleton.

Most importantly, he had the framework, the story. He had been intimately involved in Australian sport's most tumultuous and controversial episode. A decade on, the public remained obsessed with Bodyline.

What he wrote would have extra weight since Harold Larwood had made known his view that Fingleton was among the most courageous of all of the Australian players who faced Bodyline.

But did Fingleton have the courage and discipline needed to turn the characters, events and iconoclastic thoughts swirling around in his head into a popular book? Or was he just a newspaperman, fated never to become an author? He was concerned that despite his wide reading and equally broad general and literary knowledge he might not be up to the challenge. Not many people knew he had not even been to high school.

As Fingleton began the first draft of his first book, *Cricket Crisis*, he needed reassurance. He wrote to Neville Cardus, who was now living in Sydney, for advice.

'I never encourage people to write unless I feel there is a sound reason,' Cardus replied. 'The world is full of scribblers. But Jack, you have the gift, and I am certain that you need only develop it to arrive at a point of some distinction here; for frankly there is disappointingly little decent writing in the Australian press.'

As to Fingleton's request for some advice on style, 'I can only repeat—write something every day. And read as much as you can of good essay writers—Hazlitt, Lamb, Robert Lynd and so on. Always try to get a few metaphors into a passage—no, I don't mean far-fetched or obviously poetic ones; but rather humorous or expressive. Part of the art of vivacious writing is to use a familiar word in an unfamiliar context.'

Fingleton was encouraged, and when he'd finished a few chapters he sent one to Cardus. Cardus wrote back in February 1943 to say he had 'read and re-read it, and I'm still rather pleased'.

> If you 'keep it up' the book will be well removed from the average. There are vivid things in it, seen clearly and conveyed to us in the right words. But for English readers, avoid as much as possible (without taking the personal touch out of your writing) phrases such as the 'cable buck was passed'. Colloquialisms are good up to a point. 'Ballyhoo' is accepted. But no 'film' echoes.

Fingleton took note, and continued working away. But there was more to this task than writing. This book wasn't just a compilation of memories, but a history, too. That would require research. And there would be numerous characters who were well known to the public, particularly Bradman and Douglas Jardine. They would have to be convincingly and accurately portrayed.

As part of his historical investigations, Fingleton tracked down the origin of the term Bodyline. The general consensus was that the Melbourne *Herald*'s Hugh Buggy was the first to actively promote the term, which he used in an article on the first day of the opening Test of the 1932–33 series. A former Australian Test player, Jack Worrall, had also referred in the Melbourne weekly *The Australasian* to 'half-pitched slingers on the body line'. This had attracted the attention of a young journalist, Ray Robinson, also with the *Herald*, who tried to insert it in a headline, only to be overruled by the news editor, who 'saw no news-value in the new word'. He did, however, consent to its use in the story itself.

Fingleton wrote to Buggy in an effort to work out who deserved the credit. Buggy—who, like many journalists during the war, worked with the Government Censor—said he 'never laid claim to having been the coiner of the word "bodyline" although the distinction has been thrust upon me many times'. He had 'always strenuously disowned it'. Besides, he'd heard 'some talk that Claude Corbett used it earlier'.

In his ball-by-ball report of the First Test for the *Herald*, Buggy said, he wrote that 'Larwood in his sixth over bowled on the line of the body. Later in writing "telegraphese" I remember writing: "Larwood after lunch resumed at the Randwick end again bodyline." Whether I was the pioneer or not I am uncertain.' Buggy noted that the *Herald* had used the word in a double-column summary of his ball-by-ball story: 'This summary was a string of highlights culled out of my stuff by [Ray] Robinson.'

Fingleton next sought out the West Indies' most illustrious player, Learie Constantine. In one Test, in England in 1933, his team had adopted similar tactics.

The West Indians had targeted Jardine, who despite numerous hits to the body had refused to show any pain as he scored his one and only Test century.

In his letter to Fingleton, Constantine explained how the West Indies team had come to attack England with some of its own medicine: 'That bodyline test at Old Trafford 1933 was I believe an agreed arrangement between our captain, Jack Grant, and some of the influential people of the MCC . . . but after a tryout the death-knell of the whole process was sounded.' Constantine didn't want this information 'passed on to newspapermen'.

Fingleton's research also took him to the Prime Minister's office, from which he sought approval for a certain paragraph he wanted to use. Fingleton was a great admirer of John Curtin, a former journalist and avid cricket fan, whom he'd met many times during his cricketing days. During the war he got to know Curtin well. As part of his work in censorship and intelligence, he was involved, along with the PM's longtime advisor Don Rodgers, in determining what could and could not be reported from Curtin's press conferences.

In September 1943, Fingleton asked if Curtin had any objection to his mentioning the PM in several paragraphs of his book. Because of his work with the Government, Fingleton had knowledge of many cables sent between high-ranking politicians in England and Australia.

Fingleton had an extra card up his sleeve: his mother-in-law was at the time standing for Parliament as a Labor member for the federal seat of Wentworth. At the start of his letter, Fingleton wrote: 'My mother-in-law might yet be with you' in Canberra, and added, 'if she does get there no win has been harder earned'.

(Jessie, attempting to be Australia's first woman member of parliament, lost the poll by only a few thousand votes, but succeeded in achieving a massive twenty percent swing towards Labor.)

Fingleton then transcribed the paragraphs he wanted permission to include:

> The synonyms of cricket, as Sir Pelham [Warner] terms them, become very boring at times. There was an occasion in 1942, after Japan had taken Singapore and Java, when raids on the front-doors of Darwin and Port Moresby heralded an imminent invasion of Australia. Some luminary of the Dominions office sent the following airy cable to the very harassed Australian Prime Minister, John Curtin—'At the moment the Empire team is batting on a sticky wicket and the Axis fast bowlers have had some success. Our best bats are still to go in and the score will in time show that we can give as well as take punishment.'
>
> John Curtin was a first grade cricketer of other days in Perth. He kept his interest in the game, was always pleased to meet and mingle with players and was a frequent visitor to dressing rooms when a big game was in progress but, surely in the dark affairs of nations, there is a time and place for everything! I could never pluck up courage to ask the war-time Prime Minister what he thought of that cable but I should not be surprised if it had a very short innings on its way to the waste paper basket.

Fingleton asked the PM if this was 'treading on English corns rather hard'. Within days, Curtin's private secretary Eric Tonkin replied, advising him not to mention the telegram. Fingleton got out the black pen.

Shortly after, he made a dreadful error. He had more than half the book finished, frantically typing away with two fingers, when he decided to ask another expert to cast an eye over it. His former editor, A.R.B. Palmer, had offered to give Fingleton the benefit of his experience. Fingleton duly sent the manuscript to Palmer via Army Post. It never arrived. It was lost somewhere between North Queensland and Sydney. Worse, Fingleton had forgotten to make a carbon copy. He was shattered. All that work wasted! He would have to start all over again. But he'd learned his lesson. From that day on, Fingleton made—and meticulously preserved—carbon copies of every manuscript, letter and note he wrote. For weeks, Fingleton was in deep depression as he pondered whether he could summon the energy to rewrite the book. Maybe the loss of the manuscript was a warning that such a pursuit was sheer folly.

Adding to the strain were heavy demands at work. The Army had assigned him to a most unusual—and exasperating—job, that of press secretary to the former Prime Minister, William Morris (Billy) Hughes. The government wanted someone who could effectively contain this political loose cannon. This was no mean task—Hughes went through advisors and press secretaries as often as hot breakfasts. The 'Little Digger' was notoriously cantankerous and reputed to be a nightmare to work for. He was one of Australia's most formidable leaders, but hardly loyal. He had repeatedly changed political parties and been expelled from a number of them. A brilliant orator and aggressive wartime leader, Hughes was shunned by many as a political rat. Fingleton described him as a 'cranky, irascible, ruthless, gnome-like Welshman . . . who could have given tips to Machiavelli. A famous man who was a big bastard to work for.'

Fingleton was being kind.

After leading the nation during the First World War, when he had been at the centre of the conscription debate that divided the country, Hughes, now head of the United Australia Party, was upsetting people all over again.

Curtin was particularly worried by Hughes's repeated attacks on American General Douglas MacArthur, who had come to Australia as Supreme Commander of Allied Forces in the South-west Pacific. Hughes took an instant dislike to MacArthur, whom he saw as an egotistical cowboy. Fingleton knew that Curtin had been 'getting a lot of flak' from MacArthur about Hughes. The Little Digger 'used to go on the air each week and give the American particular stick; in Billy's estimation, MacArthur was a dud who could do nothing right . . . The general, who was a very vain man, tired of this abuse and told Curtin that if he didn't shut the little so-and-so up, he, Curtin, could get another Allied Commander for the Pacific and pretty quick too.'

Fingleton's unenviable task in Canberra was to try to 'curb the venom' of the Little Digger, and in particular stop him criticising MacArthur during his radio broadcasts.

Thus began 'three tumultuous months' in Hughes's office. The containment policy didn't work. Hughes continued to abuse MacArthur, arguing, among other complaints, that 'All he's done in life is lose the bloody Philippines.'

Fingleton's first day with Hughes set the tone. The new advisor was forced to work until 3 a.m. because Hughes wanted every statement the volatile Labor MP Eddie Ward had ever made on the subject of coal. The next morning Fingleton 'very proudly' handed the statements to Hughes, who immediately threw them in the wastepaper basket.

Not long afterwards, Hughes asked Fingleton what had happened to all the Ward statements. Fingleton told Hughes he'd already given them to him. That was news to Hughes.

'Do you think I'm a bloody fool?' he said.

'No, but you must think I am,' Fingleton said, steeling himself for the sack after just one day. To his surprise, Hughes kept him on.

★

One benefit of the Canberra job was that his wife and infant daughter could at last come to live with him. But the move wasn't easy for Philippa, who suffered extreme culture shock.

She had, after all, had a privileged upbringing. In the Street household, servants did the cooking and cleaning. Now Philippa had to fend for herself. But she learned fast. It was difficult, and at times she felt terribly isolated, but she somehow coped, teaching herself the basics of housekeeping and cooking, while being a doting wife and mother as well.

Fingleton, meanwhile, struggled to keep up with his boss's mood swings.

Hughes was notorious for sacking his staff. The one who deserved the prize for the shortest period in his employ was a private secretary, 'rich with degrees', who had been in the position only a few hours when Hughes asked him to do a menial job.

'After all, Mr Hughes, I am your private secretary.'

Hughes bellowed: 'Ah, brother. You mean, you were.'

Among the dubious pleasures of working for Hughes were his tantrums and his dreadful driving. To travel with Hughes to Sydney and back—as his staff were often required to do—was to put your life in his terrifyingly erratic hands. Hughes was adept at driving on the wrong side of the road. On one trip, a press secretary, after being tossed this way and that in the back seat, was about to throw up.

Hughes's secretary called out to the near-deaf driver: 'Mr Hughes, I'm afraid Morris is going to be sick.'

'Bloody sissy,' Hughes said as he stopped the car. As the press secretary was violently ill on the side of the road, Hughes gunned the engine and left him behind. Morris had to walk in the rain to Goulburn and catch the train. He got his revenge, though, later becoming world famous as the author Morris West.

Fingleton was smarter. Each time Hughes said he was about to drive to Sydney, he would book himself a berth on the train.

Since Fingleton was employed by the Army, Hughes could not sack him outright. But that didn't protect him from Hughes's tongue-lashings.

When the tirades got too much, Fingleton retreated to Country Party leader Arthur Fadden's office.

'It's no good, Mr Fadden,' a distressed Fingleton would say. 'I can't stand this old twerp any longer.'

'But don't tell me that he is getting you down. You stood up to Larwood—you should be able to stand up to Billy,' Fadden answered. 'You're not going to let this old so-and-so beat you, are you?'

'Larwood was different; he only came at you from the front. W.M.H. comes from all angles at once.'

At times Fingleton would have to call for reinforcements. His first pick was usually his old cricketing buddy Bill O'Reilly, because for some reason Hughes tended to respect well-built men.

Fingleton would telephone O'Reilly and say, 'You had better come down. The old bloke's being impossible again.'

O'Reilly would arrive. Hughes would suddenly grow quiet, and say, 'He's a fine type of man, you know.'

Fingleton eventually gave up and sought a release from Hughes's office, but not before he had collected a treasure trove of information and anecdotes about one of Australia's most controversial politicians.

In later years, Fingleton would delight in telling Hughes stories. His favourite revolved around Hughes playing on his supposed deafness.

A group of Canberra pressmen were attempting to get some information out of Hughes on a proposed sugar deal. As he came out of the Cabinet room, one of them asked: 'Mr Hughes, anything to tell us about sugar?'

Hughes as usual feigned complete deafness. 'Oh, well, you see, the Arbitration Act.'

'No, no, Mr Hughes,' they cried. 'Sugar . . . anything to tell us?'

'Well the Navigation Act . . .'

One of the larger men stormed towards Hughes, telling his colleagues, 'I'll make the old bastard hear.'

He cupped his hands and bellowed, 'Mr Hughes, anything to tell us about sugar?'

'Oh, well. I have two things to say. In the first place, I am not an old bastard and in the second place, I have nothing to say about sugar.'

After leaving Hughes's staff, Fingleton was transferred back to censorship work.

In this role he would attend Prime Minister Curtin's press briefings. The PM would tell the newspaper proprietors what was going on, and it would then be up to advisor Don Rodgers and Fingleton to decide what could be printed and what was off the record. It was uncomfortable work for Fingleton, who opposed restraints on press freedom, but in wartime priorities changed. Still, whenever possible, he attempted to work on the side of the journalist.

Working so closely with Rodgers and the Prime Minister, Fingleton found his respect for both growing.

His connections with the Sydney press proved invaluable when the leading newspaper proprietors, unhappy with what they deemed unfair censorship, in April 1944 ran blank spaces on their front pages to show where important information had been censored by the government. In retaliation, the NSW branch of the Censor's Office, headed by Horace Mansell, after several clashes, ordered that all *Sunday Telegraph* copy be submitted to it for approval. Editor Cyril Pearl submitted a page-one proof that prominently displayed an editorial titled, 'Free Speech is the Basis of Democracy'. When Pearl later told Mansell that the *Telegraph* had begun printing papers with blank columns, the agitated censor said, 'You will be in very serious trouble if you allow those papers to go out.'

At the time, Fingleton was working temporarily in the Censor's Sydney office. Mansell urgently dispatched him to the *Telegraph* offices to get copies of the first edition. When Fingleton arrived at the dock, he was met by Frank Packer, his one time fellow cadet journalist. Packer offered him a chair while he waited. Even though the hum of the printing presses could be heard, no newspapers appeared. Packer and other executives kept assuring Fingleton that it wouldn't be much longer. But it was not until after 1 a.m. that Fingleton received a copy, and when he delivered it to Mansell, the Censor sent a group of Commonwealth police to seize the entire edition.

Fingleton was far happier when he returned to Canberra in late 1944. Apart from rejoining his family, he was able to do genuine journalism again as a political reporter for Radio Australia. He combined this with his Department of Information duties. The Department's archives contain numerous secret reports written by Fingleton in 1945.

They include Ben Chifley's first press interview as Prime Minister in July of that year. After being congratulated by reporters for taking over the leadership after the sudden death of Curtin, Fingleton wrote, Chifley 'lit his pipe, thanked the press, and said that he wished it to be understood at the outset that he did not want himself incorporated from time to time in sensational press statements'.

He had often found that somebody walked along the corridors and said 'Good morning' to a press man, that might easily appear in the afternoon as a sensational statement from the Minister concerned. Mr Chifley added that his remarks, of course, did not apply to any present. He wanted it to be understood, however, that if he told them things not under his name, it was not to appear over his name. He would not promise that he would give them clear statements of what was intended to be done . . . but he would see that they were not led up the garden path. He would tell them if they were wrong rather than tell them what was the right thing.

As with Curtin, whose death deeply upset him, Fingleton was impressed with Chifley. He particularly admired his fairness in dealing with the press, his common touch and strong sense of humanity.

When the war ended in August, Fingleton returned to journalism as a radio and freelance newspaper reporter in the Canberra press gallery.

But an even bigger priority was recreating that damned lost manuscript and getting his first book back on track.

15

His Masterpiece

Fingleton's early months in the Canberra press gallery were accompanied by a frenetic rhythm. It was easy to track him down. You simply followed the sound—the incessant tap-tapping of his two-finger typing.

In his cramped office on the Senate side of Parliament House or at the dining-room table at home, Fingleton, between filing political reports for Radio Australia, would bash away for hours at a time on his *Cricket Crisis* manuscript.

It was difficult, and he had few guideposts. Fingleton was heading into the unknown, taking a novel approach to cricket writing. Diving deep into a contentious subject, he covered it both as a participant and as an observer, adding trenchant analysis and often biting wit. Many times he thought of giving up, but Philippa would persuade him to keep going, even ordering him to get back to the typewriter. Whenever she could, she also tried to lighten his burden by making the atmosphere at home as conducive as possible to writing.

This was no easy task. By the time Fingleton re-started his book, Philippa was caring for two small children, Belinda, who was three, and Jim, who had just turned one. She was also pregnant with their third child. While Jack tapped away, the Fingletons also moved from their home in Reid to the dress-circle suburb of Forrest. But between the chaos of child minding and moving house, Philippa did all she could to ensure that her husband wasn't disturbed. He needed that support, because he was under growing pressure to get the book finished.

Losing the original manuscript was a body blow. Then came the news that a rival book was in the works. Journalist Ray Robinson had been writing about cricket between the wars, inevitably touching on the Bodyline series. And unlike Fingleton, he had a publisher lined up.

When Robinson finished his manuscript, he showed it to Neville Cardus, who was so enthused he posted it to his London publishers, William Collins, recommending that they buy it. Collins agreed.

When Fingleton also approached Collins in 1945, he found it was a case of first in best dressed. Collins wrote to Fingleton in 1945 to explain that as the Bodyline subject had angered so many people, 'it might be inadvisable to bring it up before the public'. Once Robinson's *Between Wickets* was in the process of being published, in 1946, Collins' editors saw little mileage in another book covering the same period and many of the same personalities. They were also concerned that Fingleton had given too much emphasis to Bradman, 'and perhaps in too strong phraseology'.

'He is a popular hero, as you know, with every schoolboy, and possibly too with many fathers, and while we quite agree that one might say your remarks regarding his super-excellence as a batsman makes most interesting reading, we would again stress that we consider it should be handled in a very diplomatic and indirect manner.'

Fingleton was suspicious. Sir Pelham Warner was known to

be close to Collins, and he thought they were also afraid of offending the former England manager, 'whom I do not let off lightly'.

It was also galling that Robinson—a friend but also a professional rival—had found favour with Collins at Fingleton's expense. That wasn't surprising, however. Robinson was sweet natured, meticulous, knowledgeable and passionate about the game. The 40-year-old was admired by generations of Test cricketers.

Fingleton was more cynical, hard-edged, and caustic. He didn't hesitate to point out Robinson's chief weakness as a cricket writer—he had not played the first-class game. Ever the gentleman, Robinson did not respond. Fingleton wrote to a friend, 'I am not afraid of him as he is not at all known in the cricketing world, but I would like to beat him all the same.'

In July 1946, the Cassell publishing house accepted Fingleton's manuscript, and had it in bookshops by the end of the year. Robinson's book had come out three months earlier, and contained a short introduction by Sir Pelham Warner. Fingleton was one up on him there: he convinced Cardus to write a foreword to his book, and thought it more appealing than Warner's effort.

Despite Fingleton's fear of being overshadowed, *Cricket Crisis* won immediate acclaim and soon became a cricketing classic. It remains the most authoritative first-hand study of 'the Bodyline storm'.

Admirers of *Cricket Crisis*—and many have named it their favourite cricket book—praised its wit, artistry and wealth of deeply informed fact and comment. Most assumed the writer was well educated, certainly not someone who had left school before his teens. *Cricket Crisis* is a tribute to the intelligence and self-education of Jack Fingleton and the support of his wife, to whom it was dedicated.

As Cardus notes in the Foreword: 'The honesty of every page is as straight as Fingleton's bat, and with the pen he is not afraid to attack; but his inborn realism always keeps his eye on the ball, so that he knows exactly where his strokes are going; there is next to no vague footwork, and in not more than one chapter does he give a possible chance.' Usually critical, Fingleton turned a blind eye to this explosion of cricketing metaphors.

Fingleton the writer was not unlike Fingleton the cricketer: trenchant, committed, fearless. Where Robinson composed carefully, weighing each phrase, Fingleton wrote exactly what he thought. He just let it flow. He refused to pull punches. And he was prepared for the consequences.

Cricket Crisis presented a trenchant, ground-level view of cricket that many fans had not seen. Bradman, in particular, came across for the first time as a three-dimensional human being. Gone was the sickly-sweet coating applied by countless fawning admirers. Instead, Fingleton showed that, like everyone else, he had flaws; that far from being loved by fellow cricketers he was disliked by some. With a keen journalistic eye, Fingleton cut through the gloss of Bradmania, revealing the truth behind the legend.

He also cut to the core of Bodyline, explaining that it 'was nothing more nor less than a revolution against Bradman'.

The book is divided into two parts. The first covers Bodyline. The second, subtitled 'Other Lines', intersperses chapters on Fingleton's favourite players, including O'Reilly, Grimmett and McCabe, with snippets from his diaries of the tours to South Africa in 1935–36 and England in 1938, and observations on a variety of subjects, including Australian politicians and critics.

Bradman, whom Fingleton calls 'the problem child of cricket', is the focus of the Bodyline section. Fingleton explains why he was a loner, why he was such a devastating batsman, why he was so suspicious of others, including, clearly, the author, and why he was treated in turn with disdain. That Bradman was clearly affected by, even scared of, Bodyline, is clear. At a time when Bradman was such an Australian idol, to say so took considerable courage.

Fingleton also scrutinises Douglas Jardine. His view of the England captain is far more benign than that of many Australian fans. He admits that he even liked him. Some of his sharpest barbs are reserved for Pelham Warner, the England manager. Warner's claim that Fingleton was to blame for the Woodfull leak was in fact a prime motive for the book. Warner comes across as a clever, careful politician who could always negotiate his way out of trouble. Fingleton also looks at Harold Larwood, with enormous respect for his cricketing prowess. Fingleton refuses to place all the blame for Bodyline on Larwood, explaining that he and Jardine 'each did a job, and the great pity of it, in the final analysis, is that two such eminent and gifted cricketers should have departed from the game under such an unmistakable cloud'.

The book is studded with great anecdotes. Of Larwood, Fingleton writes:

> Larwood was a professional cricketer, and it is a fair deduction that he bowled as he was ordered. He was greatly upset when Oldfield was injured in Adelaide. He had no great personal liking for Bradman, whom he considered conceited; but Larwood, in his nature, in his outlook on life, was rather a meek soul. There was his quiet reply at Ballarat when an irate busybody crossed Larwood's name off a list which had just been posted at the Englishman's hotel showing the team for the morrow.
>
> 'I hope,' said the foolhardy soul to Larwood, 'that you never play cricket again.'

Larwood did not break out into a fury. 'You say that,' he said quietly to this fellow, 'when cricket is my life, my means of livelihood.'

The reviews were glowing. Congratulatory letters came from readers as exalted as Ben Chifley and Robert Menzies. Philippa sent a telegram to say she was 'thrilled with my copy. Your wife a very proud little girl. Wife of a famous author. Congratulations and all my love.'

C.L.R. James described *Cricket Crisis* in a letter as 'the best account' of Bodyline, and in his own acclaimed cricket book, *Beyond a Boundary*, called Fingleton's work an 'excellent and necessary book on the bodyline controversy'. On one key point, however, he disagrees with Fingleton. Bodyline, in his view, was not just a quest to overthrow Bradman but also 'the violence and ferocity of our age expressing itself in cricket'.

After James finished writing *Beyond a Boundary*, he asked Fingleton to look over the manuscript. Fingleton offered praise and suggested improvements, writing, 'there is much with which I don't agree—the bodyline series for instance (I wonder if you know I played in that one) but that is just a matter of opinion'.

James did not change his account, explaining to Fingleton that he wanted 'to show that bodyline was a symptom of degeneration in "it isn't cricket" which continues to this day, and that degeneration I relate to the declining standards of morals and values in the world at large'.

Cricket Crisis did not delight everyone, of course. It hit nerves, notably Bradman's. The Don told friends he was disgusted that Fingleton had all but called him a coward.

Cricket Crisis kicked off a new phase in the Bradman–Fingleton feud.

In his autobiography *Farewell to Cricket*, Bradman fired back, questioning Fingleton's qualifications to criticise him. Fingleton, he wrote, 'cast very grave reflections on my tactics. It may be well to remind readers that his last three Test innings against Jardine's men yielded 1, 0 and 0, whereupon he was dropped from the Australian team.

'In the same three innings I scored 177 runs at an average of 88.5. These figures scarcely give Fingleton any authority to criticise my methods. Apparently I had to make a century every time and also be hit more often than anyone else to satisfy the taste of some.'

Fingleton replied at length in his book *Brown and Company*. He had set out to 'analyse rather than criticise him,' he explained, 'but I did re-quote opinions of Bradman which [Jack] Hobbs and [M.A.] Noble expressed at the time. They were certainly very critical of Bradman. One said that you would slap a schoolboy if he exhibited such methods; the other said he was letting Australia down and he criticised Woodfull for not checking him in his style of play.'

As Hobbs and Noble did not play against bodyline and therefore made no runs against it, perhaps they too, on Bradman's logic, should not have dared to criticise him. D.G.B. does me honour in comparing me with himself, even in the matter of making ducks, but using his same logic, which seems pie-eyed to me, his scores preceding the ones he mentions concede my right to criticise him as much as I like.

Against Jardine and the first flush of bodyline, and with both of us batting twice on a sticky pitch, Bradman, previously to the scores he mentions, made 3, 10, 36, 13, 18, 23 and 0. I made 29, 53 not out, 119 not out, 18, 26, 40 and 83. His average to this stage, then, against Jardine's team, was 14; mine was 73. Confining it to Test innings, his was 0 and mine was 50. When I was dropped from the Test team, his average, for all the help of that 88.5 which he stresses, was 31; mine was 46.

Bradman refers to centuries and hits. He made one century in all the games of that season against the Englishmen and those who played in those games will permit themselves a wry smile when he mentions 'hits'. Some batsmen received more hits than were good for themselves or their cricket but, mainly because of some odd weavings and shiftings before Larwood even bowled the ball that tour, Bradman received exactly one hit! It was those tactics that led Hobbs and Noble to criticise Bradman so strongly.

As a journalist who played Test cricket, I am, I suppose, by profession, more analytical than most other cricketers who've written books on the game, but I like to think that my premises are justly formed. Most of my impressions of Bradman against bodyline were formed at the other batting end.

But Fingleton wasn't finished. He soon had more ammunition to use against the Don.

Fingleton at the time was spreading himself thin. Apart from his radio work, which included providing cricket commentaries for the ABC, he freelanced for several media organisations.

For South African newspapers he covered a variety of Australian issues as well as the local cricket scene. Indian newspapers were also keen bidders for his services. When the England team arrived in Australia for the 1946–47 tour, Fingleton asked Sir Raghunath Paranjpye, the Indian High Commissioner, if *The Hindu* would be interested in carrying his reports. The editor immediately cabled its answer: 'Yes.'

By the late 1940s, Fingleton had worked his way up to what Philippa described as 'the best job in the world', spending part of the year at home in Canberra tussling with politicians, and the rest following cricketers around Australia or overseas and getting paid for it.

He was reluctant to write for Australian newspapers, remarking that they 'are not noted for their generosity'. He thought they also treated their journalists poorly. With a successful book under his belt, he no longer had to worry about keeping Australian newspaper editors contented. He could make better money writing for international ones, all of whom were unendingly interested in his cricketing views generally, and Bradman copy in particular. And the tour of Wally Hammond's team was the ideal venue for assessing whether Bradman, now approaching his forties, was still the czar of the local sporting scene or whether he was losing his edge.

Not for the first time, it wasn't certain that Bradman would make himself available to play England. He had been ill with fibrositis and gastritis, and was also trying to establish himself as an independent stockbroker in the wake of the controversial collapse of his boss Harry Hodgetts's firm. In the biggest financial scandal in South Australian history, Hodgetts was in 1945 declared bankrupt, with liabilities of £82,854 and 238 unsecured creditors, including Test cricketer Arthur Richardson, retired Governor-General Lord Gowrie, and Bradman. Hodgetts, found guilty of fraud and false pretences, was sentenced to five years' jail.

Within days, Bradman was operating a new business from the same offices, and with full access to Hodgetts's client list.

Bradman had been striving for some time to become a respected member of the Adelaide Establishment. But many of the blue-bloods in its ranks turned up their noses at sportsmen. The Hodgetts debacle, and questions over the extent of Bradman's involvement in it, did little for his social or professional status.

Although the affair cast a cloud over Bradman in the eyes of the business community and the social elite—especially Stock Exchange and Royal Adelaide Golf Club members—his stockbroking business gradually found its feet. His clout in Australian cricket also increased when he took over Hodgetts's seat on the Board of Control. But whether his involvement would be strictly off-field was still in doubt. The England tourists were surprised by how gaunt the Don looked. Bradman himself doubted he was well enough to endure lengthy Test matches, but eventually he agreed to play, combining his role as one of the three Test selectors with the captaincy.

If Bradman was hoping for a gentle return after his eight-year Test hiatus, it was not to be. Instead he found himself at the centre of another cricket controversy, which swirled around the question of his sportsmanship. This time Fingleton was not on the opposing side, but from his perch in the press box, he was still close enough to offer his observations.

The Test series began in friendly enough fashion, but that soon changed. Bradman had won the call in Brisbane and decided to bat. He found the England attack extremely tricky, and showed it: England captain Wally Hammond thought he 'began like a schoolboy'. After making 28 unimpressive runs, Bradman attempted to chop a ball from Bill Voce wide of the slips. It instead flew to Jack Ikin at second slip and chest high. Ikin took the catch, and all of the England players assumed Bradman was out. But umpire George Borwick said it was a bump ball. Bradman was given not out.

Hammond was disgusted that Bradman did not walk, and at the end of the over he walked over to him and said: 'A fine fucking way to start a series.'

It was also a fine way for Bradman to regain his form. He went on to score 187, helping Australia to a comfortable win in the First Test.

In the press box, most were astounded that Bradman had remained at the crease. As Fingleton wrote: 'Former Test cricketers in the Press-box involuntarily shouted "he's out", and that was the general Press-box opinion, an opinion, of course, which is not infallible. Inquiries made some weeks afterwards, however, provided conclusive evidence that it was a catch Ikin made, and not, as Bradman obviously thought, a bump ball.'

O'Reilly, sitting near Fingleton in the press box, was equally convinced that Bradman had been out, and that umpire Borwick had been 'caught napping'.

Fingleton often wondered what Bradman's future might have been had he been out for 28 and not 187. Early in the innings, he noted that the Don appeared to 'be in great mental distress'. He took Bradman's part in the controversy, saying he may not have realised he had given a catch. 'In all my experiences with Bradman,' he wrote, 'I never once had the slightest reason to doubt his sportsmanship.'

The Ikin incident gave a sharp edge to the Test series, and ensured that newspaper editors were eager for any copy Fingleton could give them. His close contacts with current and past players made him one of the few journalists who knew what exactly was going on in the Australian dressing room. One of his best sources was Keith Miller, who provided Fingleton with good intelligence from inside the Australian team.

Miller was one of several players who, as in Fingleton's day, had their differences with the Don. The detractors may have not been so plentiful this time, but they were there and, knowing of Fingleton's own testy relationship with Bradman, often passed on interesting titbits.

Miller, a swashbuckling fellow with an outsize personality and matinee-idol looks, was the ultimate free spirit, and it was only natural that the Second World War fighter pilot would be at odds with his reserved, authoritarian captain. Miller also struggled to comprehend the restrictions imposed by numerous cricketing officials, in particular those close to Bradman, such as Bill Jeanes.

After a long day in the field during the Fourth Test, Miller was relaxing in the Adelaide Oval dressing room with a glass of beer when Jeanes told him to hurry up and get into a taxi headed for the team's hotel. Miller said no, he was staying right where he was, and a heated argument erupted. Jeanes reported Miller to Bradman, and the next morning he was summoned to the Don's Adelaide office.

Bradman was apologetic, saying Jeanes was ill and that Miller should forget the incident. But the paceman was disgusted to have been treated like a naughty schoolboy sent to the headmaster's office. He confided the incident to Fingleton, on condition that he not write about it. Fingleton advised Miller to be wary of both Bradman and Jeanes, but reassured him that he was such a valuable player they would never think of dropping him.

There was still a general feeling that Bradman was trying to get back at England for its earlier misdeeds. Fingleton described Bradman's captaincy during the 1946–47 series as having 'an element of mercilessness that recalled memories of Jardine'. It wasn't exactly leg theory, but England was subjected to its fair share of bumpers.

> As for the spirit, I don't think the 'goodwill' series helped one iota, and in this Bradman must accept his share of responsibility. He was a good and a shrewd leader, but not a generous one. It was Bradman's job to win for Australia, undoubtedly, but he could have made one or two gestures to such an opposing side. Particularly should he have ordered his fast men, Lindwall and Miller, to cut down the big crop of bumpers. It seemed to me, however, that Bradman, when confronted with an MCC cap, could neither forget nor forgive the bodyline tour.

Bradman's tactics—most controversially, he was accused of playing for a draw in Adelaide—upset many, including numerous former Test players. Fingleton reported that Herbie Collins, now writing a newspaper column, had fronted Bradman behind the Members' Pavilion at Adelaide Oval.

'I have written an article for my Sydney newspaper about you,' Collins began.

Bradman nodded.

'In case they don't print it in full, I'll tell you the theme of it. I've suggested that cricket would be a better game now if you got out of it.'

Miller was another who was less than excited by Bradman's approach. He resented the way the captain pressed him to bowl faster and be more aggressive towards certain England players, such as Bill Edrich, whom he wanted to 'grind . . . into the dust'.

Miller, who knew what real war involved, found Bradman's belligerence distasteful. His remorselessness may have won Australia the Ashes, but Miller wondered at what cost.

The following season found Fingleton again travelling the country, this time covering the tour of a depleted Indian team. *The Hindu* was particularly interested in the lead-up to, and achievement of, Bradman's 100th first-class century, during an Australian XI match against India in Sydney. But the juiciest story occurred off the field. On the eve of the Fourth Test against India in Adelaide, Bradman attended a Legacy Club luncheon. When the invited guest speaker, India team manager Peter Gupta, was delayed, Bradman took his place. Within hours, what he said to the fifty-odd guests was emblazoned across the front page of the Adelaide *News*. The Test skipper and selector, it seemed, had made some interesting comments on players whom he was considering for the Ashes tour of England later that year. He was especially disparaging about Australia's spin bowling candidates. Bruce Dooland, in his view, was suffering from 'touritis', and his obsession with getting into the touring squad had affected his bowling. He was unimpressed with Canberra's Fred Johnston. And while he was happy with Colin McCool, Bradman still 'did not think anyone ever expected him to develop into another Grimmett'. Summing up, Bradman lamented: 'At present we have no spin bowler who is really outstanding.'

When Bradman saw *The News* he was enraged. He told several media contacts the comments had been made at a private function and he had expected them to remain private. The Melbourne *Sun-Pictorial* quoted him as saying that the publication of his comments without his permission was a breach of journalistic etiquette. In any case, he added, he had been 'misreported'.

The News wasn't going to let Bradman get away with that. The following day, the journalist who had been at the function, Colin Hay, insisted his report was accurate. Hay said he had spoken to Bradman, 'who has known me on the cricket field and as a newspaper man for ten years, outside the dining hall'. He went on: 'He knew I was representing *The News*. At no time did he request that any of his remarks not be published. As the points he made were of such moment, I considered it my duty to give a factual report of his speech.'

Hay also approached Bradman in person. The Don reiterated that fairness demanded 'under the exceptional circumstances of my talk yesterday that you should not have used anything that I said . . . I filled the breach as an act of courtesy, and I don't think any of my remarks should have been published.'

The editor-in-chief of *The News* laughed Bradman off, saying his 'conclusions on journalistic ethics are, to say the least, peculiar'. Bradman had not said at the beginning of his address that his remarks were not for publication, and 'if he simply forgot yesterday to declare his remarks private, then he should not employ the old familiar practice of "blaming the reporter"'.

The local branch of the Australian Journalists' Association was also upset by 'complaints about remarks concerning Adelaide newspapermen alleged to have been made by the South Australian captain'. The AJA noted that this was not the first time Bradman had complained about reporters. He had also been offended when remarks he had made at a meeting of the Federal Institute of Accountants were reported. The AJA wrote to Bradman asking if he had made his complaints of misreporting directly to the newspapers and if he could give instances of this. If he could not substantiate allegations of general misreporting, it said, he should withdraw his statement. The issue petered out, but not before it had widened the breach between Bradman and the Adelaide media.

Fingleton ran with the story, telling his Indian readers that 'for the first time as a cricket legislator, Bradman today put his foot in things when he unburdened his selector's soul . . . Interesting as Bradman's opinions are, more interesting is the fact that he is the first Australian selector in history to breach oyster-like silence on the eve of a selection of a touring team.'

He related how 'Pressmen in the Adelaide hotel tonight watched Bradman's co-selectors—Dwyer and Ryder—read Bradman's story on the front page of an Adelaide newspaper. Fingleton said 'it was obvious that they were amazed at the indiscretion of their co-selector' in revealing which players were and were not secure for the English tour.

> No selector ever before thus far committed themselves. Previously, the selectors have observed the unwritten rule that they will not discuss such matters. There is also a written rule that selectors make no comment to the press or make broadcasts on the likely members of the team. The question that is being relayed to Board officials in the Eastern States is whether Bradman has disqualified himself from the selectorship.

Fingleton continued the attack in a dispatch the following day. After explaining that the Board of Control had confronted the

Bradman controversy with 'tight-lipped silence', he commented that the Don had 'made a very bad blunder'.

'The point is not whether any remark of Bradman found their way into the Press, but whether he made any such remarks about likely players to England to anyone at all, other than his fellow selectors. That is where he blundered.'

Fingleton was particularly miffed by Bradman's apparent dismissal of Fred Johnston, a player in whom he'd taken a personal interest. Fingleton kept a close eye on the Canberra cricket scene, and had been impressed with Johnston's leg spinning talents. He thought Johnston, a Sydney teacher who had been transferred to Canberra, was being wasted in local cricket and could be an asset for the NSW Sheffield Shield team. He contacted his old NSW teammate, now state selector, Alec Marks and asked him to come to Canberra, stay at his place and watch Johnston play. Unfortunately, Marks's visit coincided with torrential downpours, and the weekend's grade matches were called off.

Undeterred, Fingleton went to Plan B. He invited Johnston to his house and organised a makeshift pitch. Johnston bounded in from the street and down the driveway, bowling to Marks, who stood in the garage with bat in hand. After facing Johnston for several overs, Marks picked him for the NSW team. Johnston went on to take more than 100 wickets for NSW.

Fingleton was irked not just by Bradman's off-field behaviour but by his batting during the India series. In one dispatch he said the Don was now 'purely an orthodox batsman who scores mainly off indifferent bowling'.

Less than three weeks after the Legacy Club blunder, the Australian team for England was announced. Colin McCool made it. Bruce Dooland and Fred Johnston didn't. Bradman's views about Australian cricketers had clearly not changed. Nor had his views of his main detractors—as Fingleton was to learn in the brutal opening weeks of an England summer.

16

Laughing at the Gods

If Fingleton had any hopes of healing his rift with Bradman while following him around England in 1948, they were dashed by a provocative newspaper article.

It was Bradman's farewell tour, and he was feted like a king. The anticipation was almost overwhelming. In a typical piece of hyperbole, Neville Cardus wrote: 'Cricketers in England will rejoice that the last rays of Bradman's splendour will fall on the greenest fields in the world.'

Fingleton, as ever, took a grittier view. In a preview article on the tour for the London *Daily Mail*, he wrote that Bradman, now forty, had lost none of his lust for victory. He was obsessed with finishing this tour unbeaten. Fingleton recalled the Don's old nickname, the Bowral Boy, which dated from his teen years, when he played on the Bowral village green in dark trousers and blue shirt:

Somehow we of his playing generation feel that Bradman has missed much in the changeover from the Bowral Boy to Mr Bradman. There are things for which we count the game most blessed that Bradman seems to have missed. We have always had a spirit of comradeship between us that, in my personal experience, has been unknown to Bradman. He thinks we are jealous and resentful of him. He's wrong. A lot of us only think he has sacrificed much for runs and records.

After reading the piece, Bradman decided to boycott Fingleton for the rest of the tour. He informed other officials that Fingleton would 'not receive any further privileges on the tour as far as I am concerned'. He twisted the knife again after the tour. In *Farewell to Cricket*, he took issue with 'one of the most openly bitter articles about me'. He did not name Fingleton, merely referring to him as 'an ex-cricketer, well known to both sides'. 'The whole thing reeked of personal spleen, naked and unashamed,' Bradman wrote. He claimed that teammates, opposition players and officials had come to him 'expressing their disgust at what was obviously a personal tirade against me . . . Their references to what they thought of this critic were better expressed verbally than in print.' Bradman noted that Fingleton had 'made a special study of my alleged weaknesses, and whenever the opportunity arose, would labour my shortcomings (according to him) on wet wickets'.

Fingleton was unfazed by Bradman's boycott. Bradman wasn't especially close to any Australian pressmen, so he was unlikely to be scooped on a big story. Besides, Fingleton's good relationship with many of Bradman's players ensured that he knew what was going on behind the Australian dressing-room door. Several other pressmen on the tour shared his feelings about the skipper. He was surrounded by 'cobbers' such as O'Reilly and Tom Goodman, working for the *Sydney Morning Herald*, Ray Robinson (the Sydney *Sun*) and Arthur Mailey (the *Telegraph*).

He also had an abundance of work to keep him occupied. As well as reporting for a number of newspapers, he was doing radio broadcasts and preparing his second cricket book.

The Orient Line
brochure outlining the
itinerary of the 1938
Australian team's sea
voyage to England.

R.M.S. ORONTES
20,000
TONS

CAPTAIN: Captain G. G. Thorne, R.D., R.N.R.
STAFF COMMANDER: Comdr. F. J. L. Butler, R.D., R.N.R.
FIRST OFFICER: Comdr. H. Petit-Dann, R.D., R.N.R.
PURSER: H. N. M. Herapath.
SURGEON: B. Muir, M.R.C.S., L.R.C.P.
CHIEF ENGINEER: G. D. S. White, M.I.Mar.E.

ITINERARY

BRISBANE	dep. Wed.	Mar. 2	PORT SAID	Sat.	Apr. 9
SYDNEY	,, Wed.	Mar. 9	NAPLES	Wed.	Apr. 13
HOBART	,, Sat.	Mar. 12	VILLEFRANCHE	Thur.	Apr. 14
MELBOURNE	,, Tues.	Mar. 15	TOULON	Fri.	Apr. 15
ADELAIDE	,, Thur.	Mar. 17	GIBRALTAR	Sun.	Apr. 17
FREMANTLE	,, Mon.	Mar. 21	SOUTHAMPTON	Wed.	Apr. 20
COLOMBO	Wed.	Mar. 30	LONDON	Thur.	Apr. 21
ADEN	Tues.	Apr. 5			

Bill Brown, Les Fleetwood-Smith, Jack and Bill O'Reilly wave from the deck
as the *Orontes* sets sail.

The 1938 Australian team to tour England. Jack is second from right in the back row.

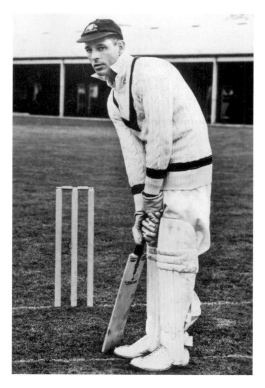

Jack in full pose on the 1938 tour of England.

Jack and Don Bradman greet England's Frank Woolley (left) during the 1938 England tour. To the right is the Australian team manager Bill Jeanes.

Jack hitting through the covers against Worcester in 1938. Bradman is his batting partner.

Jack and Philippa on their wedding day, 17 January 1942, in Waverley.

Jack in his Army uniform.

Jack and Philippa at Waverley Oval showing off their firstborn, Belinda, in 1942.

On their way to England in 1953. From left: Belinda, Grey, Larry, Philippa, Jack and Jim.

Some years on and Jack is on another Ashes tour as a journalist. It didn't stop him donning the pads.

The Jack Fingleton golf swing.

Jack Fingleton, the journalist.

Receiving his OBE from Governor General Sir John Kerr in 1976.

Jack with a couple of his hero Victor Trumper's bats.

Playing to the crowd when appearing on *Parkinson* in Australia.

If the tour proved successful, publishers had told him, they wanted a book chronicling Bradman's last hurrah. The success of *Cricket Crisis* had made Fingleton a marketable author.

Adding to the pleasure of the tour was the chance to revisit England. Fingleton was an unabashed Anglophile. He loved British pomp and ceremony, the village green, the traditions. But London in 1948 was vastly different from the city he'd visited ten years before. The devastation of the Blitz was visible everywhere. 'All the way up from Tilbury we had seen the pitiful remnants of bombed-out buildings and homes', he later wrote. 'London still looked magnificently good in April of 1948. It had been battered and purged but it was still pulsating in resilient manner.'

The struggle to recover from the war was apparent even on the cricket field. When Australia was playing at Worcester, one spectator saw the groundsman sprinkling sawdust near the wicket. ''Ere, go easy with yon sawdust,' he called out. 'Why, yon man is wasting full month's ration of ruddy sausage meat.'

'You had to taste English sausages of 1948 to appreciate that,' Fingleton observed.

Far more appetising was the sight of the Australian team beating all and sundry. Bradman and most of his players were in fine form, inspiring enthusiastic copy. The team was on a mission to prove it was Australia's greatest.

Once again, however, the issue at the top of everyone's mind was whether England could contain Bradman. The Test series began at Trent Bridge, and Bradman was soon in command, scoring another century. England then set out to stifle him by bowling outside his leg stump to a leg-side field. Fingleton wrote that 'these English tactics did not seem to impress Bradman'. At the end of play, Bradman was unbeaten on 130. That night, Fingleton and O'Reilly met a group of England players past and present. Over a drink, O'Reilly told the England paceman Alec Bedser that he wasn't impressed with the placement of his leg-side field. If Bedser wanted to get Bradman out, he said, he would have to adjust his field. Bedser was intrigued, and O'Reilly drew him a diagram.

Next day, Bedser adopted the O'Reilly plan, moving Len Hutton from leg slip to fine leg, about 12 yards from the bat, in position for the leg glance. Mid on was moved to become a short leg. Shortly after, Bradman leg glanced a ball straight to Hutton, who caught him.

'Bedser, grinning hugely, gave a wave of appreciation to O'Reilly in the far-off Press Box,' Fingleton wrote, 'and even three minutes later this momentous cricketing news had gained the outside world because a passing engine-driver exultantly whooped a cock-a-doodle-do on the whistle.' Bradman soon heard of Bedser's wave to the press box, learned of Tiger's involvement in his dismissal, and privately accused O'Reilly of treason. That did nothing for their already tense relationship. Fingleton came to Tiger's defence, stating that 'any bowler is fully entitled, in the interests of the game, to tell a fellow slave what he thinks of things'.

Fingleton also noticed that Bradman and Miller appeared to be keeping each other at arm's length. The captain who 'holds more field conferences than any captain I've ever known,' he wrote, 'had remarkably few' with his key paceman throughout the tour. Again, it all revolved around the excessive number of bouncers Miller was bowling.

Still Bradman, hell bent on beating his old foes, could do no wrong in the public eye. The Test and county victories continued to pile up, and everywhere Bradman went he provoked near-hysteria.

Fingleton described the Don's arrival at the crease in the Fourth Test, in Leeds:

Bradman received a remarkable reception, the like of which I have not seen approached on any ground. Thousands of people lined up many deep three-quarters of the way to the pitch. With three policemen as a bodyguard, Bradman came to bat down this long lane, his green cap faintly showing every now and then among his adulators. He was enthusiastically clapped, patted and pummelled as he walked along.

Bradman emerged from the lane to a thunderous applause which continued for the rest of the way in the middle. The Australian acknowledged it with a merry rising of his cap, but this seemed insufficient so he gaily waved his bat to the crowd. This, surely, will always rank as the greatest tribute paid any cricketer, and, be it noted, this was not, like Hutton, Bradman being welcomed on his home ground. He was an Australian in England but, more than any cricketer of modern days, Bradman belonged more to the game of cricket than to any country.

Fingleton was just as enthused by the spirit many of the younger players showed. He doubted whether he had 'ever seen a more pleasing innings' than Arthur Morris's Test century at Lord's. He also liked the precocious attitude of the baby of the side, Neil Harvey. As for Keith Miller, he acknowledged that he was 'the supreme believer in Miller as a cricketer . . . He has given me joy in the game unapproached by others.'

Fingleton was also keenly appreciative of England's most talented, above all paceman Dick Pollard: 'His hair is red, his face is ruddy, his flesh is pink and you see much flesh on his arms because Dick rolls his sleeves up higher than anybody else in the game . . . Off field, he plays the piano splendidly.' Fingleton liked cricketers who were well balanced, good all-rounders. Single-minded zealots irritated him. He much preferred players with broad general knowledge and a sense of fun.

And he always welcomed surprises.

By the time the Australians walked onto the Oval for the

Fifth Test, they were ahead 3–0. The Ashes had been won, with England's batting—rated by Fingleton 'the poorest in modern memory—no match for the visitors'.

The only fascination left in the series was whether Bradman could score the few runs he needed to finish with a 100–plus average in Test cricket. His average at the start of the Test was 101.39, so four runs were all it would take to keep him over the century mark. As Bradman headed out to the wicket, he looked supremely confident. After all his last three Test innings at the Oval had been 232, 244 and 77.

Fingleton takes up the story:

> The reception he received must have been embarrassing for him. It lasted all the way to the middle, and there [Norman] Yardley had assembled his team and called for three cheers for Bradman. This the English team gave heartily and Yardley shook Bradman by the hand. Bradman took guard, looked about and settled himself. [Eric] Hollies bowled him a good one which Bradman played off the back foot. The next was pitched slightly farther up. It drew Bradman forward, he missed and the ball crashed into his stumps. And what a roar there was from the crowd!
>
> This was one of the strangest experiences I have ever known on a cricketing field. One moment the crowd was acknowledging Bradman lavishly in his farewell appearance in Test cricket against England; that noise had barely died on the afternoon air when it was rent again with the crowd shrieking at Bradman's dismissal. As the game gives, so the game takes away! Bradman looked back at his stumps, seemed not able to believe what he saw there, turned slowly and very, very slowly retraced his steps to the pavilion and a sympathetic reception. The game that had given him so much had denied him at the very last Test appearance.

Bedlam broke out in the press box. What a cruel end to the hero's last stand: a final Test innings duck and an average of 99.94—tantalisingly short of the three figures Bradman yearned for. Cricket had humbled its greatest conqueror. Amid the furor, Fingleton and O'Reilly were beside themselves. E.W. Swanton thought they would both have a stroke, they were 'laughing so much'. And why not? They were laughing at a god with feet of clay. Laughing at the fact that even the mighty Bradman could fail. Laughing at an old antagonist who'd just got his comeuppance.

Bradman and his supporters put it down to spite. Bradman told his biographer Charles Williams that O'Reilly's mirth had nakedly exposed 'the disloyalty I had to endure during my early years as Australian captain, a disloyalty based purely on jealousy and religion'. But he reserved special ire for Fingleton. He, in Bradman's view, 'was the ring leader. He conducted a vendetta against me all his life and it was most distasteful because he was a prolific writer of books and articles. Conversely, with these fellows out of the way the loyalty of my 1948 side was a big joy and made a big contribution to the outstanding success of that tour.'

In making those remarks Bradman conveniently forgot how often Fingleton had written of him with praise and admiration.

But if Bradman resented their reaction, some of his teammates thought nothing of it. After the series, acting captain Lindsay Hassett invited Fingleton and O'Reilly to accompany the team on their bus to Birmingham.

'It was quite like old times as we joined in the team songs,' Fingleton wrote. 'It was a touch of kindness that we greatly appreciated—and, as far as I could see, contaminated no one.' And, as he dryly observed: 'This would not have happened with Bradman.'

Then it was over. On 10 September 1948 Bradman was dismissed for the last time on English soil in a first-class match.

He and his team had done what they set out to do—go through the tour undefeated. They become known as 'the Invincibles'. And the Bradman mystique intensified.

Fingleton was no sooner home than William Collins, who had knocked back *Cricket Crisis*, were pressing him for a book on the tour, which they wanted to have on sale by the start of the following Australian summer. And where previously they had been hesitant to overemphasise Bradman, this time they wanted all Bradman, all the time.

Another feverish period of writing began with Philippa struggling to keep three young children out of mischief as her husband ploughed through the reams of typing paper. Fingleton came up with a title early—*Brightly Fades the Don*, a play on the title of the Russian novel *And Quiet Flows the Don*. The publishers were enthusiastic.

So Fingleton again sat down to analyse the Bradman phenomenon—and once more provided a detailed and vigorous assessment. As Fingleton's good friend the British journalist Michael Parkinson would later say, Fingleton was Bradman's 'most ardent supporter and sternest critic'.

Fingleton's respect for Bradman the cricketer was enormous. Indeed, many of the finest tributes Bradman received came from Fingleton's pen. Bradman the man was, well, a man, with flaws like any other.

As Fingleton wrote in *Brightly Fades the Don*:

> Together with all other cricketers of our generation, I salute him as the greatest player of his age, the greatest attraction the game of cricket has known. He did not make the friends in the game which others did but, possibly he reasoned, he would not have been the player he was had he allowed his concentration to be upset in the slightest manner. He brilliantly and

decisively achieved the objective he set himself when he found his feet in first-class cricket—and that was to be, by far, the greatest run-getter and the greatest holder of records the game has known. And, in doing that, he gave to the man-in-the-street the greatest possible value for his admission money and he brought to cricket the most pronounced publicity the game had ever known.

Once again, Fingleton's inside knowledge and personal contacts with players gave his book both gravitas and a light and humorous touch. It was studded with lively anecdotes from those on the scene, like the one about Bradman's return to the dressing room after his final dismissal in England:

> English cricket was free, at long last, of the Bradman plague, the Bradman scourge, the Bradman blight, call it what you will. On this lovely September afternoon, the cricket world far removed from that outside world of trouble and limitless and abortive peace talks, Bradman yielded up his batting ghost for the last time to English cricket, and his remark on returning to the pavilion, made in all good humour, was typical of the man.
>
> On his entry, a sleepy Lindsay Hassett stretched on a form.
>
> 'Ahhuum,' yawned Hassett, 'what happened? Did you chuck it away?'
>
> 'Well,' said Bradman, with a wide smile, 'I worked it out that to average a hundred for every innings I have had in England, I would have had to make about 500 not out—and this game, as you know, is limited to three days.'

One less flattering tour story Fingleton decided to leave out. It concerned the time Bradman was asked by Australian Government officials to hand over a cheque for £10,000 from the state of NSW for the restoration of Canterbury Cathedral. Bradman was suddenly difficult to find. Eventually the prominent Labor politician H.V. Evatt tracked him down in a match against Kent. The captain's first words were: 'What have you done about that taxation matter for me?'

Bradman had wanted the Australian Government to approach British Treasury figures and, considering how much he had done for Commonwealth relations, urge them to be lenient on him over the tax on royalties from his forthcoming book. Fingleton believed Bradman was eventually 'charged only a very nominal sum. That would have meant lots of money to Bradman as he would have not only have got big royalties from *Farewell to Cricket*, but also would have made much out of its serialisation.' Fingleton wrote to Evatt for details, 'as it created a precedent that could help me in my own royalties'.

Whether Evatt replied is unknown.

Fingleton's main emphasis, of course, was cricket, in particular the 1948 tour. But here, too, he wasn't afraid to question accepted wisdom. Just how good, for example, had that Australian team been? Many hysterical words had been written about this team. Fingleton took a step back and offered some perspective. Certainly, he wrote, winning twenty-three and drawing eight of their thirty-one tour matches had been a great feat, and the commentators had grounds for calling the team 'the best of all time'. On the other hand, however, England had been in unusually poor shape. Fingleton thought it arguable that the 1930 Australian team had been better: 'On good pitches, it would have been difficult to oust the 1930 batting side which had Bradman himself at his very greatest, and the second most prolific scorer in Ponsford in modern cricket history. It had, too, Woodfull, Jackson, Kippax and McCabe. This 1930 side, of a certainty, would have been far superior to the 1948 one on a wet pitch, for instance.'

(Some years later, Fingleton received a letter from the 1948 tourist Bill Brown, who provided the insight that Australia had 'caught England just after the war with a new ball rule made to order for our quickies'. Brown explained: 'It was undoubtedly a strong side but apart from Bedser there was not a great deal in the English attack and certainly no speed of any description to hit back with. As for team spirit, I feel it didn't come anywhere near the '34, '38 and South African sides in this respect.')

Fingleton also answered the critics who claimed he and his cronies only ribbed Bradman out of envy:

> Much has been said and written of the 'jealousy' of those who played with and against Bradman, but those best qualified to speak are those who played with him, and I have never met a single first-class cricketer of Bradman's age who was not ever ready, indeed eager, to declare that the game of cricket had never known his like before. He had his critics, and will always have, I suppose, for his somewhat indifferent, cold and unfriendly attitude towards most of those with whom he played, but not one, I replied, has ever denied the greatness which rightly belongs to Bradman. On good pitches, he stood in a class of his own as a scoring machine; and, moreover, the game has never known one to approach, yes, even approach, his miraculous consistency. When you boiled Bradman down, when you analysed his eyesight, his footwork, his judgement, his range of strokes, there was still something left in which he was always superior to all others, and that was consistency.

Only twice had Fingleton ever seen Bradman rattled: 'Once was during the bodyline days and the other whenever a "sticky" pitch happened along.' Otherwise, 'Bradman's mind was always cool, calm and analytical and, in its sphere, was as great a taskmaster of the body as man could possess. His mind gave his body no rest. His mind called the tune and his body, gifted as it was in peerless footwork, eyesight, judgement and a perfect dynamo of ceaseless energy, danced to it. The only times the dance became agitated were against bodyline and on sticky pitches.'

Fingleton didn't hesitate to record how Bradman had his favourites in the team, 'particularly when it came to bowling out the tail-enders . . . Those not in the beam of his smile often received scant opportunities, so that this English tour was not a happy one for some. So weak was English cricket in 1948 that Bradman could well have given the "Ground Staff" more opportunities without risk of defeat, but he had set his heart on an unbeaten record and never once took a risk with it.'

Fingleton also noted that, in truth, Bradman's batting on that final tour was 'only a shadow of what it had once been'.

But no one reading *Brightly Fades the Don* could be in any doubt of Fingleton's respect for the Don's achievement or his unique place in cricket history.

Before the book went to press, Fingleton asked Labor MP and writer Les Haylen to look over the proofs. Fingleton wrote to Haylen that Bradman 'likes the good stuff; but, like the big Alsatian, can't take it'.

Haylen recommended that he tone down the emphasis on Bradman. 'The very fact that you are a good writer and Bradman is not (not even the ghost of a good one) makes it imperative that you select your weapons carefully,' he wrote. 'You have used the rapier in the book—you must keep that style of legitimate restrained comment. Further, it's your book—don't let it be Bradman's by over-featuring.'

The Bradman focus remained—the cons as well as the pros.

Bradman publicly took the book in the right vein, even complimenting Fingleton on it. But parts of it obviously irked him. And Harry Kneebone, a journalist at the Adelaide *Advertiser* and an ally of Bradman's, was disparaging. Under the headline, 'Bradman's Enemy—Jealousy', he wrote: 'There are people who inflexibly hated Bradman. The core of this anti–Bradman feeling was a group of former players—some of those who went to England in one or more of the 1930/34/38 tours.' Kneebone said that when he had asked Bradman the reason for this bad feeling, the Don replied, 'Jealousy.'

The reviews, however, were overwhelmingly positive, and Fingleton received glowing letters of congratulation, including one from John Arlott, who judged *Brightly Fades the Don* 'possibly even better than *Cricket Crisis*'. The *Times Literary Supplement* was unreserved in its praise, calling it 'the best written cricket book since the war'.

A small sour note was that the publishers had put on the back cover an advertisement 'which lauded Ray Robinson's *Between Wickets* to the skies—described as the "best on cricket written by an Australian so far",' Fingleton griped. 'Maybe it is, but it seemed more than odd to me that this, at least, controversial opinion, should be flagged out at the back of mine . . . Good chap and all as Ray Robinson is, I don't relish the playing of second fiddle to him, and I don't think I should be asked to.'

But the pro-Robinson blurb didn't seem to dampen public interest in the book. It sold steadily from the day it appeared in the stores in June 1949. Fingleton was happy with his second publishing success. But he was less content with the prospect of remaining in the Canberra press gallery.

He enjoyed a good relationship with the Prime Minister, Ben Chifley, and his press secretary, Don Rodgers. The pair passed on interesting inside information to Fingleton, including details of the sudden disappearance of a *Sydney Morning Herald* political reporter. The journalist, who was having an affair with a member of the PM's staff, had been stealing documents from Chifley's office and passing them on to Opposition politicians. A trap was set. A juicy document was strategically placed in the office, but the name of a key figure mentioned in it was deliberately misspelt. The document was duly pilfered, and the reporter dictated its content direct to copytakers at the *Herald*. The following day, the Chifley staff saw the story and noticed the misspelling. The reporter was summoned to Chifley's office. The PM drove him out of Canberra, stopped the car on the Yass road, and told him he had two choices—leave Canberra at once or have his misdeeds revealed to his superiors. The journalist was heading to Sydney within hours.

Fingleton was one of many who liked Chifley's no-nonsense approach to life. Shortly after returning from England, he asked Rodgers if there was any chance of joining the PM's staff. Rodgers said Chifley was interested. He regarded Fingleton as 'a fair, objective and conscientious political writer who would be an asset to the Canberra staff,' the secretary noted. As well, 'he regards you as the best cricket commentator in Australia'. If Fingleton wanted to come on board, he would be No. 4 in the office.

Fingleton had also asked if Bradman had ever expressed interest in a political career. Rodgers said, 'Bradman nibbled at us in Mr Curtin's day. My own view is that he would be foolish to go into politics.'

After much reflection, Fingleton decided to stay put. As far as some observers were concerned, however, he was already a formidable figure in political circles.

One story told of that time is of a U.S. diplomatic official who, passing Parliament House in a taxi, noticed Chifley helping Fingleton to restart his car. It seemed that Fingleton's car had broken down and, seeing the PM's car drive by, he'd flagged it down and asked Chifley to give him a push so he could clutch start it.

The U.S. official was astounded at the sight of the Prime Minister, sleeves rolled up, putting his shoulder to the back of the car while Fingleton ran beside it with his hands on the steering wheel, ready to jump in.

'Is that who I think it is?' the official asked the taxi driver.

'Sure is . . . That's the great Jack Fingleton.'

'No, is that who I think it is pushing the car?'

The cabbie replied almost nonchalantly: 'Aw, yeah, that's Chif.'

The American shook his head and mumbled: 'What a weird, weird country!'

Soon afterwards, Fingleton was asking Chifley's office for help on another pressing matter.

One of the highlights of his 1948 England trip had been going with former England wicketkeeper George Duckworth to meet Harold Larwood for the first time since Bodyline.

Whereas Bradman continued to dominate the cricketing world, his nemesis Larwood was by now well out of the public eye, running a confectionery shop in a Blackpool side street. Fingleton was the first Australian cricketer he'd met since the summer of 1932–33, and Larwood gave him a guarded welcome. Fingleton wasn't surprised: 'Not only was I one of the "enemy" of 1932–33 but I was a newspaperman, and Larwood had memories of how he had been publicised over the years by the stunting gentry of my profession.'

Larwood made it clear he didn't want to say anything Fingleton the writer might use. Fingleton stressed that this was a personal visit. He was not here in pursuit of a story; he simply wanted to meet again one of the most important figures in his life. It was a goodwill visit, and he hoped to show that for some at least, the bitterness of Bodyline had been forgotten.

Gradually, Larwood's mood warmed.

A pinch of snuff shared between Duckworth and Larwood (Fingleton declined) finally broke the ice. They soon began talking about Bodyline and Bradman. Larwood confirmed that Pelham Warner, under the misapprehension that Fingleton had leaked Bill Woodfull's dressing-room remarks to the press, had promised him a pound 'if you can bowl Fingleton out quickly'.

He did, producing a delivery which Fingleton described as the best bowled to him in his career. 'When I came off the field, Sir Pelham was waiting there at the door with a pound note in his hand,' said Larwood. 'Ah, well, those days are gone for ever, but here's a pound note. Let's all go and have a drink and we will say it is on Sir Pelham.'

Fingleton and Duckworth's visit fuelled Larwood's interest in moving to Australia. Fingleton doubted that Larwood would make such a huge change, and not just because he had a large family. After all, not so long ago Australians had regarded him as a national enemy. But Fingleton assured him that Australians were very forgiving people, and said that if Larwood should decide to emigrate he would help if he could.

In 1950, Fingleton, working in his Parliament House office, received an urgent telegram from Larwood: 'Leaving Orontes London tomorrow stop Can you arrange accommodation for self wife five daughters eldest daughters fiancée stop Also jobs signed Larwood.'

A letter arrived some days later.

> We have decided pretty quick to take the plunge, our fate is in the hands of the Gods, but I don't think we have done wrong, it will be a wonderful venture for the children, and as you know I adore them.
>
> Well Jack I am leaving it to you, to just fix us up temporarily with accommodation, you know, a quiet Hotel, or anything like that, for a few days, until we can sort things out.
>
> June (my eldest daughter) is bringing her young man out with her to settle down too (so it looks like an Australian wedding).

No matter what happens, we are relying on you to book us rooms, or anything like that for a few days, and then we can talk.

Fingleton showed the cable to Chifley, who contacted Tom Watson, of Tooths Brewery in Sydney. He converted a hotel in Kingsford so it could accommodate Larwood's large family. The rate was £14 a week for two months. Larwood later discovered through Fingleton that Chifley had paid half his accommodation bill, but at the time the PM insisted that this remain a secret.

Larwood expressed his gratitude to both Chifley and Fingleton. 'Had you not come . . . into my shop . . . I would never have come to Australia. Coming to Australia is the best thing I have done in my life.'

But at first he was apprehensive. What sort of reception would he receive from those who still looked upon him as the scourge of Bodyline?

He need not have worried. Australians embraced Larwood, and Fingleton was only one of a large group of well-wishers who greeted him when the *Orontes*, the same ship that had brought him over for the Bodyline series, docked in Sydney in 1950.

When Larwood and his family had settled in, Fingleton invited him to Canberra and organised a meeting with Chifley at Parliament House.

Larwood shook Chifley's hand, and in his strong Midlands accent said: 'Mr Chifley, I would like to thank you very much for what you have done for myself and my family. You have given us a wonderful break in life and we want to express our appreciation to you.'

Chifley looked at Larwood, then at Fingleton. 'What did he say, Jack?'

Fingleton translated.

Chifley replied, in his rasping, nasal voice: 'It's very nice to have you out here, Harold. I hope you settle down all right. Things go well for you?'

Larwood looked at Chifley, then at Fingleton. 'What did he say, Jack?'

17

Not Even a Singleton

Fingleton was a hoarder. He kept everything—copies of letters received and sent, articles, clippings, any information that might come in handy in his journalistic work. His tiny office in Parliament House was cluttered with piles of newspapers, files and boxes. He would also often write notes to himself, jotting down facts and arguments on contentious issues.

Some of this information was used; some wasn't.

One of the most interesting of Fingleton's personal notes concerned the rift between Keith Miller and the recently knighted Sir Donald Bradman.

The much gossiped-about rift between the two men became a public issue in March 1949, when the Australian selectors, Bradman, Jack Ryder and Chappie Dwyer, named the team to tour South Africa—and Miller was excluded.

It was an extraordinary decision. 'Australian cricket is reeling today under the Miller blow,' Fingleton wrote in the Sydney *Sun*. 'On playing ability I would unhesitatingly place him today in the top six cricketers in the world.'

Clearly, at least two of the selectors thought less highly of

Miller, and Miller assumed that one of them was Bradman. They had had their run-ins on the 1948 tour, when Bradman's ferocious focus came into conflict with Miller's laid-back, hedonistic attitude. His night-time wanderings during that tour were legendary: he was even rumoured to have dallied with Princess Margaret.

Miller and Fingleton also wondered whether hurling a few bouncers at Bradman during a testimonial match had worked against Miller. Bradman had looked daggers at him at the time, as he did in another game when Miller threw his wicket away with cavalier batting.

Bradman repeatedly denied that he voted against Miller's inclusion on the tour, but Miller and many of his teammates were sceptical. They knew the Don was a master at covering his tracks.

Eventually Miller had a reprieve. When Bill Johnston was injured in a car crash, he was sent to South Africa to replace him. But Miller never stopped trying to find out which selectors had initially crossed him off the list.

As Miller told Fingleton, his first hint that something was amiss had come at a lunch at the Cricketers' Club in Sydney on the day the touring squad was to be announced. Miller ran into Chappie Dwyer at the bar, but Dwyer wouldn't look him in the eye.

Later, in South Africa, he told Dwyer, who was also the team manager, that *Sun* sports editor Johnny Moyes had received a letter from Bradman of which he'd shown Miller the last section. It read, 'I hope Keith doesn't think I had anything to do with him being dropped from the tour of South Africa.'

Dwyer replied: 'Did the little bastard say that?' For his part, Dwyer denied voting against Miller's inclusion.

If both Dwyer and Bradman were telling the truth, Miller concluded, he'd been dropped on the say-so of 'poor old Jack

Ryder . . .' Since that was impossible, 'Someone was telling me a bloody lie along the track.'

This issue prompted an exchange of letters between Dwyer and Bradman, each reassuring the other that he hadn't revealed his vote to Miller.

Finally Sid Barnes, a 1948 tour teammate of Miller and Bradman, provided the background. In his often controversial *Sunday Telegraph* column, he wrote: 'Bradman, through various channels, has several times denied that any dispute with Miller was responsible for the latter's non-selection for Africa. 1948 teammates of the pair, myself included, were never taken in by such protests.'

Barnes said that during the Second Test, at Lord's, Bradman had thrown the ball to Miller, and 'Miller, who had announced his intention of not bowling in the game because of some injury or other, kicked the ball back to his incredulous captain. I did not catch the comment which went with the action, but I'm assured that Miller curtly advised Bradman to have a go himself.

'Bradman picked up the ball and—this I did hear—replied: "You'll keep."'

Barnes said Bradman 'was as wild as a battery-stung brumby with his star all-rounder'.

Fingleton's note on his clipping of the column reads: 'Barnes, for obvious reasons, hasn't told the full story. In the dressing room that evening, Bradman grumbled apropos of Miller not bowling . . .

' "I don't know what's up with you chaps. I'm 40 and I can do my full day's work in the field." And Miller replied: "So would I—if I had had fibrositis during the war!"'

Barnes too had his share of run-ins with players and administrators. After the 1948 tour, when he'd had a lucrative business selling anything and everything to the still-rationed English, he decided he could make better money writing about the game than playing it.

When Fingleton covered England's tour of Australia in 1950–51, he found Barnes as lively a character in the press box as he had been on the field. One of the highlights of the summer was the day the ever-mischievous Barnes sat down beside Cardus. As Fingleton told the story: ' "Look here, Neville," Barnes said. "I've got an idea. What about me slipping a carbon paper into my copy today for you and you can do the same for me tomorrow? We both write the same sort of stuff." '

It was the only time Fingleton ever saw Cardus 'stumped for a word'.

That England tour, led by Freddie Brown, might not have had the excitement of other cricketing ventures Jack had been involved in, but he—and publishers Collins—found enough interest in it to warrant a third Fingleton book. So, in between filing copy on the series for various overseas newspapers, he worked away on *Brown and Company*.

It wasn't quite a classic, but it gave Fingleton the chance to make some telling observations and administer some typically cheeky digs.

And Fingleton the journalist uncovered plenty of fresh detail about the England captain, in particular his experiences during the war. Brown had joined the Army, been sent to North Africa, and was captured at Tobruk in 1942. He and fellow Bodyline tourist Bill Bowes spent three years as prisoners of war in Italy and Germany. They'd been fed near-starvation rations, and ended up 'grovelling in the refuse for something to eat'. By the time they were liberated by American troops, Brown had lost four and a half stone.

Yet despite their deprivation they had organised cricket and rugby matches for their fellow POWs.

Fingleton admired Brown enormously, describing him as 'the most popular captain that England had sent us in living memory'.

The Australian captain, Lindsay Hassett, was also a close ally of Fingleton's, so he found the dressing room a far more hospitable place than during the Bradman days. Hassett's impish delight in being an 'infinite tease' had alienated some Australian officials, who'd been reluctant to make him captain. He'd squeaked in as captain for the South African tour the previous year 'only by the last vote of the Board of Control'. But Fingleton always sprang to his defence, all the more eagerly because Hassett was the first Catholic since Warwick Armstrong in 1921 to lead his country's cricketing side.

It was a happy summer for Fingleton, surrounded by Australian and English friends, including Cardus and R.C. Robertson-Glasgow, and sharing all the off-field gossip. He learned, for instance, why Bill Edrich was a glaring omission from the England squad. According to Robertson-Glasgow, Edrich had 'made enemies among the pussy-foots' and 'drank at the wrong time', notably indulging in a binge near the selectors during a Manchester Test match.

Despite the absence of Edrich, England—whose team appeared the weakest ever sent to Australia, rallied after losing the first four Tests to win the final one in Melbourne. Unlike so many recent Australia–England Test series, this had been a happy one. The grim, win-at-all-costs period of Bradman had passed.

Fingleton was thrilled to find an England dressing room welcoming Australians once again. 'I walked into the English dressing room to shake Brown by the hand. Pipe in mouth, he was still grinning. It was good to see it; and good to know just what this win would mean back home in the villages, hamlets and cities this same evening. England had been taking it on the chin, in many ways, for years past; it was good and proper to see England dishing it out for a change.'

★

The following season, Fingleton was provided with a different cricketing chore, helping to get another game off the ground—through the introduction of the Prime Minister's XI match.

Chifley and Labor had been replaced in 1949 by the conservative Liberal Party, led by Robert Menzies. Fingleton's politics had not limited his political friendships. He had a longstanding and amiable relationship with Menzies, who was fascinated by cricket. It was his abiding passion, and for many years he had sought out Fingleton at Parliament House for the latest cricket gossip.

Menzies also admired Fingleton's journalistic skills. Fingleton made the most of that, often steering the conversation away from cricket so he could fish for interesting personal detail to flesh out his political reports. After Menzies became PM the private meetings became more frequent. Fingleton discovered Menzies was a lonely man. Menzies enjoyed company, and with Fingleton, in the seclusion of the PM's office, he could talk about what really enchanted him. It was a relationship envied by many in the Canberra press gallery, the bulk of whom Menzies did not trust.

But Fingleton also knew he had to tread warily. Bert 'Doc' Evatt, Chifley's successor as Labor leader, was just as obsessed with cricket and similarly eager to have Fingleton's ear. This forced Fingleton to 'be diplomatic to steer my course between [Menzies] and the Doc on cricket. Each was jealous of the other and would say to me: "Of course, he doesn't know anything about the game. All theory." '

Fingleton just kept nodding.

In 1951, Menzies bumped into Ian Emerton, the deputy clerk of the Senate and president of the ACT Cricket Association, in the parliamentary library. Emerton expressed disappointment that Canberra had been overlooked that summer as a venue for the touring West Indian side. Menzies suggested that perhaps a game against a Prime Minister's XI might solve the problem.

'I know most of the Board [of Control]. Leave it to me,' Menzies said.

A short time later, Emerton saw Fingleton in the library and asked for his help. Could he pressure Menzies to follow up that Prime Minister's XI idea?

Fingleton took the familiar path to Menzies's office.

When he told the PM he supported the plan and could help recruit players, Menzies became more interested. With Fingleton by his side, he telephoned Bradman in Adelaide to ask if he would lead the XI. Bradman refused.

Menzies thought that had scotched the idea, since without Bradman there would be little public interest. Not so, Fingleton assured him.

The PM contacted the Board of Control, saying the Government would cover all expenses and that any profits would go to charity.

Amid a subsequent flurry of phone calls, Menzies continued to dither. In a personal note in his files, Fingleton wrote: 'It was on and off thrice. On one Friday evening, it was definitely on. Saturday his secretary rang to tell me it was off. I went to the Lodge after golf and talked a very unwilling PM into it again, for the third time. Ever since he has spoken of how "when I got the idea of this match" . . .'

Fingleton helped Menzies pick his first team, inviting old mates such as O'Reilly and Hassett to Canberra, along with other Australian representatives—Neil Harvey, Sam Loxton and Ian Johnson—and New Zealand Test batsman Martin Donnelly. The West Indians would certainly have a competitive game to start off their tour. Menzies made Fingleton captain of his XI. The match would take place at Manuka Oval.

Fingleton's links with the oval were strong. As a member of a Sydney team, he'd been involved in the first match ever played at the ground, in the 1930 Easter Carnival. As well as having briefly served as president of the Australian Capital Territory Cricket Association, Fingleton had captained the first Sheffield Shield team to play at Manuka, when NSW visited Canberra in March 1935.

As he, Menzies and West Indian captain John Goddard headed to the middle of the oval for the historic toss, there was high drama in the pavilion. The organisers had just been told they were barred from using Parliament House glasses and cutlery for the official luncheon. Nor could Parliament staff man the bar at the ground. The stern Speaker of the House, Archie Cameron, had refused permission, claiming an old law forbade the loan of property outside the building. The organisers rushed to the Lodge and the Cabinet rooms, and managed to find enough cutlery to keep everyone happy. Volunteers ensured the beer flowed.

Losing the toss and put into bat, Fingleton opened with Hassett. It went downhill from there.

Menzies had secured a deal that no player in the Prime Minister's XI would be dismissed before scoring. But someone forgot to tell umpire and former Test paceman Ernie McCormick. Then again, McCormick might just have ignored Menzies' instructions on purpose, to get one back on his 1935–36 South African tour colleague.

The first ball faced by Fingleton was an outswinger from John Trim, which he edged to Everton Weekes at second slip. Weekes, who had broken Fingleton's record for successive Test centuries, took the easy catch. Fingleton looked at McCormick, who was wearing a garish golf cap, as if to demand a second chance. But McCormick pointed him to the pavilion.

Fingleton's first-ball duck was a source of great mirth during the lunch break, when the West Indian visitors rubbed in the ignominy. After Fingleton feigned an attempt to strangle McCormick, Weekes, sitting across from him, remarked, 'Don't worry, Jack; you may have lost your record for successive centuries but you've now got another. You must be the only batsman in the world who has got out first ball in a Festival Match.'

Fingleton gave Weekes the sickliest of looks.

Donnelly saved the Prime Minister's XI innings with 72, giving the West Indies 229 runs to beat. Then rain, thunder, lightning and a dust storm hit, forcing a premature finish with the West Indies on 2/142.

All headed to Hotel Canberra for the official dinner, where Fingleton had to face further ridicule. Menzies finished the dinner with a poem.

What, Fingleton
Not even a singleton
O what a fruitless journey
Thanks to a singularly slow piece of thinking by Ernie.

Menzies later wrote to Fingleton that he thought the match 'a splendid occasion' and was determined it wouldn't be a one-off affair. For the rest of his sixteen-year tenure, playing the Prime Minister's XI was an integral part of every touring cricket team's schedule.

Menzies and Fingleton were an interesting combination, a resolute conservative and a man from a strong Labor clan. Menzies continually ribbed Fingleton about his background and the numerous left-wingers in his family. Fingleton tried to insist that he was neutral, but Menzies was convinced he really favoured Labor.

The subject of Jessie Street came up more than once, and Fingleton proudly stood up for her against Menzies's digs. Jessie's open admiration for the Soviet Union's granting full equality to women convinced some she must be a Communist. Philippa and

Fingleton robustly defended her against the charge, but Menzies, who on taking office in 1951 tried to ban the Communist Party, couldn't resist taking a shot at Fingleton's famous mother-in-law.

In 1951, Ian Fleming, then the foreign manager for the *Sunday Times* in London (his first James Bond book was a couple of years in the future), asked Fingleton to join the paper as a foreign correspondent. Fingleton readily agreed, and his relationship with the illustrious paper continued for decades. The Argus newspaper group in South Africa was also eager for any copy Fingleton could provide. He now had a good, steady income. As well as the Argus group and *Sunday Times*, he was freelancing for India's *Sports and Pastimes* and *The Hindu*, the *Straits Times* in Singapore, the *Sunday Mirror* and *Truth*. Better still, with the foreign newspapers keen to take his sport reports, he could combine his work in the Canberra press gallery with following whichever important cricket team was in the country.

As long-time political correspondent Rob Chalmers explained: 'When Jack would go away on long cricket tours, or even when he was in Sydney, he'd give me the task of earning a few bob taking over the job of being Australian correspondent for the Argus papers. He would tell me that what they were interested in, apart from cricket, is anything to do with Aboriginals and sharks.'

Fingleton's next big assignment was the Australian tour of England in 1953, and there were plenty of outlets keen to take his reports. He had also signed a deal for another tour book.

It was now high time, he thought, to reward his biggest supporters. As he walked up the gangway of 'the water-coach to London', accompanying him were Pip and 'our progeny, Belinda, James, Grey and Laurence . . . which shows what can come of shipboard romances'. Their dog, Rontes, stayed at home.

For the children, the boat trip to England was a memorable adventure. The Australian cricketers treated them as part of an extended family. Sid Barnes would 'shout' the Fingleton children drinks at the bar, while Lindsay Hassett, Keith Miller and Ray Lindwall were constant companions.

'Arthur Morris, whom I later met through business, told me how much the Australian team enjoyed my brothers' and my rendition of "My Dear Old Pals",' Grey Fingleton said. 'This was a song our Dad taught us, which is surprising because it was about three old drunks. And he always told us that he never touched a drop until he had finished with cricket. From the stories I heard later, I think he was confusing himself with his father.'

For the next six months, Fingleton showed his wife and his children, aged between three and ten, the delights of Britain, between filing reports. Late at night he would steal some time to pound away at the new manuscript, entitled *The Ashes Crown the Year*. The children grew accustomed to falling asleep to the rhythm of his two-finger tapping.

For most of the tour their father was near exhaustion, but later he rated it as one of the most rewarding times of his life. He was thrilled to have his family with him, but they soon discovered that covering cricket tours was excruciatingly hard work for the journalists involved. Aside from the endless travel, the demands of sports editors all over the globe were relentless. At least Fingleton made the book easier to finish by doing it in diary form.

But with family in tow, he made certain that the sights were seen and the moments enjoyed. London was far more colourful than in 1948, when 'the city was low-spirited, people were poorly dressed and the food was in keeping'. Now it was 'brightly painted'. They visited the gorgeous Cotswolds, and Fingleton and Pip were even in Westminster Abbey for the Coronation of Queen Elizabeth II. Menzies had organised two seats.

Fingleton was smitten.

'As I saw the Queen enter Westminster Abbey this day, I felt centuries of English tradition and history and suffering following in her train. As she left, to the ringing peals of the Anthem, I thought of England's future unfolding in front of her, and in her presence of youthful beauty and majestic bearing the doubts and the tribulations of the future seemed to fade away. And so may it be. God Save and Aid Queen Elizabeth!'

Fingleton did know when to hide his Labor ideals.

He was almost as delighted by the English pub scene, where the 'dominating theme', he wrote, was 'companionship'. He loved the regional accents, especially the Yorkshire dialect. He even (almost) got over the fact that one night on the Yorkshire Moors he and Arthur Mailey had to sleep in his car because they couldn't find a hotel room.

He and O'Reilly also played social cricket matches, and he took Belinda and James to Lord's, where his daughter 'spent most of the afternoon swopping waves with [Ray] Lindwall on the balcony [rather] than watching the cricket'. After stumps, he kept the children entertained for half an hour while waiting for the Australian players to re-emerge from the dressing room: 'When I was playing Test cricket with Hassett I never thought the day would come when I would be lined up to see him come out. Nor did he!'

They went to Oxford, and had dinner with Douglas Jardine. Keith Miller took great delight in joking with Jardine about 'bumpers'. In a profile of Miller for the *Sunday Times*, Fingleton recalled 'how he bowled a vicious bumper at His Cricket Eminence in Sydney that surely cost him selection for South Africa'. Later, watching Bruce Dooland, the former South Australian spin bowler who had moved to England, excel against Australia at Trent Bridge, he suggested facetiously that Bradman, who was on his way to England to be a £10,000 guest columnist for the *Daily Mail*, should write his first column on 'Why Dooland was not thought good enough for the 1948 Australian team for England'.

But aside from the sight-seeing and socialising, Fingleton had a competitive Test series to cover, whose outcome lay in doubt until the final dramatic encounter at the Oval. It went England's way—Australia's only loss, but enough to require that they hand over the Ashes. The Australians provided plenty of entertainment. But England held up at the critical moments, and their win triggered wild celebrations. It was described by Fingleton as 'England's finest cricketing hour in long memory. As an Australian, I paused to salute it.

'This has indeed been a year among years, but, for many Britishers throughout the island and the world, after the Coronation came one event of outstanding importance. The Ashes Came Home. The Ashes, indeed, Crowned the Year—and great merit and thanks to [England captain Len] Hutton and Hassett for contesting them in such a friendly manner.'

Not so friendly were the demands of the Collins editors, who wanted the book finished before the Fingletons returned to Australia. The family headed to the Sussex countryside, where Fingleton embarked on an all-out slog through the final chapters. Pip kept the kids quiet, and their reward would be a visit to the local pub, a meal, and traditional games. At last Fingleton handed over the manuscript, and they set off by sea back to Canberra.

18

Keeping Up the Attack

The Don wasn't the only Australian captain who got under Fingleton's skin. Ian Johnson did too.

Fingleton didn't think much of the Victorian as a spin bowler. When Johnson missed the 1953 England tour, he wasn't surprised. He believed, like many, that Johnson's bowling action was suspect and that most of his victims were tail-enders. And Bradman had not been involved in selecting the 1953 touring team.

When Johnson became Australian captain, in 1954, Fingleton believed a major reason was his assiduously cultivated friendship with Bradman. In taking the helm, Fingleton believed he had, with Bradman's support, elbowed Miller aside, 'even though Miller far outshone him as a captain in Shield games and as a performer'. Again the Don's shadow loomed.

A new captain was needed because of Hassett's retirement following the 1953 tour. That Johnson was clearly a far inferior player to Miller didn't matter—least of all, Fingleton thought, to Bradman. Other Test cricketers agreed that Johnson was a great speech maker. Fingleton saw clues that Miller had no chance of being Test skipper in an Adelaide *News* article in March 1954. The article revolved around two pieces, one by an anonymous 'former Test star' and the other by a 'former Test critic', debating who should captain Australia. The former critic pushed for Miller on the ground that he was the most imaginative of the candidates. But the former Test star was dismissive of Miller. He strongly favoured Johnson, even though many thought the spinner's Test career had ended. The star, who identified himself as a South Australian, complained that NSW always tried to dictate Australian cricket and that South Australia had been relegated to a minor role. He noted that Miller had openly criticised Johnson in the press and had taken delight in bowling bouncers at him. In the star's view, Johnson's omission from the 1953 England tour was a mistake that could have been avoided if 'Bradman, Dwyer and Ryder [had] been the Australian selection committee'. (Bill Brown and Phil Ridings were on the committee with Ryder instead of Dwyer and Bradman.)

Fingleton was all but certain the 'former Test star' was Bradman. He wrote to the Adelaide *News*'s editor, Rohan Rivett, in search of answers. It so happened that Rivett had commissioned Bradman to cover the previous year's Ashes tour for *The News*.

'One writer, a former Test star, refers to himself in the article as a South Australian,' Fingleton wrote, 'and both writers are said to have seen "most of the Test matches of the past 25 years". I've gone over the South Australians in that category and Sir Donald Bradman seems to be the only one who would qualify. He wasn't, of course, either a Board member or a selector when the article was written (both most interesting incidentally) and was perfectly free to write for newspapers. Would you be willing to reveal the position for me? I seem to recognise the "Rivett" touch in the second [article].'

Rivett refused to help, replying that both articles 'were published in strict confidence and I would be going back on my word if I broke faith now . . . In your own guidance, I can only say that you are right off the beam in a major part of your conjecture.'

That didn't stop Fingleton.

When the Board of Control, with Bradman back on the selection panel, gave the captaincy to Johnson, Fingleton was even more convinced he'd been the 'Test star'.

Bradman and Miller, of course, 'had been operating on different wave-lengths since 1948,' Fingleton wrote. 'There was an immediate clash of outlook, temperament and personality.' But Fingleton soon had the opportunity to get back at Johnson and Bradman. Johnson's early months as Test captain were a roller-coaster ride. The First Test against the touring England team ended in an emphatic 154-runs victory. Then came the second Prime Minister's XI match at Manuka Oval, at which umpire Fingleton was attired in a pith helmet. England won that game and, with their intimidating new paceman Frank Tyson, went on to win the next two Tests.

In an open letter to the Australian selectors Bradman and Ryder, Fingleton wrote in the *Daily Mirror* that a change of captaincy for Australia was imperative.

> You were two of the selectors who turned down Keith Miller for South Africa. Remember that? When I proffered that personal feelings had much to do with it you, Don, told me I should write something that I knew something about. Well well. Anyway we eventually get Miller to South Africa and they thanked us for it. Now, how about recommending Miller for the Test captaincy in Adelaide? He wouldn't let you down, and if you two recommended him, the Board must say 'Yes.'

The selectors ducked Fingleton's missile, instead sticking with Johnson for the Fourth Test in Adelaide, where Australia lost for the third time in a row. England won the series 3–1, and Fingleton knew exactly whom to blame. It was plain cricket politics.

Johnson had the advantage of being a Victorian, he concluded, 'and the Australian captain down the years has gone mostly there'. He went on: 'Some Victorian officials and newspapers consider it a matter of pride that they should provide Australian captains. And the Victorians are pretty smart in cricket politics. One has only to look at the number of men they always get in an Australian training side to appreciate that.'

But Fingleton argued that Johnson was also given a leg-up because of his friendship with Bradman.

> Bradman said that the selection committee, of which he was not a member, made the mistake of not picking Johnson for England in 1953, and he should not only be chosen for England in 1956, but be captain. But there have been some astounding selections by committees of which Bradman has been a member. These are some of them—Grimmett and Tallon not chosen for England 1938; Dooland not chosen in 1948 and Miller not chosen [for] South Africa 1949.

Fingleton was unflagging in his support for Miller. But the selectors were just as stubborn, naming Johnson as captain for the upcoming West Indian tour. Bradman was obviously pushing hard. He even went so far as to publicly explain why Johnson should remain skipper. Among the reasons were 'a sterling character, with a keen sense of humour'.

Fingleton was surprised by Bradman's decision to go public. In a *Daily Mirror* article headlined 'Bradman Astray in His Judgement', he wrote that he had 'never before known a selector defend his work in public and I was under the impression that selectors and board members, like players, were not allowed to write for the Press'.

'No one doubts Sir Donald's great knowledge of the game,' he wrote, 'but it sometimes seems that he allows his personal feelings to sway his judgement of some players.'

O'Reilly was stirred by Fingleton's fighting words, writing to him: 'The little fellow had his chin right out, and I was delighted to see that you hit it squarely. You will doubtlessly be dubbed a member of the movement and ostracised from the inner groups in no small order. What matter?'

Bradman did not respond to Fingleton's criticism, but his close scrutiny of Johnson certainly had an impact on the Test skipper. Johnson hit back at his detractors during a radio interview after he arrived in the West Indies. Fingleton and O'Reilly had been critical of the make-up of the Australian squad sent to the West Indies, arguing that more young players should have been blooded, especially since Australia were heading to England the following year.

Johnson told the interviewer that O'Reilly and Fingleton had 'made absolutely no effort to be constructive'. Instead, they'd been 'entirely destructive . . . I can safely say they are doing not one bit of good to the game in Australia.'

Johnson was clearly not aware that numerous players thought Fingleton and O'Reilly were right. Several sent Fingleton anti-Johnson letters during the tour. Miller was, understandably, particularly derogatory. He even revealed that he had come close to putting one on Johnson's chin during the Test series. Behind his back, Johnson's teammates called him 'Myxomatosis', joking that he always appeared to put himself on to bowl when the rabbits—the weak tail-enders—were batting so he'd have a better chance of bagging easy wickets. Several in the team agreed with Fingleton that Miller should be leading the team. Johnson and Miller, far from bosom buddies, had several on-field spats.

Miller shared Fingleton's view that Johnson, the ultimate diplomat, had charmed his way into the Test team and the captaincy, and that he was getting his instructions from Bradman. Just before the Fifth Test, Miller wrote to Fingleton from Antigua that Johnson had 'bull-shitted his way along, which after all is what they love here, but without prejudice he's done a fine job as an ambassador'.

Miller said that in the Fourth Test, at the end of the fourth day's play Johnson had replaced Miller with Ray Lindwall shortly after he had dismissed Everton Weekes and Collie Smith. A livid Miller muttered to Johnson, 'You couldn't captain a bunch of bloody schoolboys,' and threatened not to bowl again in the Test—whereupon Johnson suggested they sort it out behind the grandstand after play with an old fashioned fist-fight.

Miller wrote to Fingleton that after having six runs hit off his over, Johnson told him: 'He was going to put Lindwall on. Ray's back was stiff and suffering from cramp. I told Ian I thought he was wrong, but he ignored my idea.'

That night, Miller 'was cranky and got stuck into him [Johnson] in front of the boys . . . I told him not to get me or any of the other lads to bowl again when Weekes, Worrell or Wolcott were really set. Johnson used to bowl at them before they got their eye in, then when about 30/40/50 would retire smartly.

'Anyway, Jack, I gave him the works about gripping the last few wickets and let him know the boys knew.' Miller added that Johnson, sensing he lacked support, had 'since changed his Hitleristic attitude, which at the start of the tour made us all cranky'.

They all rallied, won the Fifth Test, and finished victors 3–0 for the series.

Fingleton had considered going on the West Indies tour, but in the end was glad he didn't. In August 1955, his mother Belinda travelled from Sydney to visit her son and family in Canberra.

Shortly after arriving, Belinda complained of a slight pain, which led to a precautionary visit to the local hospital. The hospital staff, although not concerned by Mrs Fingleton's condition, decided that she should stay overnight, telling her that she would be leaving in the morning. However to the surprise of all, Belinda died that night. Her death hit Jack hard, as the pair were close. Some years later, he dedicated his autobiography *Batting from Memory* to her, describing it as a 'tribute to the memory of a wonderful mother'. Like her son, Belinda Fingleton was a tough, proud character. Jack admired her for it—and for her courage in keeping the family together after their father died. His favourite memory of her was of the time he introduced her to Menzies at Canberra Airport.

Menzies pointed at Jack and joked, 'I suppose you are not proud of this chap!'

She gave him an ear full. The proud wife of a state Labor MP had never thought much of the Liberal leader. She was far more impressed when, on a previous trip to Canberra, Jack organised for her to meet Ben Chifley, whom she idolised.

It took Fingleton a long time to get over losing her.

Even though Johnson now had a Test tour triumph under his belt, Fingleton continued to argue that Miller was the right man to lead Australia to England in 1956. In the *Daily Mirror*, Fingleton picked Miller as his tour captain and Johnson as vice-captain, though he also put Johnson in the category of spinners who 'mostly don't spin'. All the same, Fingleton seemed resigned to seeing Johnson named captain.

> He is pleasant to deal with and will make a good tongue of the first few weeks in London with all the speech-making, but then comes the playing grind through the counties and the five Tests. The hard-heads of the north, for instance, will expect deeds not words.

By right of succession, we should now have Miller's team—and he is even more popular in England than in Australia—but we won't have Miller's team because politics and, I fear, a little jealousy, will debar it.

Fingleton was so convinced that Johnson was a chucker he tried to persuade the PM of it. In conversation in Parliament House in February 1956, they discussed which spinners should go on the Ashes tour. Menzies wanted Johnson. Fingleton liked Johnny Martin. Menzies was also keen on South Australia's John Wilson. 'I like him too, but he throws,' Fingleton said. 'And so does your friend Johnson, every now and then.'

Johnson was again chosen as captain. Fingleton covered the tour once again. He got all the gossip from O'Reilly, who was a shipmate of the players. It didn't sound like much fun. 'This team is dull,' O'Reilly wrote. 'No sign yet of character of any kind. The chief impact from the ship company's angle is their inaccessibility. Blokes like Harvey, Benaud and Davidson and others who hide themselves in corners should be hoisted over the side. Ian's [Johnson's] reputation is still unsullied. The two managers must be working hard somewhere. One sees them only when the tucker bells blare.'

Fingleton joined O'Reilly to accompany the team through a contentious series. The Australians believed wickets had been doctored to suit the England bowlers, in particular spinners Jim Laker and Tony Lock. The pair were almost impossible to face on the turning wickets. Fingleton was one of many journalists who protested. He spat over the cable wire: 'If a team is invited to a series of five-day Tests then the pitches should be prepared accordingly.' The Ashes remained up north.

There would be no tour book this time: Ashes failures didn't sell too well. Instead, Fingleton began working on another idea—a collection of essays on subjects ranging from character profiles of players to the strains of reporting on Test cricket. Writing this book involved even more juggling than his previous ones, not least because Philippa was pregnant again. In December 1956 she gave birth to their fifth child, Jacqueline May Anne. Fingleton was thrilled. As his daughter Belinda recalled, 'Dad wanted another daughter. He would talk about how little Jacqui was up in Heaven, waiting to come down. And when Jacqui was born, he went along the hospital corridors, waving a bunch of gladioli and exclaiming to Pip: "You little beauty. You did it."'

When the new father could find a free hour, he tapped away at his book. The essay format gave him the chance to eulogise his favourite cricketer, Victor Trumper; offer biting anecdotes about the game; and set down typically pungent comments on a variety of topics, including Bradmania. Fingleton said the aim of the book was 'to do some sort of justice to players of other days', notably Trumper.

Menzies wrote the Foreword, and revealed that he'd given Fingleton special treatment in his role as a press gallery correspondent. After putting forward 'awkward questions to me with a slightly quizzical air' at press conferences, he said, Fingleton generally 'starts to leave with the others. But every now and then he turns back, by request, and we have ten glorious minutes on cricket.' And, of course, several more 'awkward questions' about other subjects.

After reviewing several chapters of the book preparatory to writing the Foreword, Menzies found Fingleton in the parliamentary library and asked, 'How long did it take you to write this tripe?'

'There goes the Foreword,' Fingleton thought, and asked, 'You don't like it?'

'Yes, I do, very much.'

The book titled *Masters of Cricket*, focused on some of the most interesting characters of Australian cricket—men like Warren Bardsley, who was almost kicked out of the Visitors' Gallery when Federal Parliament was sitting because he was talking too loudly to Fingleton; and paceman Tibby Cotter, who was feared because he gave every sign of wanting to kill batsmen. He told how Warwick 'Big Ship' Armstrong had grown as a cricketer at about the same rate as he grew in girth—like a graceful young gum tree—gradually transforming itself into a huge Moreton Bay fig. Armstrong apparently did not think much of Bradman, whom Fingleton described as 'Caesar-like', or of many other players for that matter. Nor did another Australian Test luminary, Herbie Collins. As for Bill Ponsford, Fingleton revealed that he did not relish the prospect of playing under Bradman's captaincy. 'Accordingly, those closest to Ponsford were not really surprised when he packed away his cricket gear and took out his fishing rod.'

Bradman remained a touchy subject. During the 1956–57 season, a testimonial match for O'Reilly and Stan McCabe was played at North Sydney Oval. Many big names were there. One wasn't: Fingleton wrote himself a note which accompanied the manuscript, that read:

> Sir Donald might have made another little gesture had he agreed recently to play in a light-hearted Sunday afternoon match in Sydney to aid the McCabe–O'Reilly Testimonial game. No doubt he had valid reasons why he couldn't join in the tribute to two of our greatest players (greatest in many senses). His presence would have been acclaimed by everybody and he was still apt with the bat as he showed by making 83 in an Adelaide Stock Exchange match the very next week. As it was, McCabe and O'Reilly found satisfaction in the fact that the ground was crammed to capacity—without the Don.

In *Masters of Cricket*, Fingleton reflected on how Bradman, by that time deeply entrenched in cricket administration, 'dominates the game in this country. Surely it is not a good thing that any one man, however competent as a player, should have overriding powers in a national game. The fact (or so it seems) is that Sir Donald Bradman does virtually what he likes in Australian cricket.' Calling for change at the top, Fingleton wrote that Bradman should welcome several members of his own generation 'to discuss and debate affairs and players with him,' because 'many of us question his judgement at times, and also his likes and dislikes'.

Not surprisingly, Bradman's mate Ian Johnson also received a backhander. While noting that Johnson was a 'most likeable person', Fingleton wrote that his poor record in England had proven the detractors right. 'The official determination to maintain Johnson as captain and not have Miller, no matter what happened, did Australian cricket more harm than O'Reilly, Fingleton or any other critic could possibly have done.'

Fingleton also took the rod to journalism, expressing concern about ghost-written columns and captains' encouraging pressmen to 'call upon them in the dressing-room'. His complaint was simple: 'The journalist who is "fed" material can't always afford to be objective.' And the sensationalistic player diary, invariably put together by a ghost writer, causes immense harm in the team dressing room.

England's Ashes visit in 1958–59 provided plenty of material for yet another book. It was a highly controversial series, marked by allegations that numerous Australian players were illegally throwing the ball. Fingleton's large web of contacts on both teams provided him with inside information and a stream of gossip. England had been in South Africa, and Fingleton's friend George Duckworth told him the locals had 'slung all sorts of women at [captain Peter May]—but he preferred his ale'.

Another contact on the England team told him that one of their leading batsmen had lost form on tour because of the turmoil that erupted after he managed 'to get two girls in the family way at the same time—no mean feat'.

On the field, too, 'There was much more smoke than usual on this tour,' Fingleton said.

It primarily arose from the 'chucking' controversy that gave Fingleton the cheeky title for his book: *Four Chukkas to Australia*, a play on the polo term. But there were also dramatic changes in Test captaincy, umpiring disputes, and selfish play that threatened to kill the game.

And there were media battles. The press box was constantly in uproar. In one Test, when Colin Cowdrey was given run out, 'one Fleet Street gentlemen stormed out of the box [in protest], screaming abuse on all and sundry and doubting the ancestry of Australians in general. We don't, as a rule, mind this so long as the genealogist has a smile on his face as he says it—but the scream-ing one departed in haste and out of sight down nearby steps.'

Fingleton also felt too many non-experts were invading the press box. Most were there to ghost write the experts' comments. 'Much of what appears in the Press of both countries these days is blatantly dishonest in that it is not written—and often is not even conceived—by the person whose name appears over it.

'I can imagine no more dishonest place than the modern Press-box for an Australian–England Test match. Some men whose names are blazoned over columns and columns of syndi-cated material sit there the whole summer and never write a single word! How can responsible newspapers, so full of rectitude in their editorial columns when they detect a public misdeed, encourage and perpetuate such a farce? It is a plain deception of innumerable newspaper readers.'

Australia had in 1957 made the extraordinary decision to appoint the youthful Ian Craig as captain ahead of Neil Harvey and Richie Benaud. However, just before the 1958–59 series, Craig fell ill with hepatitis. Benaud replaced him—and ushered in a new era in Australian cricket.

Fingleton had doubts about Benaud. He thought Harvey, despite 'lacking the social graces and making no effort to make himself popular with the top brass', would have made a good skipper. And he wondered whether Benaud's journalistic background would limit his longevity. Local administrators had delighted for decades in keeping the press at arm's length.

While Benaud was in South Africa in early 1958 with the touring Australians, he had written to Fingleton saying he was now a C grade journalist with *The Sun* and wanted to make journalism his career. 'I do really like the job and find it most interesting,' Benaud wrote. 'I tried for four years before they would give me a transfer from the accounts to the editorial on *The Sun*, so you can see that I am quite keen.'

Fingleton was not sure how a journalist would fare as a Test skipper, but he was intrigued. As soon as Benaud became captain, he impressed Fingleton with his savvy handling of the media. Benaud was always prepared to be interviewed, didn't play favourites, and 'was of infinite value to many Pressmen who sometimes needed a new angle, a new story'.

In his new role Benaud immediately came under pressure. The English press were claiming some of his bowlers were throwers, or chuckers. Fingleton agreed. He thought the Australian opening bowler Ian Meckiff had 'a most unusual action'. 'Generally he is passable, but I do not like his very fast ball, which is delivered with a very suspect jerking action. I think that ball should be "called",' Fingleton wrote.

Another player was even dodgier. The Australian opener and occasional spinner Jim Burke had, according to Fingleton, 'the worst throwing action I have seen in cricket'. Fingleton was astounded that Burke had bowled in England, South Africa,

Australia and New Zealand without being 'called'. 'If I were his captain, I would never ask him to "bowl",' he wrote.

Others in the state teams also had dubious deliveries. Fingleton believed South Australia harboured the most. Among his files is a note that reads:

> At the MCG after the 57/58 Test had a drink with Phil Ridings and Gil Langley, two South Australian (Bradman the third) selectors. Phil complimented me on my writings. Said I had been proved right many times. In conversation, he said to Langley: 'Cut it out Gil, you know we have been picking chuckers in our state team for years.' Gil agreed.
>
> In early June 1960 or late May 1960, Rohan Rivett, editor in chief of the Adelaide News, was in Canberra. He asked my opinion of Meckiff. I told him I had no doubt he had thrown in the Second Test at Melbourne. Rivett said a friend, Hooker, had watched Meckiff through strong binoculars in this same game and thought likewise. 'Anyhow,' he concluded, 'Bradman has a film which shows Meckiff throwing. Bradman knows Meckiff throws but seemingly is prepared to hide behind umpire's white coat who won't call him.'

Around that time, Fingleton appeared on ABC television with O'Reilly, Ray Lindwall and umpire Mel McInnes to discuss the ramifications of chucking. McInnes admitted that on one occasion, England spinner Tony Lock had deliberately thrown a ball in Brisbane, 'but I missed it'. He also said he believed umpires should give bowlers the benefit of the doubt.

Fingleton said he was 'staggered' at McInnes' admitted laxity in implementing the throwing law, adding that Australia's Jim Burke was the most blatant exponent of chucking he had seen. He said he also thought Lock had thrown the ball deliberately on several occasions. Fingleton believed the McInnes comment underscored the prime reason for the spate of suspect bowlers: the level of umpiring in Australia was unacceptably poor, and far too lenient.

Fingleton later wrote to the *Sunday Times'* Pat Murphy predicting that Bradman would 'hit the high spots' when the ABC broadcast the show. 'They invited him to be on . . . but he declined. A pity. O'Reilly and I would have bowled him up a few. But he gives only prepared statements and appeared on commercial TV on tele-recording with right to edit out anything he didn't like. He is a big fish in a little pond.'

Fingleton had been informed by his contacts in the England team and management that they 'blamed Braddles [Bradman] for the continued playing of the chuckers'. McInnes often travelled with Bradman during the series, and the England team suspected collusion. They also thought McInnes 'too dictatorial'.

When the disgruntled England players and pressmen left, many in Australia hoped the 'chukka' controversy would depart with them. It didn't.

It instead became an even more contentious issue for the likes of Fingleton, Bradman and certain Australian umpires. Fingleton thought local officials from Bradman down had sat on their hands for far too long, and predicted that 'the full repercussions of this Australian summer have yet to come'.

It wasn't long before he was proven right.

19

A Game for Cool Fools

Fingleton and O'Reilly were up on their feet, madly clapping, hollering their delight. Tiger was in such a state he had forgotten where he was and knocked over his work table, sending his typewriter crashing to the floor. Fingleton was hooting and laughing loudly. All around them, normally staid pressmen were prancing about, roaring and applauding as one. The rickety old Gabba press area was wobbling on its foundations.

In front of the players' rooms, Sir Donald Bradman, caught up in all the excitement, had unconsciously rolled up and shredded the afternoon paper. Umpire Col Hoy said the wife of a well-known Brisbane specialist 'came up to me, clutching me, shaking me and in a voice chock full of emotion, said, "Col, I got so excited, I wee'd myself."'

Nearby, in the West Indian dressing room, skipper Frank Worrell asked for calm and said, ever so slowly, 'Man—this is a game for cool fools.'

It had been one incredible afternoon—and it could not have been timelier. After years of dry, lifeless cricket, in December

1960 the Tied Test between Australia and the West Indies had revitalised the game. Even crusty old commentators like Fingleton and O'Reilly were beside themselves. Suddenly, though, it occurred to them that the rest of the world would want to know exactly how this incredible finale had come about. O'Reilly picked his typewriter off the floor, hoping enough keys were still functioning for him to compose a sensible sentence for the *Sydney Morning Herald.*

Fingleton sat down at his own typewriter, looked at his watch, realised he was right on deadline, rolled in a piece of foolscap paper and started banging:

BRISBANE, Dec. 14—In the greatest Test match in the history of cricket, Australia and West Indies today drew the first Test—737 runs in all. Never have such fantastic scenes been witnessed as here in the last over by [Wes] Hall when three Australian wickets fell. At ten minutes to 6, with nine runs wanted by Australia for victory and with four wickets left, [Alan] Davidson, hero with [Richie] Benaud of a remarkable fight-back against the clock, was thrown out by [Joe] Solomon.

[Wally] Grout met Davidson halfway to the wicket. The clock showed six minutes to 6. Grout went helter-skelter for a run on the seventh ball from [Garry] Sobers and made it amid pandemonium. Sobers gave his last ball against Benaud everything he had. He literally pelted it into the pitch to keep Benaud at the other end so that Hall could bowl the last over against Grout. And Benaud, avid to get the single to keep the strike, could do nothing about it.

Hall the magnificent fast bowler, who had bowled his heart out in one morning to give the West Indians their great chance, slowly rolled up his sleeves and prepared to give the last over everything he had. He roared it in at Grout who could not get his bat to it. The ball hit him in the midriff and he doubled up, but Benaud had sprinted off. Grout recovered with the West Indians dazed and they got a single with the ball almost in the block hole. But the very next ball, Benaud was caught behind by [Gerry] Alexander.

Hall had six balls to go. [Ian] Meckiff hit the next in the middle of the bat. The next he missed and the ball went through to the wicket-keeper.

Grout called and they ran the cheekiest of singles. Alexander pounced on the ball, threw it at the stumps at Meckiff's end and missed. Meckiff would have been out by yards.

Australia needed four runs with four balls to go. Then happened something almost unbelievable. Grout spooned Hall's next ball high to the leg. The West Indians ran at the catch from all directions but [Rohan] Kanhai positioned himself perfectly under it. And then came Hall to take the catch over Kanhai's head—and dropped it! The poor West Indians stood dumbfounded. The Australians got one run and needed three to win. Meckiff made a desperate swish off the next ball and connected.

The ball flew to the leg-boundary and the crowd roared. Australia had won! But the lithe [Conrad] Hunte chased the ball like an Olympic sprinter, stopped it on the fence and with a miraculous throw from 120 yards away had it back like a bullet to Alexander.

Alexander took it and threw himself at the stumps. The batsmen were running for three—the winning run. Grout dived at the crease but Alexander beat him. Up went the umpire's finger. Out went Grout, covered in dust, and in came [Lindsay] Kline, who had been abed with tonsillitis. The clock showed three minutes after 6.

Two balls were left. Kline pushed his first ball to the mid-wicket and he and Meckiff scampered off madly. Solomon dashed in, picked up cleanly and threw down the stumps and

the game was over—the greatest Test ever surely and the first in
history to finish in a tie.

Writing about cricket under deadline had not been this much
fun for a long, long time, if ever. The crowd had just witnessed
five classic days of play, that combined sophistication, poise,
stupidity, chaos, comedy, high drama and almost unbearable
suspense. Better still, commentators Alan McGilvray and Keith
Miller had left the ground early and returned to Sydney believing the Test would end in a boring draw. But Fingleton and
O'Reilly stayed—to witness and record every classic moment.

It brought rewards and sore heads. They worked hard to get it
all down, and then celebrated into the night. After several years of
doldrums, cricket was thrilling again.

ABC commentator Michael Charlton recalled the day—
and night—in a letter to Fingleton. One of his most vivid
memories was

> how we all caught the early plane to Sydney the next morning
> in the dawn after the long celebrations at Lennons [Hotel]. I
> can still see O'Reilly suffering intensely, shielding his eyes
> against the tropic dawn with his hat pulled over an unshaven
> face, stretched out in a deck chair on the verandah of the
> terminal building, and when some official from Ansett or TAA
> approached him to talk about the Test finish, saying: 'By jeezers
> if anyone tries to talk to me I'll 'it im in the bloody ear role.'

The thrill of those five days was so great that publishers Collins,
sniffing a bestseller, commissioned another book from Fingleton.
They needed it within a few weeks so they could get it out as
soon as possible. Fingleton was stiffened to the task by a letter
from Richard Hughes, the renowned Australian journalist then
based in Hong Kong, raving about his Tied Test report. 'I have

read and re-read it, and it shall be passed on to all cricket lovers in our fair colony. I can say only that your description matched the game.'

Jack's eldest son, Jim, remembers those days well. He and Grey were at home in Canberra listening to Charlton, Johnny Moyes and Clive Harburg call the final overs. And at the end of the series (the next four Tests also had their share of drama), their father commandeered the kitchen table to get a 25,000-word manuscript on its way to an eager publisher. The boys knew when to get out of his way.

Jim was already accustomed to seeing his father under pressure. When he attended matches with him he would watch after stumps as he furiously wrote three or four stories for different papers. Jim would take the copy to the cable operator, who would give the youngster a pained look. Fingleton didn't have the best relationship with cable operators, as his hastily composed stories were invariably littered with typing mistakes. While the operators tried to decipher the copy, Fingleton would brush off their complaints. It was the job of the sub-editors to fix it all up, he would say. 'That's what they're paid for.'

The book may have been a rush job, but it gave Fingleton the chance to analyse the series and put it all into perspective. The reason it was so monumental, he concluded, came down to the spirit of both captains—Worrell and Benaud.

The principal cause was the simple, the unsophisticated, the generous, the essentially carefree and good cricketing behaviour which Frank Worrell and his happy band gave to Australia from the moment their tour began.

So did Richie Benaud and his men rise to the West Indian challenge and in doing so they sloughed off the degeneracy into which England–Australia cricket has, in recent times, descended.

Fingleton was now a strong Benaud supporter. As he wrote to R.C. Robertson-Glasgow: 'He is not a money-grabber and treats all his blokes alike. Shares and shares whereas the noble knight of my time never looked beyond No. 1.'

Fingleton titled the book *The Greatest Test of All*, but as he wrote in its foreword, he could have equally called it 'Cricket Reborn'. The Brisbane Tied Test had 'breathed new and lusty life into the ailing spectre of a once great game'.

And stopped the nation—as Fingleton discovered the morning after the Test, when he returned from Brisbane to Canberra. Work was impossible in his office, because 'my fellows crowded in and plied their questions . . . They told me how everyone had hung on their radios the evening before. One said that some sixty or so members of his club had herded around the radio—and the bar was completely deserted. For many Australians, not to have a beer in their hands at six o'clock in the evening was almost as historic as the tie itself.'

Fingleton said he had heard of 'streams of cars' in Sydney and Melbourne 'pulled in to their kerbside and parked while the car radio was turned up for the benefit of dozens along the streets'.

> Not many saw it—a crowd of only 4,000—but hundreds of thousands listened to that last tumultuous hour and tens of thousands in Brisbane had watched it on television . . . Yet neither wireless nor television could give the picture of that demented finish. It had to be seen to be believed and, of a truth, those few who saw it could barely believe that what they saw was true. It all seemed fantastically impossible—drama piled upon drama to an excruciating climax.

As usual, Fingleton finished the manuscript before deadline, and the book was a steady seller. Although not as popular as *Cricket*

Crisis, which sold more than 15,000 copies in the first few months of release, *The Greatest Test of All* had, within weeks, boasted sales figures above the 4000 mark. It wasn't long before it was nearly impossible to find in bookshops, prompting Fingleton, not for the first time, to complain to the publishers about them being conservative with their print runs, and that they had distributed it to the wrong parts of the country. Nothing irked Fingleton more than being told by friends that they had entered a reputable bookshop to be informed that it had either sold out, or they did not have any copies. That generally prompted a heated Fingleton letter to the publishers.

There was drama at home, as well, of a less pleasant kind. Fingleton's enormous workload, added to the long periods he spent away from Canberra, had put his marriage under strain. In a letter to a friend in August 1961, Fingleton noted: 'My wife, battling with five children, certainly thinks I'm away too much—so do I.'

He was in England at the time, covering the 1961 Ashes tour, and life on the road was getting tougher. He was in constant demand, juggling newspaper writing with broadcasting and television appearances. This might have made him a popular media figure in Great Britain, but at the cost of intolerably lengthened work days. Fingleton said he felt like a grasshopper jumping 'to and from the television, wireless and Press boxes'.

He was also in a professional bind because of conflicts between the *Sunday Times* and the BBC. The BBC wanted him to be part of its Saturday commentary team, while the *Sunday Times* believed his lengthy stints in front of the BBC microphone were affecting his work for them. It thought the BBC was using its man 'on the cheap'. Time and again, the 'one exact phrase' that would have been perfect for the newspaper would slip out on the radio instead. The BBC took a high and mighty stance, arguing to Fingleton that it didn't like its commentators having news-paper commitments.

As he needed both jobs to make his touring financially viable, Fingleton attempted a compromise. He would stay off the radio for the final session of Saturday's play and focus on his newspaper work. The paper and the BBC agreed to the plan, but they—and Fingleton—remained uneasy.

Fingleton was also having serious problems with his fellow radio commentators, Alan McGilvray and John Arlott.

Fingleton was always suspicious of McGilvray, believing, with some justification, that he was less than a straight shooter and overly protective of his position as Australia's leading cricket commentator. McGilvray looked down on others, especially younger members of the ABC broadcasting team. During the Oval Test, McGilvray and Fingleton had a tiff over how Ted Dexter had been dismissed. Shortly afterwards, Fingleton had breakfast with Arlott and asked him why he refused to be on air as the same time as him. 'No, no, no,' Arlott replied. 'It was McGilvray who "did" you. Not me.' Arlott explained that when BBC officials had asked McGilvray what the trouble was on air, McGilvray had blamed Fingleton. The head of outside broad-casting, Charles Max Muller, had declared that Fingleton would not broadcast for the BBC again, but had later been overruled. This information put an end to the already sour relationship between Fingleton and McGilvray.

Not that Arlott and Fingleton were bosom pals either. Arlott believed Fingleton was often far too blunt in expressing his views on-air. Arlott loved the colour; Fingleton loved the cut and thrust of it all.

During the breakfast when Arlott told Fingleton about McGilvray, he also explained why he was sometimes unsettled by the Fingleton factor.

'But you do take the piss out of me at times,' Arlott said.

For the first time ever with Arlott, Fingleton got the last word, 'John, you do leave yourself open at times.'

Fingleton later wrote to a friend that he found himself in continuous low-level 'conflict' with Arlott: 'He was supposed to relinquish the microphone to the three experts at the end of the over, but John often found it difficult to yield the mike.' McGilvray also received a serve for being 'very self-opinionated at times'.

Fingleton hated it when other broadcasters failed to hide their allegiances. He believed journalists should always be straight down the middle, and he stuck doggedly to that ideal. Author David Frith recounts the time when Fingleton was on the air and his fellow commentator suddenly announced, 'We need 4.75 runs per over.'

Jack paused for a second, and then asked, 'Weeee? WEEEEE? Who's weeee?'

The co-commentator eventually summoned the courage to say: 'England.'

Fingleton, true to his even-handed principles, had also suc-ceeded in getting under the skin of the Australian team. After Australia had been overwhelmed in the Third Test at Leeds, Fingleton was asked by one of his sports editors at home to 'put the boot in'. He responded, stating that the Australian side was on the 'point of disintegration'. The article was duly sent to the team, and Benaud, on the first morning of the Fourth Test, pinned it on the dressing-room door. It clearly found its mark: several days later the team was celebrating a form turnaround and a 54-run victory.

Yet at the end of the series, Fingleton was able to put all the worries and conflict aside and write a glowing overview for the 1962 *Wisden Cricketers' Almanack* entitled: 'An Enjoyable Visit to Britain'. An Australian Test series win helped, and with the matches 'almost devoid of incidents,' it was 'the happiest tour of England I have known'.

When England toured Australia in 1962–63, there were fewer happy moments, notably Fingleton's omission from the guest list for the Prime Minister's XI dinner. He was fairly sure this had something to do with the fact that Prime Minister Menzies had convinced Bradman, at the age of 54, to captain his eleven. Menzies no doubt thought that it would not be wise or diplomatic to have one of the Don's most vehement critics too close at hand.

Some weeks after the match, Menzies bumped into Fingleton in a Parliament House corridor. After an exchange of pleasantries, Fingleton said, 'I feel I should tell you that I thought I might have been invited, even to the Pavilion, for your Prime Minister's match. You will know that we had a hard job, in the first place, in getting this match.'

'But you were at the dinner,' Menzies said, ill at ease. 'Somebody down the line . . .'

'This was the first dinner I missed,' Fingleton told him.

'But all my old captains were to be there, I can remember saying, Jack Fingleton for the dinner.'

In Fingleton's notes recording the encounter he remarked that Menzies 'was lying and making a poor fist of it'. Inviting his old captains was also 'baloney', because Lindsay Hassett and Ian Johnson had not been invited either. 'Well, I feel pretty bad about it,' Fingleton wrote to himself. 'This is my home town and all the chaps know it. However, I don't suppose you can think of everything.' He finished by observing, 'Most gratifying to be able to tell him face to face what I thought of it. I have never seen him so rattled.'

There was a distinct lack of harmony, too, when South Africa toured in 1963–64. Once again, the chucking issue erupted. International cricket officials had at last decided to get serious about weeding out suspect actions. This saw numerous players, including South African Geoffrey Griffin, called for throwing. Meckiff, with his distinctive cocked-arm delivery, again found himself under intense scrutiny, and before the First Test of the South African series in Brisbane it was rumoured that he could be targeted. The South Africans, surprised that Meckiff had returned to the Test team, were convinced he was going to be called.

The atmosphere at the pre-Test cocktail party at Government House in Brisbane was somewhat edgy. The three Australian selectors—Bradman, Ryder and Dudley Seddon—stood in different corners and seemed to stay as far away from each other as possible. Observers wondered whether they'd had a disagreement. Within days, a consensus had formed that the trio had been at odds over Meckiff's selection for this Test. It was revealed that the issue had even been discussed at Board level. Queenslander Clem Jones, a Board delegate, had objected to Meckiff's selection on the ground of his dubious bowling action.

It all came to a head when the South Africans began their first innings, and umpire Col Egar, from square leg, no-balled Meckiff for throwing his second, third, fifth and ninth deliveries. Captain Benaud immediately removed Meckiff from the attack, ending his international cricketing career.

Was the calling of Meckiff premeditated? How much of a role did Bradman play in his being kicked out of Test cricket? Egar has dismissed the claim that Bradman had instructed the umpires as 'absolute rubbish'. Bradman also repeatedly denied the allegation.

However, some were not so sure, including Fingleton. Even Clem Jones was convinced that Meckiff's being called had been planned well before the Test, and that it was Bradman who had told the umpires to do it.

As Fingleton later wrote:

Oddly there was a period when Adelaide was the home of a clutch of chuckers but once it was determined to rid the game of these, they quickly faded there. I often wondered whether Ian Meckiff was caught up in this movement.

One got the impression that selectors Ryder and Seddon, now both dead, had chosen Meckiff over Bradman's wishes. Bradman and Benaud, the Australian captain, were seen constantly together in Brisbane before the match. I asked Richie once whether he was surprised that Meckiff had been no-balled. He looked hard at me for a moment and then replied, 'No'.

At the time, Fingleton wrote to the *Sunday Times* sports editor: 'If you got those three idiots from the local asylum they could not have made as big a mess of things as Bradman, Ryder and Seddon did at Brisbane. I am inclined to think now it was all collusion between Bradman and Egar putting their heads together and Benaud not altogether being surprised when it happened.'

Benaud has repeatedly said he did not know Meckiff was going to be called until it happened. When it did, he maintained, he felt numb.

Fingleton's inside contacts also tipped him off that Bob Simpson was 'certain to lead Australia in England next year,' as he wrote in the *Sunday Times*. Fingleton told *Sunday Times* executives that Simpson had a good relationship with Bradman. Sure enough, Simpson was at the helm of the Australian team chosen to tour England in 1964. As with Benaud, it took some time for Fingleton to give Simpson his imprimatur. As he explained, at first he had 'doubts about the success Simpson will make of the job. He is pretty hungry.' With Simpson's opposite number, England skipper Ted Dexter, however, Fingleton was on good terms. He was so enthused with Dexter's style of play that two seasons earlier he had written him a lengthy letter setting out how he should go about facing Benaud. He should not play Benaud from the crease, or hit across the ball: 'Benaud's hand must be read. He has withheld his bosie and flipper, but if his hand can't be read, the ball can be as it comes down the pitch,' Fingleton wrote.

And no, Fingleton wasn't being unpatriotic. 'I've played and watched too much cricket to be nationalistic about things, and personally I can watch a lot of you in the middle. I don't chase into dressing rooms—I think my Press brethren do far too much of this, incidentally, and allow themselves to be used.'

As always Fingleton wanted to be, and was, his own man. But that had its consequences. On his next England jaunt, there were more dramas in store.

20

Flourishing Roses and Lost Golf Balls

By the mid 1960s, Fingleton's profile as a cricket commentator was as high as his profile as a player had been. His articles
in the *Sunday Times*, an unpredictable mixture of reporting,
anecdotes and biting comment, were widely admired for their
distinctive style, their wit and the depth of knowledge they
displayed. Judging from the number of fan letters he received, he
had an enormous following, boosted even further by regular
spots on BBC radio and television. He was known throughout
the U.K. as a cheeky, straight-to-the-point Aussie.

He returned the affection. He regarded England as his second
home and visited as often as he could. In 1963, he was there as a
guest of the British Central Office of Information. Another
journalist on the trip, Max Fatchen, recalled that on their first
night in Britain, the tour hosts arranged an evening at the opera.
The Australians sat jet-lagged in the best seats, and Fingleton
nodded off. When the singing erupted in a torrent of high notes,
he woke up, looked around, and asked, 'Who's out?'

As he got ready to leave on another Ashes tour in 1964—this
time accompanied by his eldest child, Belinda—he assumed the

three-legs of his media tripod were stable. In fact, they were decidedly shaky. His television spots were about to go. Despite having been a staple of the BBC's television coverage of the 1956 and 1961 Australian tours, he was to be replaced by Richie Benaud. To friends, Fingleton adopted an ironic tone: 'They have superseded me with Benaud (on TV),' he wrote, 'much more glamorous and presentable, I must say.' But the loss grated—and with BBC officials, he didn't mind showing it. He wrote to Charles Max Muller, the head of outside broadcasts, that he was astounded he was no longer wanted. 'I found your news most depressing. Why am I not to do any television?' Given the positive press articles and 'hundreds of letters I have received from viewers' after his 1956 and '61 appearance, 'I had the impression that I had done a good job. I think it is a poor reward to be put off like this.'

He was even moved to complain to BBC director-general Sir Hugh Carleton Greene. While he conceded that Benaud was 'a good choice', he added: 'The point I would like to make about your BBC TV is that they seem to be lacking in any appreciation of the hard work done for them by people. Perhaps the camera gives them an exalted opinion of their importance, but I do feel they are lacking in the personal contact and appreciation that go with ordinary things in life.'

(Carleton Greene did not reply, but Fingleton got back at him a few years later, when he visited Australia and Fingleton interviewed him. His admission during the interview that there were 'queers and commies' in the BBC was duly dispatched by Fingleton to the *Sunday Times*, which ran the story over four columns. Carleton Greene was not amused.)

The BBC commentator Brian Johnston tried to placate Fingleton, writing that 'you obviously feel very badly about the way you have been treated,' but the first choice for television 'was yourself'. Pointing out that Fingleton was unavailable for the BBC on Saturday afternoon because of his *Sunday Times* commitments, Johnston said that Saturday was 'a tremendous day' for television, and that it was felt that 'we must have the best on that day and not a substitute . . . TV must have a team and this must be the same team for every day of every Test.'

Fingleton was convinced the real reasons for his dumping lay elsewhere. Clearly, the BBC officials were eager to bring on Benaud, but he also believed they had not forgiven him for criticising the broadcaster's political coverage in a letter to the *Sunday Times* editor the previous year. In his reply to Johnston, he referred to that letter, saying 'there was a lot of what we Australians call "bull" in it, and so far as the BBC TV is concerned, I must say that you are an odd lot of bastards.'

Fingleton said he was disappointed that it had taken two months for the BBC to tell him he had been dropped, adding: 'If anybody asks me why I am not wanted on TV this coming summer, I shall tell them I wasn't wanted.'

Johnston insisted the sole reason was that he wasn't available on Saturdays; otherwise he would have been 'the 100% first choice for television'. But Fingleton didn't buy it.

He was now confined to BBC radio commentaries, but soon he was in trouble there as well. The incorrigibly blunt Fingleton continued to get his fellow commentators offside. His on-air relationship with Arlott was unsteady, and he shared Arlott's dislike of McGilvray, who irritated him. He once wrote to Sir Robert Menzies that he found McGilvray 'not the easiest person with whom to work . . . I "built" him up in England in 1953, when he was unknown, over the BBC. He has an odd disloyal way of returning my gesture.'

He also believed McGilvray was a poser and 'tall story-teller', who would imply falsely that he had played in important matches.

The BBC producers eventually had enough of the friction. After the First Test, Fingleton was handed an official letter complaining that the commentators were completely ignoring the producers and, when given written instructions while on air, were denigrating them by saying, 'I have been told,' 'I have been ordered,' and 'I have been asked.' When off air, they were allegedly making too much noise at the back of the broadcast box.

Taking this as another clear warning that he was no longer wanted by the BBC, Fingleton focused on his *Sunday Times* work. It was hardly the most lively Test series to report on, involving four draws and one outcome—an Australian Ashes triumph via a win at Headingley. The lacklustre character of the series was underscored during the Fifth Test, when Fingleton and Neville Cardus were returning to their hotels after having dinner in Soho. Their cab came to a standstill, surrounded by hundreds of theatregoers leaving the West End. Suddenly, a gentleman began hammering on the front of the cab with his umbrella. The driver leapt out and knocked him out with two punches.

When they got going again, Fingleton asked him why he had taken such drastic action. 'I've been watching that Lawry all day down at the Oval,' he replied. 'I'm in no mood to put up with any more bloody nonsense.' Cardus and Fingleton knew exactly what he was talking about. Watching Bill Lawry at the crease, poking away, could be torture.

For Jack, the highlights of this trip were elsewhere.

On an excursion to Rome with Belinda, he got 'ringside seats' in St Peter's Basilica for a Mass celebrated by Pope Paul VI when he 'slipped some lira' to an attendant. Corruption was justified occasionally, he later said, even in the Vatican.

They also attended a big Fingleton family gathering in Ireland that turned into a long night of tall stories, laughter and reminiscences.

Before they left on the Ashes trip, Fingleton's elder brother Les had died. He had become a notable Eastern Suburbs sporting and political identity. A first-grade cricketer, he was secretary of the Waverley club, a NSW Sheffield Shield team manager, and a delegate to the NSW Cricket Association. He was also an interstate bowls representative, a NSW and Australian handball champion, an excellent golfer, and secretary of the NSW Gun Club. And as if all that weren't enough, he was Mayor of Waverley and stood several times for election for the federal seat of Phillip.

As Jack would often say, a stroll down a Waverley street with Les would take hours, because everyone knew him, and wanted to talk to him. Les invariably saw the good side in a person's character, prompting him to be a friend to virtually everyone.

Les suffered from diabetes, but his death was still unexpected. As he was one of the most popular figures in the Eastern Suburbs, it was not surprising his funeral attracted hundreds of mourners.

After Fingleton returned from the England tour, he faced another death—his brother Glen died unexpectedly. During the Second World War, Glen had been a conscientious objector. He told authorities: 'I'll send money and work to feed the troops, but I will not kill anyone.' During and after the war, Glen worked on the wharves. Concerned about the plight of his fellow workers, he became a notable union organiser, organising the mechanical branch of the Waterside Workers' Union. Communist infiltrators attempted to take over the branch, but Glen resisted. For that, he was physically attacked, and suffered constant threats that his house was about to be bombed.

Elected as a union representative, Glen travelled to Geneva for an international conference. But after he refused to back Communist factions in several important votes, the union delegates would not give him his ticket home, and Glen was stranded in Europe. His only hope of getting back to Australia was via England, and so he worked his way through France, despite not knowing a word of the language, and hitchhiked to London.

At Australia House he met up with the grandson of one of the Fingletons' original neighbours at Bondi Junction, who organised for Glen to get home as a '£10 migrant'.

Glen remained a passionate union man and secretary of the WWU's mechanical branch. But in June 1965, after delivering an emotional speech at a stop-work meeting in Glebe, where he was imploring the men to return to work, he collapsed and died.

Like the rest of the family, Jack was inspired by Glen's courage and commitment. When Andrea, a well known Sydney radio announcer, implied that his brother was one of those commies working on the wharves, Jack soon put her in her place—and even threatened legal action.

Jack's youngest brother, Wally, had a flourishing sporting career in his youth. He was also making his name as a journalist. Then one wet day, a bout of boredom led him into an entirely different vocation. He recalled: 'I had a day off, and as I was a mad surfer, I was going to go to Bondi. However, it was pelting rain, and instead went to Jack's bookshelf at home to get something to read.

'I picked up a book called *Blazing the Trail in the Solomons*, which Chappie Dwyer, who ran the Catholic Emporium in George Street, had passed on to Jack.' The book was a biography of a priest who had lived in the Solomon Islands. 'After reading the book, I said to myself, this is what I want to do. I wanted to do something worthwhile for others.'

After seven years of study, he was ordained as a Marist priest in 1944. Soon afterwards, he achieved his goal of becoming a missionary to the Solomon Islands, where he lived for the next twenty-seven years, often in primitive conditions. Father Wally Fingleton eventually had to return to Australia on doctor's advice when he seemed likely to lose the sight of one of his eyes. Since then, he has been involved in different parishes throughout NSW and Queensland.

When Fingleton came back from overseas, he faced a new phase in the long-running rift with Bradman. Fingleton had written to the Don in June 1964 to say how delighted he was that members of Bradman's family had made him so welcome when they had seen each other at Lord's. He had hoped the letter might mend their relationship.

Bradman replied:

> Your letter was not unwelcome (though you seemed to expect it might be). Perhaps it was a strange quirk of fate that this friendly gesture on your part was kindled by my family being so nice to you at Lord's. Why shouldn't they be? They are normal, natural people who treat others as they find them.
>
> I am willing to accept your gesture in the spirit that it is offered. If you have been hurt or upset by people in England saying to you: 'Of course you and Don are the worst enemies,' I can only reply that you should not be surprised. Your writings and comments over the years could scarcely have created any other impression. Most certainly this view was not caused by acts or deeds of mine but I could scarcely be unaware of your attitude nor could I be expected to react kindly to it, especially as I believe you have no justification. But as you have rightly concluded, life rolls on and there is not too much of it left, I am quite happy to forget the past if that is how you want it.

A peace pipe appeared to have been produced, but this letter still deeply hurt Fingleton.

'Dad used to get very upset about Bradman,' daughter Belinda said. 'I remember him talking to my mother when I was a teenager. My parents would often discuss his articles. He was particularly upset by the reaction to a letter he sent to Bradman. He did rely on Bill O'Reilly to provide support at times.'

Jack was astounded that Bradman could not see any justification for his feeling negative towards him. Had he forgotten what had occurred during their playing days? Had he forgotten how he worked against Fingleton before the 1934 England tour? And the 'dressing room leak'?

So Fingleton's letter did little to restore calm.

Life at home in Canberra wasn't exactly tranquil, either. Fingleton kept up his demanding work schedule, pushing aside the piles of newspapers and files in his tiny office at Parliament House to try and get some work done. Piles of newspapers were continually collapsing around him, and he often had to rearrange everything just to get enough space for his typewriter.

At home, Fingleton was an old-fashioned Catholic father, loving but strict.

The children according to one family friend, 'chafed at the bit' under his watchful eye. Any male who came near his beloved 'Bin' got a look stern enough to ward off the less confident. When she went to Europe with him, he knew how Jessie Street must have felt on the *Orontes* all those years ago, when he was pursuing her daughter.

But there were advantages to having Fingleton as a dad. For one thing, they were able to meet some of Australia's best-known cricketers. Keith Miller and his wife Peg, Len Darling and Lindsay Hassett all slept under the family grand piano when they stayed over in Canberra.

For relaxation, Fingleton played golf, with almost as much passion as he felt for cricket. A member of the Royal Canberra Golf Club, he was for some time a low-handicap player and won his share of club championships. His proudest feat was a par round around the Royal Canberra course, but as he grew older, his handicap grew. It didn't stop his ritual of playing each Saturday.

He was an assiduous student of the game, using his scorecards to make notes on his shots, and jot down ideas on how to improve them. But he refused to get tuition. 'There's no need for lessons,' he would exclaim on the tee, shortly before fading the ball towards the rough.

According to his golfing partners, Fingleton hated to lose a ball. On Sundays, he often played in a mixed foursomes event. The deal was that after the game the men would shower and then go into the lounge, where they were expected to buy drinks for their partners until the presentations.

But often, after putting out on the eighteenth hole, he would say to the others, 'I'll see you later. I'm just going back down the fairway to see if I can find that ball.' He would spend the next half hour wandering around the course, while the other members of the foursome grudgingly paid for the drinks.

At the golf club, as at Parliament House, he invariably wore a rose in his buttonhole. An enthusiastic rose grower, he had several varieties in his garden, and on his way out would cut one to adorn his lapel. If he missed his morning rose he'd head to the rose gardens behind Parliament House, talk to the gardeners and cadge a bloom from them.

His gentlemanly manners extended to an intense dislike of swearing. Any colleague who swore in front of him would be cut off sharply. 'He was regarded in that way as somewhat slightly eccentric by the younger blokes, who were continually swearing,' press gallery denizen Rob Chalmers said. 'They soon realised he very much objected to such language.'

Fingleton could be impatient, caustic and opinionated. He abhorred fence-sitters. His waspish tongue upset, intimidated and even frightened people. A colleague put it bluntly: 'Jack was a very agreeable man, but he could be a shit as well.'

During the Vietnam War, another member of the press corp introduced Fingleton to a member of his family who was in the

Army. Fingleton abruptly said he would never allow his own son to join the Army. He was serious. His son Grey was eligible to be called up for national service. Fingleton believed the war was senseless, blamed Menzies—to his face—for Australia's unnecessary entry into it, and said that if Grey's birth date came out of the conscription lottery he intended to refuse him permission to join the military.

As he wrote in his autobiography, 'One did not have children, nurture and educate them, for such an illogical war.' Anything illogical irritated Fingleton, who never suffered fools lightly.

He was also an intensely private man, for all his friendships. On latter tours, when he was no longer accompanied by old teammates, he often retreated to his hotel room, refusing to join any journalistic rat pack. Some who knew him thought he was the 'prickliest man of all time—in the cricket sphere anyway', and some wondered whether his insecurities and thin skin could be traced to his humble background. But once you had him in company he was always entertaining, a fount of anecdotes.

And he was always willing to help the newcomer, never forgetting how important mentors had been to him as a young journalist. Provided a cub reporter had the courage to front up to Fingleton, he would help him. Alan Ramsey, one of Canberra's most respected political correspondents, was one who sought him out. When he came to Canberra in 1966, the unabashed Fingleton fan made a point of meeting 'the great man'.

'The thing about Jack was . . . it was the name. The Fingleton name,' Ramsey recalled.

He was the bloke down the hall, who worked in this little dog box. It was just a door, and almost nobody had ever been in there. We didn't see him much because he would be away on cricket trips, and then he would just show up.

· And as he didn't appear that often, I used to keep an eye out for Jack, because I loved talking to him. I found him a man of grace, knowledge and great good humour. He was one of the most genuine people I ever knew.

It was a very different press gallery then, and it was a very different Canberra. The gallery was much smaller, almost totally male, clubby, and more elite. When I first started, not many of the blokes would talk to me because I was a young blow-in. I really didn't want to get into that clique, and they didn't want you in it anyway. That's why I liked Jack, because he was different. Jack was not a member of that day-to-day clan.

Fingleton's clan at home was by this time disintegrating. The strains in his marriage had reached breaking point. Philippa had grown tired of the isolation, of her husband's long trips away, of the small-town parochialism of Canberra. The age difference was another factor. She wanted to return to Sydney, all the more urgently because her mother Jessie's health was failing. In 1967, Pip moved to Roseville, on Sydney's North Shore.

The separation was kept well out of the public eye. Both Jack and Pip wanted to keep it private. Few outside the family were aware of it; only his closest colleagues were informed and told to keep it to themselves, because Fingleton, at least, still thought reconciliation was possible. At every important gathering, Mr and Mrs Fingleton would show up, and they both remained doting parents and grandparents. Belinda explained that despite the marriage problems, the children had a happy home life. 'We enjoyed great family bush picnics, beach holidays, the rosary every Sunday night, family sing-a-longs around the piano where Dad would play brilliantly by ear,' Belinda said.

'Dad also had a magnificent tenor voice. As he had such a great dry and quirky sense of humour, Dad would enthral all the children with stories he made up as he went along. And to all his grandchildren, he was a much-loved "Grandpère".'

(Fingleton's children excelled academically and at sport. Jim and Larry became doctors—Jim with a Doctorate of Philosophy from the ANU, and Larry was a highly respected surgeon. Grey and Larry both played representative rugby at school, while Larry was also a competent cricketer. Jack, who was particularly close to Larry, believed he could have gone further in his cricketing career. Belinda was a competent swimmer and made the ACT women's netball team, while Jim was an ACT rugby representative. Jacqui, who moved with her mother to Sydney, has enjoyed a flourishing life, including working as a Qantas air-hostess and an involvement in politics.)

After the separation, the family remained the top priority. Jack made certain he had a strong and loving relationship with all members of his spreading family. He was also there for them when they needed advice or guidance. Although concerned that his work was tugging him away from his family, his spirit remained relatively buoyant. He never lost hope of reconciliation. Jack even told close friends he stayed with on one England tour that he was contemplating giving away covering cricket if there was any chance it could save his marriage. Nonetheless he and Pip were a couple no more. Now, approaching 60, Fingleton was on his own.

21

A Solitary Existence

Writing is a lonely occupation. To stop one going completely crazy, the writer needs others to bounce ideas off and help release frustration. For Fingleton, Bill O'Reilly was that foil, especially when they were away covering the Australian team on tour. They supported each other in the press box and during those meandering periods between matches. So in the 1960s, when O'Reilly gave up touring and confined his *Sydney Morning Herald* cricketing columns to domestic games, Fingleton fell into a mild depression. He knew O'Reilly's absence would put him in the spotlight more, but that had its downside.

Soon after O'Reilly told Fingleton his touring days were over, Jack wrote to the *Herald*'s longtime cricket and rugby league writer Tom Goodman: 'Tiger, on his own, is always a comfort and I will miss him . . . Every night I go to bed convinced that I will turn this tour in, but in the morning I realise I have a big family to bring up and the tour really means thousands of pounds to me. The thought of leaving them all keeps me awake at night; and the knowledge that Tiger will no longer be there makes me almost crook.'

The two friends' affection for each other came through in their correspondence, which went on for decades. Their letters were lively, argumentative, full of gripes, full of cheek. There were moments of sadness. In 1968, when Stan McCabe fell seriously ill, O'Reilly told Fingleton he had visited their comrade-in-arms in hospital.

His wrists were so thin that it was impossible to believe that he was the bloke who hit Ken Farnes over the square leg boundary at Nottingham in 1938 when I happened to be batting with him.

It was the very first time in my life that I had seen a sixer hit without really trying. I bent down over the little bloke and recounted the tale of that innings—reminding him how he belted the daylights out of those bloody Poms, and brought us back out of the jaws. Those little eyes seemed to react towards a sparkle as I went along, and I was certain that I was getting through when I saw the customary twitching of the lips start moving. But he's crook—bloody crook. I would hazard a guess that his liver is rent to ribbons.

A month later, McCabe was dead. He had returned home, only to fall down a cliff at the back of his house and break his skull. Richie Benaud broke the news to Jack in England.

In other letters, Tiger and Jack exchanged views on cricketing identities. Tiger had little time for Australian officials, tagging them a 'senile range of fizzers'. After discovering that NSW cricketing czar Syd Smith had just completed fifty years in the game's administration, and that all other members of the executive had been re-elected unopposed, O'Reilly complained. 'Wouldn't it give you the dry rot?' This group had, in his view, succeeded 'in rooting the game entirely'.

Tiger also had his doubts about the man who was being called the next Bradman, NSW batsman Norm O'Neill. He didn't think O'Neill had what it took for Test cricket. 'Tired of making excuses and repeating that he has tremendous talent. He has everything it needs bar the guts and the brains. Two highly important ingredients . . .'

He told Fingleton that the new cricket writers seemed fixated on dressing-room gossip and would believe anything the players told them. As far as Tiger was concerned, they were a 'strange crop of young ne'er-do-wells' whose plan was 'to bugger the game'.

As for the new crop of cricketers, several of the best enjoyed Fingleton and O'Reilly's company, and they returned the approval. They took a special interest in Ian Chappell, the grandson of their much-admired captain Vic Richardson. They could both see a lot of Vic in Ian, but that didn't mean they would give Ian an easy ride. He had to earn their respect.

When Australia toured England in 1968, Ian scored a century at Taunton, in the same match in which his younger brother Greg, playing for the opposition, Somerset, scored a half-century. After Ian's innings Fingleton sent a message inviting him to the press box.

'Jack had previously spoken to me a few times telling me how much he admired my grandfather,' Chappell said.

On this occasion I assumed Jack was going to congratulate me on my innings and tell me how proud Vic would be. However, Jack just said, 'Hello, Ian' in his own distinctive way that made it sound like 'Een', and then proceeded to tell me how he thought Greg was a good player in the making.

Jack proved to be a good judge of batsmen and was also an excellent motivator. His comments made me realise I would be quickly overtaken by my younger brother if I didn't keep my wits about me.

Jack was also a good judge of character. On that same tour he told me: 'Een, your swearing will get you into trouble.'

Some years later, Chappell took part in a golf challenge match in which he was partnered with Rodney Marsh, against Fingleton and his close friend from the *Adelaide Advertiser*, Keith Butler. O'Reilly came along as the unofficial referee. Fingleton's relationship with Marsh had been tense. After Marsh had played his first Test in 1970–71, Fingleton sidled up to Chappell and asked, 'What's this cove Marsh like?'

'He's a good bloke—likes a beer, plays good golf, he can bat a bit and he's a much better keeper than what he showed in the First Test. Why do you ask?'

'Well,' said Fingleton, 'he got on the plane and threw his suit carrier into the luggage rack and it landed on my deerstalker hat. I told him to be careful, he could damage my hat, and he replied, "It could only improve it."'

By the time of the golf challenge, at the Victoria Golf Club, Fingleton and Marsh's relationship had improved.

The match was all square as the group headed to the thirteenth green. Fingleton had a short putt, which would have put the journos one up. Chappell was standing next to Butler. Fingleton stabbed at his putt, prompting Butler to mutter to himself, 'How could he miss that bloody putt?'

Chappell smelled an opening. As they headed to the fourteenth, he told Marsh, 'You keep Butler company. I want to have a chat with Jack.'

Coming up beside Fingleton, he said, 'Jack, you ought to hear what your partner is saying about your putting.'

Fingleton spun around and yelled, 'Butler, what have you been saying about my putting?'

While the pair squabbled, Chappell and Marsh won the fourteenth hole and held on to win the match one up.

After several rounds at the bar, the group took a taxi back to Melbourne. Chappell recalled, 'We pulled up outside the Graham Hotel, where the journos were staying, and just as O'Reilly's shoe hit the footpath, Marsh said, "Where are we going for a drink now, Tiger?" Tiger immediately jumped back into the cab, until a rather annoyed Fingleton said, "Come on, O'Reilly, the boys have to play in a Test tomorrow."

'"Don't be stupid," replied Tiger. "We used to drink before games—they can handle it." Eventually Fingleton won out, but he had to drag Tiger out of the cab.'

Sir Robert Menzies and Fingleton also enjoyed a lively correspondence. Over several decades, and continuing on well after Menzies stepped down as Prime Minister in 1966, they discussed a variety of issues from the media to cricket. Menzies would moan to Fingleton about the standard of political reporting, and Fingleton would respond with snippets of cricket news, observations about politics, and even advice.

In late 1966, he wrote from England that Menzies's Liberal Party successor Harold Holt, was 'getting stick' in Australia for saying 'all the way with [U.S. President] LBJ' when Lyndon Johnson visited Australia. 'I heard him say this on the air and it was said in a humorous manner and, as you know, the humour at times, does not read too well in print. But I think he is doing all right, feeling his way.'

They argued over cricketers, of course. After the Prime Minister listed some of his favourites, Fingleton demurred on a few of his choices: 'I could never see Arthur Mailey, delightful character as he is, in the top bracket. I played against him as a youngster, and failed to "trouble". I might have urged you to include, in an overall picture, Hutton and Miller and "Ponny" [Ponsford]. And perhaps, strangely, I find that Benaud finished his stint as no great cricketer.'

As for cricket officials, on the re-election of O'Reilly's bête noire Syd Smith, he told Menzies the crusty old official 'is again to lend the power of his bright personality to the NSWCA. Allah be with us! The look of him is enough to put the game back a decade.'

Fingleton's close South African ties made him more attuned than some cricket writers to the nuances of life and politics there. While many were demanding a sporting boycott of South Africa because of apartheid, Fingleton trod more warily. He knew that if he were to start calling for tour boycotts his association with the Argus newspaper group would be affected. He admitted to Menzies that it put him in a quandary. 'One has to be careful, in giving varied reasons why I don't think the tour can take place, not to give the suggestion that I don't want it.'

Fingleton was eager to make the apartheid issue a subject of his next book, which he planned as a collection of essays on topics from famous matches and players to 'craft, character and controversy'.

The issue of apartheid in sport had flared into an international controversy when Basil D'Oliviera, a 'Cape Coloured' who had moved to England and been selected for its Test side, was dropped in 1968 from the team picked to tour South Africa after political pressure from the hosts. When D'Oliviera was eventually included in the side, South Africa refused the team entry. The tour was abandoned and South Africa was frozen out of world sport, an isolation that would last twenty years.

Fingleton was no great fan of D'Oliviera. In an interview with the *South China Morning Post*, he described him as 'a pleasant batsman, but he is a poor field and an unimpressive bowler'. Writing to Menzies a few months later, he said he had been 'nauseated by all this guff over D'Oliviera' and was thinking of 'penning a few acid words'. He thought that by making D'Oliviera into a martyr, South Africa's action had actually been 'a meal ticket' for the player. The Marylebone Cricket Club had 'made a proper bosh of things', and the 'crypto Communists' had unfairly made South Africa their target.

Menzies replied that he also found the D'Oliviera affair 'nauseating' and said he'd discussed it with the South African Prime Minister. Menzies agreed with the PM's view that D'Oliviera shouldn't have been allowed to tour,

> not so much [because] it violates the rules of apartheid but because D'Oliviera was a sort of angel to the Cape Coloured and whenever he was given out, there would be the most tremendous demonstration, the ground would be invaded and a great deal of unpleasantness would arise.
>
> The unperceptive people who pushed South Africa out [of the Commonwealth] did not realise that the asperities of apartheid will never be modified if the rest of the world sends South Africa to Coventry, and if, as we have seen, the United Nations through its special agencies takes every opportunity of putting South Africa on the outer. People, who, with rather over-advertised virtue, boycott a nation, are doing a foolish and destructive thing.

The following week Fingleton wrote to ask Menzies if he could use 'a few lines' about Australian cricketer Grahame Thomas and Menzies's role in getting permission for him to tour South Africa in 1966.

NSW Cricket Association official Alan Barnes had told Fingleton that Thomas was of 'mixed blood'. Fingleton also understood that Menzies 'had a few words with Dr [Hendrik] Verwoerd [the South African PM] and he assured you that there would be no doubt about Thomas being received there'.

He added that he wasn't enamoured of all South Africans. 'I don't admire the tough strain of Afrikaner, who always reminds me of some Germans,' he wrote. 'They are so rigid. They are at their worst in Orange Free State. I saw a rugby match in Bloem-fontein in 1963 and it was the worst sporting crowd I have seen. They do not allow Coloreds into the Bloemfontein ground at all and after this experience, I commend the practice. The whites of that day would have polluted them.'

Menzies confirmed the Thomas story, explaining that Barnes had told him that the Board 'were a little anxious' that the South African government might raise objections, possibly after the team had arrived. Menzies thought it prefer-able to 'find out in advance', and arranged a meeting with the South African ambassador:

> I remember showing him a few photographs of young Thomas and saying to him in a slightly facetious way, that though he was somewhat dark complexioned he was no darker than thousands of fully Caucasian types to be seen on the beaches of Sydney. I told him that it was understood that Thomas had some Red Indian blood, though anybody who looked less like a hawk-faced Red Indian I could hardly imagine. The Ambas-sador told me (and of course he cannot be quoted on this matter) that he thought there would be no difficulty whatever, the objection on the part of his people being to people who presented what he called a 'negroid' appearance.

Menzies then told Barnes that the Board 'could safely go ahead and choose' Thomas. They did.

Fingleton actually met Verwoerd in Pretoria in 1966. At Menzies's behest, Verwoerd agreed to a fifteen-minute off-the-record chat. It went an hour overtime. Fingleton 'didn't take a note, and put it all in his head', but as soon as he left the PM's office, he scribbled down what he could recall for future reference. He never used the information in any story, but kept the Verwoerd notebook among his files.

After greeting the PM in Afrikaans, Fingleton asked him about 'his feelings re the natives'.

'The white people had made South Africa what it was,' Verwoerd replied. 'In the process, they have developed the native. The South African native was the best off of all the natives in the African continent. The natives in South Africa had more cars than the Communists in Russia.'

Verwoerd said he had told the Indian Prime Minister, Jawaharlal Nehru, 'I will bet you that we will educate more natives in ten years than you will in India in 100 years.' He went on, 'We have nurtured a serpent in our bosom. But I don't hate the natives. I have many good friends among them. I want to give them the right to run their own affairs in their own country. South Africa is a white man's country. The white man made it. We will not be pushed out. We know the native mind. We understand them.'

Fingleton was hardly a happily nodding interviewer, telling the Prime Minister that 'no democratic country could tolerate his detention laws'. Verwoerd replied that desperate ills required desperate measures, and that anybody 'put inside' under the detention act was a Communist. Fingleton was unimpressed with that argument. He thought Verwoerd 'had a Hitler-like zeal and has the inflexible view of a typical Dutchman on matters politic. He won't fail white South Africa.'

Shortly after the interview, Verwoerd was assassinated, stabbed to death in the House of Assembly by a parliamentary clerk.

Fingleton's correspondence with Menzies could also be bitchy. Fingleton once wrote that his mother-in-law Jessie 'made marriage for dear Ken Street a pretty turbulent affair, with her interests and activities. Billy Hughes once said to me, with some truth I'm afraid: "Your mother has a red bee in her bonnet." She would have been the first of Australia's Women's Lib who have done their sex, as I see it, much harm. Unfortunately my wife, Philippa, has a like tendency.'

Fingleton's correspondence file overflowed with names from the highest levels of the cricketing world. Apart from the scribbled ramblings of the Englishman R.C. Robertson-Glasgow, who, sadly, was gradually losing his mind, there are the almost indecipherable jottings of Sir Pelham Warner, who after the Bodyline rift became a good friend of Fingleton's, interesting snippets from *The Times*'s veteran cricket correspondent John Woodcock, who often had Jack at his home during the England tours, notes from player Alec Bedser, and the majestic handwriting of Neville Cardus. By 1970, Cardus was growing bored with the game, writing, 'Frankly I can't go every day to cricket now. Too much seam bowling.'

Harold Larwood was in constant touch. When Fingleton asked for background information about Douglas Jardine, he replied that he was a 'very stern and ruthless man on the cricket field, but I found out, that underneath all that, he was a little shy . . . When in Adelaide after Oldfield got hit, Jardine decided to open bat to face the boos. He was hit several times, but he never flinched.'

Larwood vividly remembered the Sydney Test, when 'after bowling 33 overs', he had been told by Jardine to bat with ten minutes left. 'I was furious, but Wally Hammond who was not, calmed me down, and next day took my score to 98. The Skipper afterwards told me, he wanted me to have my innings, and then have a good rest, so everything was forgiven. Truly a great man.'

Irving Rosenwater, author of the most thorough and objective biography on Bradman, informed Fingleton that the Don 'was not overpleased that I should have quoted J.H.F. so liberally, in view of the past history between you.'

Australian captain Bill Lawry provided interesting details about his team's difficult tour of India in 1969, where they had encountered crowd violence, riots, and dreadful conditions both on and off the field. Lawry had been at the centre of one infamous incident during that Test series, when he shoved an Indian photographer after a group of cameramen rushed to the centre of the ground, shouting, 'Riot! Riot! Photos!'

The team was vilified in the local press. Fingleton had written a piece in the *Hindu* defending the Australians. Lawry wrote from Madras to express his gratitude, saying he didn't want to be quoted but that the Indian press had been cruel, 'even to the stage of where they are making up false interviews'. He added, 'The crowds have been frightening at times . . . I've looked very brave standing out there, but I don't think I've ever felt so uncomfortable in all my life. When I have to hit an Indian, pressman or not with a bat, then I'll send myself home.'

Fingleton also corresponded copiously with newspaper editors. When a complaint to the *Johannesburg Star* that it was mangling his copy brought the excuse that his copy was sometimes 'too late', Fingleton shot back, 'Suggest you get somebody else to handle the next tour . . . No writer can appear to do a good job if his material is ignored, badly handled, mutilated and made subservient to agency reports and, indeed, even potted comments from London.'

His correspondence with the legendary Melbourne *Age* editor Graham Perkin was more amicable, especially when he agreed to write articles for the paper and end his long-running boycott of cheapskate domestic newspapers. Perkin relished telling Fingleton that he had lunch 'with your friends Sonia and Billy [McMahon, the Liberal Prime Minister] the other day'. He went on, 'He is really dazzling company, but I do not think I will return the hospitality for just awhile. The funny little man has convinced himself that he is a brilliant success and sees himself winning handsomely in November.'

Fingleton wasn't enamoured of McMahon either, describing him as a 'flea'.

★

Some of the touchiest correspondence was with Bradman, but by the late '60s, it appeared they might finally be ready to reconcile. Fingleton wrote to Bradman in 1968 seeking help on an article he was writing for Britain's *World Sport* magazine on 'what makes a champion', how to compare champions from different eras, and the merits of modern cricketers.

Bradman responded at length, explaining that 'generally speaking I maintain that a champion in my generation would have been a champion in any other generation'. However, comparing generations was more difficult in cricket than in other sports. There were too many variables, such as wickets (covered or uncovered), the quality of the pitches, the standard of bowling, fielding, the laws, and the equipment used. He added:

My cricket career was played with a smaller ball, larger stumps and much of it under the offside LBW rule—all in favour of the bowler—as compared with say Trumper.

But these factors need to point to the fact that S.F. Barnes was a greater bowler than his figures indicate (because he did not have those advantages). And Trumper had to bat against Barnes—I didn't. In cricket a big score may be made thanks to a muffed catch—a duck due to a partner's error in a run-out. But each equally affects a batting average. The tactics of the bowlers can play a dominating part in what happens. Bodyline was a case in point.

And in cricket, perhaps beyond all other games, spectators so often give high marks to style (where Trumper was evidently superb), personality and verve (à la Trueman or Miller or Lock) or dynamic action (à la Wes Hall). But are you concerned with style or effectiveness? As Cardus has written, the eagle is more beautiful to watch than a modern jet plane, but there is no doubt which is faster.

Obviously you wouldn't expect me to express a view of a comparison regarding myself, and anyway I wouldn't be the best judge. This is for others to say.

Bradman also passed on the news that his wife Jessie had almost died several months earlier from a pulmonary embolism and was still 'terribly ill'.

As head of the Australian Cricket Board, Bradman was involved in the decision to cancel the 1971–72 South African tour of Australia because of widespread opposition to the country's apartheid laws. Fingleton was supportive. After witnessing the crowd riots that had followed the Springboks rugby team around Australia on their winter tour, both men could see that allowing the South African cricketers into the country would only lead to further violence.

However, until then many Australian officials, including Bradman, had been eager for South Africa to tour, on the ground that politics and sport should not mix. In June 1971, the South African tour appeared a certainty. McMahon approached Fingleton and asked what he thought of a Prime Minister's XI match with the South Africans. Fingleton told him 'not to touch it with a barge pole'.

In a note recording the exchange, Fingleton wrote: 'PM very friendly. He's a sad case. So very avid to be good friends with everybody, and, in the end, he will finish by offending many.'

It didn't take long for McMahon to offend Fingleton. When the South Africa tour debate was intensifying, Fingleton approached McMahon for an interview. McMahon fobbed Fingleton off.

Fingleton reminded him that when he had become PM he'd told the press gallery his door would always be open for questions.

'Yes, but I have been very busy,' McMahon said.

'But I wanted only a minute or two with you.'

'Yes, I knew that, but I knew the type of questions you wanted to ask me, and you knew I wouldn't answer them.'

Fingleton also knew that McMahon, whom he rated vastly inferior to Curtin, Chifley and Menzies, had been just as evasive when Bradman had written to him seeking guidance on the South African issue. Eventually Bradman held discussions with McMahon and his South African counterpart John Vorster, who both advised that the tour should not go ahead. However, this had to be kept quiet, because in calling the tour off, cricket officials did not want to be seen to be acting at the behest of the government.

At the press conference in Sydney in which Bradman announced that the tour was off, Fingleton asked him, 'Do you think the tour would have been cancelled had the South African government agreed to the inclusion of two Coloureds?'

Bradman answered: 'No.'

Shortly after, Fingleton left the conference to file for his South African newspapers. He also wrote an article for *The Australian* newspaper in which he said he 'felt exceedingly proud to know [Bradman]. His studious statement cancelling the South African tour showed that he knew where to place the blame. His opinion that a gesture to loosen the country's rigid racial laws is all that's necessary to bring the brilliant South African side back to where it belongs in international cricket will hit South Africa in the right place—in Mr Vorster's government.'

Vorster later publicly queried Fingleton's South African press story, claiming that he had a letter from Bradman, via his ambassador in Canberra, in which he denied making any statement on Coloured players.

Angry that his professional integrity had been questioned, Fingleton telephoned Bradman.

Put on the spot, Bradman said, 'I was under great stress and strain that night. I have no recollection that you asked me such a question. If you say you did and I answered "No", I accept your assurance unreservedly. I would say, now, that had the South African government taken a different view to the coloureds, the tour would have been acceptable to most Australians.'

Fingleton again encountered Bradman's cleverness at playing the political game. But he was at least pleased that the poison had gone out of their relationship. Or so he thought.

Elsewhere, Bradman was making his real thoughts on Fingleton known.

As revealed in Christine Wallace's book *The Private Don*, Fingleton wrote to *Adelaide News* editor Rohan Rivett in March 1969 asking him 'to run your gifted eye' over his collection of articles and essays, which was about to be published. Rivett passed Fingleton's letter on to Bradman for comment.

Bradman's reply was to the point: 'Like his bloody cheek.'

Some time later, Fingleton wrote to Rivett again, asking him if he'd review the new book for the *Canberra Times*. Fingleton wrote: 'I don't mind how you whack it, so long as my fellow Australians know that I do write on cricket and especially in Canberra, where I have many cobbers.'

Once again Rivett passed Fingleton's request on to Bradman. Bradman saw red, and, in Wallace's words, his reply was 'excoriating about Fingleton'.

Bradman told Rivett that Fingleton's letter reeked of jealousy, bigotry, envy and ego, and said he thought it outrageous that Fingleton should ask Rivett to write a review. Bradman seemed surprised that Fingleton, whom he also accused of suffering from 'swell-headedness', had 'cobbers'.

Bradman said he 'would prefer not to even recognise Fingleton. He had spent virtually a lifetime of using me as a meal ticket for his own monetary reward and falsely attacking me by attributing to me attitudes which I did not possess.'

Bradman then referred to Fingleton's insistence that in the Bodyline lead-up match in Perth, he'd said the England bowling attack were 'going to have a pop at me' and asked Fingleton to face Gubby Allen's bowling: 'He knows full well that he can make that filthy accusation against me in that Perth game because nobody but me can dispute it. So it is one man's word against another's. It is just merely a lie—that's all. But what is the use of one making a comment that another man is telling a lie. I repeat that I prefer to ignore him. He is not worth recognising.'

So they were back to square one.

22

Insecurities

Among Fingleton's large pile of correspondence, notebooks, scrapbooks and clippings is a pop quiz on personality that he had filled out. It provides some insights into his character.

He admitted that if he was depressed or in trouble, he would get drunk 'occasionally'. He rarely gave money to beggars, preferred others to order dinner rather than doing it himself, and did not find it hard to seek advice from others. He thought man was immortal, world wars would never end, and peace would never reign on earth. Leisure was more important to him than work, and the two qualities most crucial for getting ahead in life were good judgement and guts. On whether he suffered from an inferiority complex, Fingleton replied, 'In many ways.'

He had excelled in the areas he had focused on. He had risen to the highest level of cricket. He had established himself as a respected international journalist. He had been on first-name terms with a succession of prime ministers. The most powerful men in Australia listened to him. But Fingleton remained unsure of himself. His tough upbringing had taught him never to take anything or anyone for granted. He always felt that everything could change overnight. He was forever a child of the Depression, always worried that he didn't have enough, that his life was not complete.

His family was broken. What he'd assumed would be a lifelong bond with his wife had ended. His children had moved out and moved on, leaving him in Canberra, often alone. Only Jim was still at home while he finished his studies, and, as with so many fathers and eldest sons, their relationship was occasionally brittle. Jim was a carefree spirit, a musician who had helped teach Mick Jagger to sing bush ballads when the rock star appeared in the Australian movie *Ned Kelly*. They respected each other, but Jack sometimes thought Jim should have been working harder on his university studies. Envy may have been a factor, with his children getting opportunities Jack wished he had had. His own limited education had always weighed on him, pushing him constantly to try and improve himself.

Now in his sixties, he was finding it harder to cope with the demands of touring and endlessly filing for numerous media outlets. But he still delighted in the camaraderie of the press fraternity. During the 1972 Ashes tour of England, the coming generation of cricket writers, including Mike Coward, Phil Wilkins, Dick Tucker and Norman Tasker, invigorated him with their bouts of communal singing and their healthy alliance with the players. It reminded Fingleton of happier, more innocent times.

He was also moved to offer some advice to Ian Chappell, now the Australian captain. He should have two men up close to the English batsmen when the new ball was taken, make Alan Knott take singles when he was batting, have John Inverarity and Keith Stackpole as his openers, and play Graeme Watson further down the order because 'I want you to win this one,' he wrote to Chappell.

The collection of his writings, *Fingleton on Cricket* was on sale and doing well.

On the previous England tour, in 1968, Fingleton had persuaded Belinda to travel with him again, help him file, and provide moral support. Belinda, who understood the enormous stress her father was under from endless newspaper deadlines, would drive him to the next match and, after getting permission to sit in the press box, phone both her father's and Ian Peeble's copy through at the end of the day's play.

One Saturday, when rain had washed out play at Lord's, Fingleton and Belinda returned to their London hotel. While Belinda was taking a bath, her father left the room for a few minutes. On returning, he found an intruder going through his overcoat pocket. Thinking he had mistaken the room number, he went outside to check, only to see the pickpocket flee down the hallway. Jack chased him and attempted a flying tackle, which just missed his target. The robber then avoided a Fingleton haymaker punch and fled down the staircase. Meanwhile, Belinda phoned the front desk and the hotel doorman trapped the offender. He was sentenced to three months' jail.

Complaining of a bung knee, Fingleton went back to his room and wrote a humorous account of the incident for the *Sunday Times*. Editor Harold Evans liked it so much that he ran it on the leader page under the headline: 'When rain stopped play'. A few days later came a congratulatory note from Evans, saying, 'This is the type of story we would like more often from you.'

Fingleton half-wondered if Evans was suggesting he should get robbed more often or saying this incidental piece was better than his usual cricket report.

Fingleton's involvement with the *Sunday Times* was flourishing, but not without friction. The newspaper's adventurous, analytical tone, its promotion of fine writing, high-level investigative reporting, and constant willingness to try something new appealed to him. It gave him a prominent run in its often congested sports pages, and encouraged him to write with flair.

For years, the relationship was blissful. Fingleton admitted that 'being with the *Sunday Times* has never seemed to me like work.'

Evans was a strong supporter, as was Denis Hamilton, the editor-in-chief and chairman of Times Newspapers. In 1971 Hamilton wrote to tell him he had dined with the young Rupert Murdoch, 'an extraordinary mixture of charm, energy, ruthlessness and lack of contemporary values'. Murdoch would buy *The Times* and *Sunday Times* in 1981.

However, as time went on, Fingleton became disillusioned with the newspaper's direction. During his final years with the *Sunday Times*, he complained constantly of editors who he believed did not understand cricket. He also thought the paper focused too much on stories from in-house journalists whose knowledge of the game was dubious. In his words, it had become 'erratic, aimed more at display and freak stories'. He told colleagues he thought the newspaper treated sport as a business. Its frivolous, fun side was being overlooked.

He even put out feelers to *The Guardian*, telling its editors he no longer wanted to work with the *Sunday Times*.

Sunday Times executives constantly tried to calm the wounded bear. Sports editor John Lovesey reminded him, 'You see we do all love you whatever you think.' He said it had taken him some time to 'cotton on to your style, having been brought up journalistically on a more straight-forward prose style. But having cottoned, I came to the conclusion that you are one of the most original and truly great sportswriters.'

Lovesey said one of his favourite sports articles was a Fingleton piece for the paper about Douglas Jardine and Bradman and how they never made up after Bodyline. 'I sat in front of the two in the Leeds Press Box in 1953 where some odd person had seated them together. "Good morning, Mr Bradman," would say Jardine, "Good morning, Mr Jardine," would say Bradman, and that was it for the day until the evening farewells came along.'

At first Fingleton was wary of Michael Parkinson, another *Sunday Times* writer, believing him to be overly provocative. But Jack warmed to him and they became the closest of friends. In a letter to Menzies, Fingleton described Parkinson as a 'bright boy'.

With the paper's main cricket writer, Robin Marlar, Fingleton had some disagreements. During the 1975 England tour Lovesey wrote to Fingleton to say, 'Robin will be writing to you apologising for his remark last Saturday. I sincerely hope that matter can rest there, and indeed, be forgotten.' They overcame their differences, but Fingleton never felt close to Marlar.

Fingleton's relationship with David Frith was also cool for a time. Frith, who spent some of his early years in Australia before returning to England and established himself as a leading cricket writer and editor, became friendly with Fingleton during the 1968 England tour. Frith thought that Fingleton regarded him 'as a bit of an innocent'. It was then that Fingleton passed on to Frith that Bradman was the Bodyline leak on condition that he not 'breathe a word of this while I'm alive'.

However, Frith fell foul of Fingleton in 1973, when he used the word 'mischievous' in an article explaining Fingleton's role in Harold Larwood's emigration to Australia. Fingleton argued that Frith had accused him of being unprofessional.

The freeze lasted four years, until spring returned during a cricket match between the Australian and England press at Harrogate. The players included Kerry Packer, at the time attempting to wrest control of cricket, and Ian Chappell. Fingleton was one of the umpires.

Fingleton teased Chappell when he was bowling, no-balling him on five different counts. 'It turned into a pantomime, and then Jack looked across at me,' Frith said. 'I was at mid on and he winked. I thought, "Blimey. The war is over." '

The next morning, in the Headingley press box, Fingleton came in, saw Frith, and drawled, 'Cover drive Frith.'

'I remember thinking "That's it. We're mates again." Later on, when I sat next to him, it was as if nothing had ever happened. Yes, it had been a big row, but in the end, thank God, we made up.'

Naturally abrupt, Fingleton was used to upsetting people. One of the *Sydney Morning Herald*'s most reputable and amiable sportswriters, Phil Derriman, phoned him at his Canberra house to get some facts for an article he was writing. Fingleton was less than welcoming, and the conversation was short. A few days later, Derriman received a letter from Fingleton apologising for his curt telephone manner, explaining that he had a medical check-up that day, which he'd been nervous about, and giving him in writing the information he required.

Fingleton did mellow. It just took some time. As British cricket writer Scyld Berry said, 'Jack went from being peppery to being salty.'

To overcome his loneliness at home, he would occasionally ask friends to accompany him to functions. Fingleton wrote to one woman, identified as Roslyn, explaining: 'I am in an odd situation in Canberra as I have lived on my own though married, since January 1967. I don't think much of it but have no choice. I tell you this because you should know my background.'

Fingleton's health was also growing shaky. He occasionally admitted to dizzy spells, but that did not curb his work output. Then, in late 1974, in the middle of the Australia–England series, he broke down. The long travel around Australia, stopovers, press gallery Christmas drinks, and cables from newspapers all looking for special pieces, took its toll. At home by himself one night, close to exhaustion as he worked on an article, he felt ill, dizzy and found himself constantly falling over. As the family were in Sydney, he struggled to the phone and rang his neighbours. They drove him to Woden Valley Hospital, where doctors told him he'd had a stroke.

He had no strength on his right side and found it difficult to speak. The doctors feared the worst, and explained that even if he fully recovered he would not be able to write again. Fingleton refused to believe that. As with so many other doubters and naysayers, he was determined to prove the medical profession wrong.

Within weeks, he was conducting interviews from his hospital bed, telling the *Canberra Times*, 'I want to go back to work as soon as I can. I've been here too long.'

And within months, he was back. He had several important assignments on the go, in particular researching a biography he had been wanting to write for years, on his cricketing hero Victor Trumper. He wasn't going to let a stroke interfere with that.

However, he did make some concessions to his illness. He had to rearrange his golf swing because too much of a backswing would make him fall over, and to play eighteen holes he now needed a buggy. His voice was also considerably weaker.

His colleagues in the press box found the summer pretty dull without him. Keith Miller called upon Jack to get well quick, because 'O'Reilly is walking around like a lost dog. He's even talking to himself.' Bradman hardly spoke to Miller any more, he reported, offering only a hasty 'G'Day, Nugget,' before moving on.

Calls and letters from friends helped Fingleton stay optimistic. So did his focus on Trumper. And then came news that at last official recognition was coming his way.

Fingleton was in line to be made a member of the Order of the British Empire for services to cricket and journalism. However, securing this honour was no simple process. In the end, it required four years of toing and froing between London and Canberra and the intervention of Sir Robert Menzies.

In August 1972, Fingleton told Menzies that he had learned that Times Newspapers editor-in-chief Denis Hamilton had put his name up for an imperial honour. According to Hamilton, British Prime Minister Edward Heath had approved it, 'but there is a hold-up in Canberra'. Fingleton asked Menzies if there was any way to discreetly find out whether Canberra had 'barred me', adding, 'It would be most embarrassing if they have.'

'Of course you shall have an HONOUR as a cricket writer,' Menzies assured him, 'and on an Australian list too.'

Menzies wrote to Cabinet secretary Sir John Bunting pointing out that since the honour involved an Australian, it 'would have been referred back to you'. He said that Fingleton should be recommended 'from this end and, if you need a nominator, I would be pleased to propose the recommendation. I regard him as our finest cricket writer and indeed, I will go further and say the best anywhere.'

Bunting said he would be glad to submit the recommendation. But nothing happened.

In May 1974, Fingleton wrote to Menzies again, wondering if perhaps he had been too pushy. 'I remember you once telling me here that you looked after your honours list yourself and if anyone recommended himself, he went to the bottom of the list or even off it,' Fingleton wrote. 'You also told me in a recent letter that you thought I deserved an honour and I am wondering whether you would see fit to ask for one for me in England.'

Fingleton cited several reasons, including the high regard in which Menzies was held in England, and that he wanted the honour for his family's sake. He also expressed mild annoyance that Alan McGilvray, whom he described as 'extremely garrulous and never wrong', had recently been on the honours list.

On Fingleton's behalf, Menzies wrote to the new British Prime Minister, Harold Wilson. As the present Australian Labor Government 'has decided not to propose people for any honour,' Menzies said, it would give him 'great pleasure if you were prepared to put Fingleton up for an appropriate honour in your own list'. Menzies said he thought Fingleton was one of the three best cricket writers of modern times, his only rivals being Neville Cardus and E.W. Swanton.

Wilson told Menzies he would give his suggestion careful consideration. But Wilson still had to consult the Australian Government, and 'at this point I might want to ask for your help in Canberra'.

In 1976, with a Liberal Government back in power, Fingleton received his OBE from Governor General Sir John Kerr, with Prime Minister Malcolm Fraser in attendance. Congratulatory letters came from everywhere. R.S. Whitington jokingly asked whether Bradman had proposed him. Ray Robinson wrote him a glowing tribute, listing as his career peaks: 'as a batsman going in ahead of Bradman, your courage when Voce was battering NSW, and your innings in Melbourne, when Australia were two down, in a great partnership that turned the tide in the series. And even if you quietened that typewriter after *Cricket Crisis* and *Quietly* [*sic*] *Fades the Don* they'd have amply assured your standing as an author.' His brother-in-law Justice Sir Laurence Street said he was sorry his parents were 'not alive to see this as I know that they would be very proud of your having earned this distinction, as indeed, are we all'.

In a letter of thanks to Menzies, Fingleton said the OBE had 'given me a warm glow, much like making 50 before lunch'. He said he was 'always bolstered by the thought that I tried to make [the] best of a tough job, and Neville Cardus once said to me, "Don't forget that you have it over all of the rest of us. You know what it is like to be out there in the middle of a Test taking first ball, a tremendous moment in anybody's life."'

23

The Obsession

Victor Trumper was the most graceful of cricketers. He was a team player, never selfish or greedy. Though adored, he did not seek adulation. He played cricket for all the right reasons.

Trumper was Fingleton's hero. From an early age, he had been indoctrinated in everything Trumper—not surprising, considering that he grew up in the suburb adjoining Paddington, which was Victor's domain. Fingleton recalled countless Saturday nights and Sunday mornings when discussions of the cricket at Waverley Park ended with someone reminiscing about Trumper. You were either old enough to have seen 'the greatest' play at the turn of the century, or you wished you were.

Fingleton, of course, was in the second category. He realised he didn't have the talent to match Trumper. He was far too protective of his wicket ever to be able to come close. But he always hoped that one day he could pay his respects in an area where he did have an echo of Trumper's flair and grace, the written word. The vague plan of writing a Trumper biography led him over the decades to compile any information he could on Trumper. Whenever he came across people who had known him, he would try to interview them.

In the mid 1970s, Fingleton turned the dream into a mission, and convinced his publishers Collins that a book on Trumper would sell.

It was no easy assignment. There were many gaps and obscurities in the picture of Trumper's life. One of them concerned his birth. Fingleton investigated and discovered that Trumper had been born almost five years before his parents had married. He was not sure if he should put this in the book. At the time, illegitimacy was regarded as a social embarrassment. He asked friends for advice, including Menzies. He personally wanted to mention it, he told Menzies, believing it was 'a wonderful plug against abortion' on demand. But would the Trumper family approve?

Menzies' reply was direct. 'I would not use the story you have told me. I think it would do more harm than good.' (This wasn't the first time Fingleton had asked Menzies for manuscript advice. In 1969, after looking at the draft of *Fingleton on Cricket*, Menzies urged him to cut one reference to Bradman and his wife because it 'might give unnecessary offence'.) Bill O'Reilly concurred with Menzies. The revelation stayed unrevealed.

Fingleton was determined not to write a straightforward, 'On the 12th of February, Trumper scored 163 at . . .' biography. Instead, he wanted it to flow unpredictably, like a good conversation. And instead of trying to efface himself and stay in the background, Fingleton inserted himself and his times into the book. He wanted to bring out the modern resonances in Trumper's career by comparing him with Bradman. While glorifying Trumper, he could give a fresh and not necessarily glorious perspective to Bradman's career.

The second paragraph of the book reads: 'For me, Trumper remains the greatest batsman who ever lived. Bradman could rightly be advanced against him, but whereas Bradman, in the early stages of his career, operated upon bowlers like a butcher at the abattoirs, wading deep in their agony and frustration, Trumper was like a surgeon, deftly and classically dissecting everything that was offered against him.'

Fingleton told several colleagues, including O'Reilly, that he planned to reveal the full Bodyline story in *The Immortal Victor Trumper*. O'Reilly said, 'Ignore it.' This time it was O'Reilly's advice that he ignored.

In the middle of a chapter on Trumper's technique, Fingleton not only presents a full account of the Bodyline leak but publicly names Bradman as the culprit for the first time, bitterly explaining, 'I have always held it against the Don that he did not own up and clear me.'

Later, he also reveals that after his book *Cricket Crisis* came out Bradman 'for years ignored me' because of what he had written about him.

> Then one night we were both with the English team at dinner at Government House, Perth, and throughout the evening we studiously ignored each other. I thought it all too silly and wrote the Don accordingly, and we agreed to bury the hatchet. No doubt this explanation will unearth the old feud again, but I think I owe it to myself to tell the story as [journalist] Claude Corbett told me. At least Don Bradman was a very good and observant reporter. He had every detail correct.

Fingleton reminded his readers that Bradman had cast a critical eye on Trumper in his book *Farewell to Cricket*, including the number of hundreds either of them had made in England, and explaining that 'on a percentage basis, Trumper got one century for every 9.8 innings, where I obtained one century every 3.4.'

Fingleton admitted that statistics worked in Bradman's favour. But in his view Trumper was an artist. Bradman was a machine. And unlike Bradman, Trumper was never 'runs-greedy'.

Bradman's long shadow also falls on the end of the book, where Fingleton compares the Don's scores with Trumper's. The introduction to this section reads, 'Don Bradman once asked one of Trumper's supporters: "If he was everything you claim for him, why did he not score more runs for Australia?" That question was typical of Bradman, ever figure-conscious, but he was entitled to ask it.'

Fingleton said the figures 'prove conclusively that there was no comparison between the two Australian champions. Bradman wins by the length of the straight. Bradman rightly contends that runs are the name of the game; in judging batsmanship, however, equally important is how they are made.'

The Immortal Victor Trumper is a sound and readable biography, but it is far from Fingleton's best.

He complained loudly and often about the editing of the book, in which 'years of research' had been 'just idly tossed aside'. For months, angry letters flew to and fro between Fingleton's Canberra home and his publisher's London offices. Fingleton believed his manuscript had been 'butchered'. This book, he said, had given him 'more problems and headaches' than all his others.

Lukewarm reviews did nothing to appease him.

Fingleton's close mate Keith Butler, of the *Adelaide Advertiser*, wrote to say that he had seen 'The Knight' and had 'brought up the Trumper book' shortly after it had been released. He went on: 'I sold him [Bradman] the dummy, saying it was hard to compare he and Trumper, he won by a mile on the centuries scored per appearances. Replied: "You'd better point that out to Jack." But didn't say any more.'

A rare source of pleasure during this period was convincing Harold Larwood that he should attend the 1977 Centenary Test in Melbourne. Larwood was highly reluctant, convinced that because of Bodyline he would get a poor reception from an Australian audience. 'As you know my interest in cricket these days is very low, and I have no wish to be embarrassed in front of the huge crowds which will be there,' he wrote to Fingleton. Besides, he said, 'How people can sit on hard seats, in the hot sun, day after day, is beyond me.'

Fingleton kept working away at him, thinking it would be wonderful to have one of England's most important bowlers at the historic gathering. Larwood would not budge.

Then, just before the match, he relented. And, as Fingleton delighted in explaining later, he enjoyed the Centenary Test enormously, meeting up with players he hadn't seen for decades during what was his first visit to the MCG since the Bodyline series. Fingleton was also pleased that Larwood was among those who chose not to give Bradman a standing ovation at the end of his official dinner speech. Fingleton could understand why. Bradman, he thought, had spoken for far too long.

Larwood thanked Fingleton for persuading him to go. He was 'astounded by the reception that I received and the friendliness from my old enemies', he said, adding, 'How sorry I am that I gave you so much inconvenience from the outset.' The Test 'ranks in my memory as one of the best events in my life.'

Much as Fingleton pursued Larwood, Michael Parkinson continued to pursue Fingleton to make an appearance on his popular television show. Since they'd become friends through their work at the *Sunday Times*, Fingleton had often stayed at Parkinson's home during England tours. Parkinson later wrote, 'I had admired him long before I met him. His television commentaries displayed the witty irreverence that characterised his writing. He seemed like the man you would always want to be sitting next to on a long journey; a person of opinion, wisdom and humour. And the moment I met him I knew I had been right.' They became even closer after Fingleton retired from the daily grind of journalism in 1978, shortly after turning seventy. (His retirement prompted a tribute in Parliament: Speaker Sir Billy Snedden told the House that Fingleton had been one of the most respected members of the press gallery for more than twenty-five years.)

The following year, when Parkinson visited Australia for the first time to do a series of TV interviews, Fingleton was keen to make him welcome. But he did so in typically cheeky style.

After addressing a National Press Club luncheon in Canberra, Parkinson called for questions. 'Pretending he didn't know me, Jack stood up and reduced the formality of the proceedings to a rabble,' Parkinson said.

Fingleton's question, which lasted five minutes, ribbed Parkinson for being a Yorkshire Pom, for coming from Barnsley, 'which, as everyone knew, had the highest illegitimacy rate on the planet' and also happened to be the birthplace of a grounds-man at Headingley who had robbed the Australians on one Ashes tour—on and on and on. Finally Parkinson was allowed to answer.

Fingleton wrote in this diary that night, 'Michael Parkinson— lunch. Great to see him. Gives great talk. I am in good form (!) kicking questions off by pulling his leg about Barnsley, Boycott and Yorkshire. He and his promoter want me to do TV show with Parkie. And why not? I go to airport and have beers with them. He gets terrible ear-bash, but is magnificent about it. Gives me great wrap-up as writer which is nice in front of packed audience.'

Not everyone was excited, though. At the lunch Fingleton had bumped into several of his golf colleagues, including a woman whom he had once called a hag.

'She says to me passing by—"Do I know you?"' he wrote in his diary. 'She won't in future.'

To make Parkinson feel at home, Fingleton and Keith Miller organised a lunch in Sydney so he could meet 'one or two' of their friends. When Parkinson, delighted enough to be in their company, also met Ray Lindwall, Bill O'Reilly, Alan Davidson, Larwood, Arthur Morris and Neil Harvey, he thought he 'had died and gone to heaven', he recalled.

Finally Fingleton agreed to go on Parkinson's program. Even though the other guests were high-profile actor Kate Fitzpatrick and then Australian Council of Trade Unions head Bob Hawke, Fingleton stole the show. It was a brilliant performance. He won over guests and audience alike with first-rate sporting and political anecdotes and sparkling humour. He ridiculed Parkinson whenever possible—even putting Hawke on the spot by betting him he would be an MP after the next elections. He talked only momentarily about Bradman.

Even behind the scenes there was humour. Fingleton was concerned that his stroke had left him with an intermittent and sometimes uncontrollable drawl. When he arrived at the ABC studios, Parkinson noticed that Fingleton was speaking in an unusual tone and that his top lip wasn't moving.

Fingleton, worried that his false teeth might 'chatter', had tried to prevent the problem by using a fixative. He had applied so much that he'd glued his top set to his top lip. Just before the show, assistants managed to get his teeth unstuck, so he could at least talk properly.

Fingleton was such a standout he was invited back for several more shows. Each time, according to Parkinson, Fingleton 'wound himself up into a terrible state of nerves'. Just before his second appearance, he telephoned Parkinson to explain that as the first interview had been such a success, he feared this one might be a let-down.

'I've been thinking about what I might do,' Fingleton said.

'Come up with any ideas?' Parkinson asked.

'Think so. Tell me, have you ever had anyone croak on your show?'

When he appeared on one of Parkinson's London-based programs he worried that he might have a heart attack induced by a treacherous piece of BBC fruitcake.

Suddenly Fingleton was back in demand. His telephone rang almost continuously, with long lost friends wanting to congratulate him on his appearances. He was even stopped at Sunday Mass by young women asking, 'Are you Jack Fingleton?' People asked him for autographs. He lapped it up.

There was the occasional stinging comment though: one female viewer complained that his Ocker accent was 'very hard on the ears'.

Through Parkinson, Australia rediscovered the wit and wisdom of this one-off character. The TV host wrote that he was 'saddened how little [Fingleton's] reputation mattered in his own country . . . Therefore it delighted me beyond measure when he came on my show and, simply by being himself, reminded his countrymen that he was a very remarkable and singular man. His television style, like his writing, is unique.'

Ian Chappell could not resist the opportunity to rib Fingleton, especially after he swore when describing Billy Hughes on *Parkinson*. Under a pseudonym, Chappell sent off a letter saying he now understood why modern cricketers swore so often: they were just following the example of past players.

Some time later, Chappell's curiosity got the better of him, and he asked Fingleton if he had ever received the letter. Fingleton feigned ignorance. But he said he wasn't surprised modern players used profanities so often when they couldn't tell the difference between swearing and using a word for emphasis in the context of a story.

O'Reilly expressed his 'spontaneous and wholly unrehearsed admiration for the magnificent job you did for Parkinson the other night'. He added:

> I had a sinking feeling early on that you were going to allow your highly publicised 'love' for Bradman take charge of the show. As soon as you forgot him and started to swing the cat around by the tail you went from strength to strength. I can guarantee that I was only one of thousands who were disappointed when the show came to an end.
>
> I fear not the charge of 'bullsh—' when I tell you that I am certain you proved to be the best subject by far that I have seen under Parkinson's hammer.

O'Reilly said even his 'garage man wanted a lowdown yesterday on where the hell you have been all this time'.

Fingleton sometimes wondered the same—and decided he'd better not waste his rebirth. He had so many projects he wanted to do. Not even a heart attack, during a golf game shortly after his first *Parkinson* appearance, could slow him down. After a few weeks recuperating in Sydney, he was back in Canberra, preparing for what would be his last big assignment.

24

Am I Going to Cark It?

In his final years, Fingleton would growl that cricket had 'gone to the dogs' because of media tycoon Kerry Packer and his one-day games. Packer had taken on cricket's administrators and brought showbiz to a cobwebbed game with what he called World Series Cricket. Fingleton declared war on it, lobbing one typewritten bomb after another at the abomination.

To his last hours, Fingleton was punching away, taking body hits when he had to, hitting back when he thought he was being maligned, standing his ground and making his views heard.

T.P. McLean, hailed as New Zealand's greatest sportswriter, was one of many fans who encouraged him to keep prodding away: 'You are the only real pro writing cricket. Detachment's the key. The others are either up their own or other people's fundamental orifices.'

There was so much to keep him alive and interested, and he was determined not to miss a moment of it. He finally and reluctantly stopped touring overseas or interstate, and was immediately missed. Frank Tyson, the former England pace bowler who became a respected cricketing commentator, expressed the view that the 'Australian Test match press box without the presence of Fingleton, O'Reilly and Hassett would be like *A Night at the Opera* without the Marx Brothers; form without substance, criticism without wit, irony or perspicacity.'

There was still an abundance of subjects he could attack from his Canberra desk. The Packer takeover, and the endless 'slather and whack' of one-day cricket, were big targets. He was and remained a vehement opponent of anything Packer did. But he made sure he saw the enemy up close. He attended World Series Cup matches, and bumped into Packer at the Sydney Showground. Packer could be cantankerous, and knew Fingleton was one of his most trenchant opponents, but he said, 'Hello, you are looking much better than you are writing. Come in and have a drink with us.'

The pair spent an hour together and had a predictably vigorous discussion about the rights and wrongs of what Packer had done to Fingleton's game. Fingleton was a receptive listener, but the talk didn't change his viewpoint. He didn't like the businessman's motives and kept prodding away at him. He later wrote that Packer had 'done cricket more harm than he knows', and that the game had been 'revolutionized for money and the television screen', with sad results.

But Fingleton's main goal now was getting his memoirs into some sort of shape. He had been asked to write his autobiography, and decided it should cover every part of his big and busy life, but putting the book together proved onerous. He did not want it to be only a cricketing book. It also had to include his journalistic career, his years in Canberra tussling with Billy Hughes and Sir Robert Menzies, his long friendship with Neville Cardus, and even his admiration for *Sunday Times* editor Harold Evans.

The Bradman phenomenon also required another look—in fact it consumed three of the book's nineteen chapters: 'Memories of Bradman', 'Don Bradman as I Knew Him' and

'More Memories of Bradman'. It was clear the Don carried huge weight in Fingleton's life. But Fingleton knew that if he did not provide a full analysis of Australian sport's most famous figure, he would be accused of avoiding the issue people wanted to know about.

How to handle Bradman preoccupied Fingleton. When that part of the book was finished, he asked renowned British sports writer Ian Wooldridge for his thoughts 'on the Bradman chapters'. He wrote that they had 'cost me a deal of time and worry. He is still a great hero but in many ways he was a little, churlish man and I think this comes through.'

When *The Times* decided to run excerpts from the book, he wrote to editor Harold Evans:

> It won't appeal to many traditional readers of *The Times* who idolised Bradman and resent the slightest criticism of him, but if you are deluged by letters taking his side and weighing into me, perhaps I might be sent them and given the right of reply.
>
> O'Reilly's opinions of DGB [Bradman] correspond with me. No one doubted his ability but playing under him was different to chaps like Woodfull and Richardson. One sensed [they were] playing for Australia, with Bradman it seemed like for his own personal glory. This, perhaps, was not altogether his fault but that is how players felt . . . and I did play a lot under him.

As with the Trumper biography, the editing of *Batting from Memory* was a constant battle. He was furious when he discovered that numerous stories and observations were to be omitted. 'I don't mind polishing, but I do object to decimation,' Fingleton complained to the publishers. They even bickered over the title. The editors questioned whether anyone actually batted from memory. Instead, they suggested 'Drawing Stumps' or 'Last Overs'.

Fingleton stood firm, and the publishers relented. *Batting from Memory* it would be.

As Fingleton worked the memoir, his tenth book, his correspondence with O'Reilly continued unabated, and often gave him the fire to keep pushing on.

O'Reilly wrote in 1978 that he was growing disillusioned with the Sydney Cricket Ground. 'Apart from the construction of a shit-house or two, and that monstrosity, which rejoices in the name of the Bradman Stand, they haven't done a thing to justify the existence of a Trust,' he wrote.

When Fingleton asked if he would be guest speaker at the book launch, O'Reilly readily agreed.

If he had one misgiving about the autobiography, Fingleton said, it was that he 'should have written more about my English tour of 1938 . . . I had made my point with the selectors with the South African tour and regarded 1938 in England as something owing to me and didn't make cricket my No. 1 priority. England was too much of an Aladdin's lamp for me to give all my attention to the cricket field.'

O'Reilly replied with gusto:

Your misgivings probably surrounded the fear that I might duck out of any likelihood of offending the little boy about an association with a book that will most probably give him a good kick in the guts. If that be the case then you can rest at ease. For years now I have striven to forget DGB so far as my own private life is concerned . . . To me now he is so comprehensively unimportant that I have no time to spare for him in general conversation.

In your case the matter has to come to close examination in the manner in which he had malevolent influence on your own career described in your autobiography—your missing out on the 1934 tour which surely has gone down as one of the prime selection injustices of our time. The fact that he was not a selector then cannot be used so far as I am concerned as a telling argument in his favour. Even since 1930 when he struck the jackpot, his mounting fortune was matched only by extraordinary influence and ambition. You will remember the ingenuity he used to put the Board on the spot—with writing contracts, offers from Ramsbottom—as soon as he heard the composition of the team the Poms had chosen to come here in 1932. It was apparent to anyone with half an eye that he already had a presentiment about the reason for them including four fast bowlers. Anyway to hell with all that. You are welcome to any help I may be able to give you.

Fingleton was delighted by O'Reilly's response. He replied that he was hesitant 'to ask you as I didn't want to put you on the sacrificial altar as a sacrifice to the great DGB and I am more than pleased that your summation of him corresponds with me.' Fingleton continued:

As I wrote somewhere, he was eminently fitted to be a politician, so devious and far-seeing was he.

What gave me an infinite joy was your reference to me not being chosen in 1934. That, as you know, was a good kick in the slats to me, particularly my Mother and family.

At least I have the knowledge of knowing I never ran away from my job as I saw it. And on the eve of selection his Majesty ran a story in my own paper, *The Sun*, giving me powerful 'stick' for my running between wickets. He knew then I would not be chosen but who cares? That kick in the slats was good for me in life.

I gave them my answers in South Africa. I could have done better than I did in England in 1938 but I looked on that tour as compensation and was determined not to spend it inside a cricket field. No one could have seen more theatres, ballets, operas and the insides of the House of Commons than I did and, also, I sensed anything that team was the personal glory of DGB. I remember Napper [Stan McCabe] telling me that Braddles never came near him after the Oval when we were a wandering band of cripples.

But my attitude towards him is like yours. B . . . him. I have a quiver of stories if he comes back at me.

His life wasn't all gloomy memories. Fingleton continued to encourage young players he enjoyed watching. He wrote to the Western Australian batsman Kim Hughes offering constructive advice. Fingleton was impressed by Hughes's high level of concentration and will to succeed, but believed he too often played forward. 'You just can't play swing or swerve forward,' Fingleton wrote to him. 'You must go back, using the extra yard of the crease to expend all the swing of the ball and you then know whether to play it or leave it alone.'

Hughes took it in the right vein, replying, 'It's nice to know that one of Australia's greats is taking an active interest in the development of a young Australian cricketer.'

And even though Fingleton was no longer hovering around cricket press boxes, he was still provided with all the scuttlebutt by various high-ranking spies. One passed on the juicy morsel that after the Greg Chappell underarm bowling debacle in 1981, the Emergency Committee of the Australian Cricket Board wanted to sack him as captain. However, official Ray Steele had said that Chappell was within the laws of the game to instruct his brother Trevor to bowl the last ball against New Zealand underarm, so the Board would be in trouble if they fired him. Fingleton was also told that a high-ranking state official had abruptly taken early retirement because he 'was shagging a member of staff'. Fingleton was discreet with such personal information, but he believed the underarm incident was indicative of a game which had gone to pot.

'I really loved the "mully-grubber" in Melbourne, which will shock you, but I thought it beautifully portrayed what cricket has come to—and that is cash. And all done at the altar of television,' Fingleton wrote to his Trumper confidant Eric McElhone.

In a letter to former England batsman, Reverend David Sheppard, Fingleton said the underarm debacle 'depicts the level to which a noble game has fallen'. He was equally saddened by the posturing of the all-conquering West Indians, describing some of them as being 'more racist than the Afrikaner from Bloemfontein'. He described their team as 'domineering, dominating, full of bouncers and ill feeling'.

By March 1981, the Packer circus, as many called it, had drained all the interest from cricket. In March 1981, he wrote to BBC commentator Peter West that it was 'high time I called it a day, and I really have no appetite to see a game of cricket again. Terrible thing to say but I have had such a gutful this summer of what passes for cricket and the blab of a Packer commentator that I wouldn't walk across St John's Wood to a game unless it was a chat with you on the box.'

He suddenly decided to do something about his increasingly frustrating relationship with the *Sunday Times*. He was moved to action by some puzzling sentences in the foreword Michael Parkinson had written for *Batting from Memory*.

Parkinson recounted how, when *Sunday Times* sporting editor John Lovesey first looked at a Fingleton article, he 'wondered how he might edit it'. 'To his trained eye the writing lacked form and structure, it did not conform to accepted patterns of journalism,' Parkinson wrote. 'He brooded a long time about the problem and then made a startling discovery; namely, the secret of editing an article by Jack Fingleton is to leave it alone.'

The ever-sensitive Fingleton took offence, not at Parkinson, but at the sports editor.

Fingleton wrote to Ian Wooldridge to say he was irked to learn that Lovesey had been confused by his prose style, and also wrote to Lovesey to find out what he meant. Lovesey replied that he had originally found Fingleton's 'arrangement of paragraphs rather strange', but soon realised that his writing was like the speech 'of a master conversationalist' and that it was best not to change it.

Peace was restored. Then the *Sunday Times* did not use Fingleton's article about 'mullygrubbers', and another spate of nasty letters with a Canberra postmark erupted.

In April 1981, a Fingleton article appeared in the other British quality Sunday newspaper, *The Observer*, for the first time since he had covered the 1946–47 tour for them. The article had arrived with the mail addressed to the sports desk. Sports editor Peter Corrigan thought it was a mistake and needed to be read-dressed to the *Sunday Times*. However, the covering letter told a different story.

Fingleton wrote that he wanted to work for *The Observer* because he greatly admired the 'guts' of its sports section and thought it was 'sound and sensible, not seeking stunts or display'. For the rest of that summer, Fingleton continued to write for *The Observer*. The articles served as light relief from the chore of finishing *Batting from Memory*, which he told Corrigan was driving him 'up the wall'.

But Fingleton had no notion that *Batting from Memory* would be his last book. He had also begun working on a collection of essays for Pavilion Books, a company involving Parkinson and composer Tim Rice. Harold Larwood had contributed a foreword, ghost-written by Tom Goodman, and Fingleton had also completed an essay on Larwood.

In November 1981, just before the launch of *Batting from Memory* at the Cricketers' Club in Sydney, Fingleton travelled from Canberra to stay with his daughter Belinda and son-in-law Mal Gemmell, on the city's North Shore. Although he boasted that he was in good shape, Fingleton was clearly stressed by all the effort involved in the book launch, including making certain the right people were invited, there were enough copies of the book on hand, and that he was primed for several promotional appearances, including a live morning interview on ABC Radio.

Around 3 a.m. on 20 November, Fingleton complained of serious chest pains. He was rushed to Royal North Shore Hospital, where doctors found he had had another heart attack. In the ambulance, Jack, who never lost his wry sense of humour, was his usual impish self, asking the driver, 'Am I going to cark it?'

Two days later he died, aged 73. In his hospital bed, he had at least been able to say his goodbyes. To his brother Wal, he said, 'I had a good innings.'

His book launch became a wake.

25

The Irony of It All

Some time later, a group of luminaries assembled at Manuka Oval for a celebration of the life and times of Jack Henry Webb Fingleton.

He was now in the public domain. Michael Parkinson and his colleagues had republished *Cricket Crisis*. New editions of *Brightly Fades the Don* and *Masters of Cricket* were in book stores.

Parkinson had bought in an auction Fingleton's 1935–36 Test cap—the one in which he scored his record run of centuries—as a mark of affection for his Australian mate.

He had been eulogised by many. His funeral, at St Mary's Cathedral in Sydney, drew a huge crowd of cricketers, journalists, politicians, family and friends. With Cardinal Sir James Freeman in attendance, Jack's brother Wally conducted the Requiem Mass, before the funeral procession made its way to Waverley Cemetery.

Jack had wanted to be buried in Canberra, but instead he was interred in the family plot, with his mother, father and brother Les. The procession passed close to his original family home in Bondi Junction, to Waverley College, which mounted an honour guard of students, and on to the cemetery, where it passed the gravesites of Henry Lawson, Victor Trumper and J.C. Archibald.

All over the world, newspapers published glowing obituaries. The common refrain was that cricket would never be the same again.

Bill O'Reilly, in the *Sydney Morning Herald*, grieved for the man who since 1931 had been a 'firm friend'. Noted cricket writer Henry Blofeld, in the *Australian*, said that as Fingleton had been such an integral part of Fleet Street, his death 'will be felt with as much sorrow in England as it will be in Australia'.

'His sardonic humour, his slow drawl, that infectious smile as he made or enjoyed a press-box joke will be all much missed. And he loved nothing better than a good leg-pull, too,' Blofeld wrote. Tributes in the Sydney tabloids the *Daily Mirror* and *The Sun* came from two Australian captains Fingleton knew well and who had also pursued a writing career—Richie Benaud and Ian Chappell.

From overseas, the salutes were as touching. E.W. Swanton described him 'as a cricket writer and broadcaster, the best his country has produced'.

'If he was not exactly an easy professional companion, he was certainly a stimulating one,' Swanton wrote. 'Some of those who, unwittingly perhaps, stepped on his corns, remained wary of him ever after. But if he was a bad enemy he was a devoted friend to a wide and diverse circle.'

And now a scoreboard was to be named after him.

The old MCG scoreboard, built in 1901, had been donated by the Melbourne Cricket Club, transported to Canberra, and transplanted on the Manuka hill. Fingleton would have relished the fact that transporting the stand caused enormous headaches for local officials and that getting it to the national capital was horribly expensive. Building a new scoreboard would have been considerably cheaper.

There was a speech from Governor General Sir Ninian Stephen, who explained that in Canberra Fingleton was much more than a Test cricketer and journalist: 'He was an institution.'

Then the Jack Fingleton Scoreboard was unveiled—the same one on which he'd seen his own Sheffield Shield and Test scores tallied and then for years checked from the press box.

When O'Reilly was told about all this hooha by Lindsay Hassett, who attended the function, Tiger gulped, then let out a guttural chortle. 'I can see Fingo right now doubling over with laughter. He would have loved it. As Lindsay said, fancy being named after a bit of secondhand Victorian furniture.'

Bibliography

Books

Allen, David Rayvern, *Arlott: The authorised biography*, Aurum, London 2004

Barnes, Sid, *Eyes on the Ashes*, William Kimber, London 1953

—— *It Isn't Cricket*, Collins, Sydney 1953

Baume, Eric, *I Lived These Years*, George G. Harrap, London 1941

Blaikie, George, *Remember Smith's Weekly*, Rigby, Adelaide 1967

Bradman, Don, *Farewell to Cricket*, Hodder & Stoughton, London 1950

The Bradman Albums, Weldon Publishing, Sydney 1987

Brodsky, Isadore, *The Sydney Press Gang*, Old Sydney Free Press, Sydney 1974

Brookes, Christopher, *His Own Man: The life of Neville Cardus*, Unwin Paperbacks, London 1986

Butler, Keith, *Howzat!*, Collins, Sydney 1979

Cardus, Neville, *Australian Summer*, Souvenir Press, London 1987

Clowes, Colin, *150 Years of NSW First-Class Cricket*, Allen & Unwin, Sydney 2007

Colman, Mike and Ken Edwards, *Eddie Gilbert*, ABC Books, Sydney 2002

Coltheart, Lenore (ed.), *Jessie Street: A revised autobiography*, Federation Press, Sydney 2004

Derriman, Philip, *True to the Blue: A History of the New South Wales Cricket Association*, Richard Smart, Sydney 1985

Docker, E.W., *Bradman and the Bodyline*, Angus & Robertson, Sydney 1978

Douglas, Christopher, *Douglas Jardine: Spartan cricketer*, Methuen, London 2002

Eason, Alan, *The A–Z of Bradman*, ABC Books, Sydney 2004

Fingleton, Jack, *Batting from Memory*, Collins, London 1981

—— *Brightly Fades the Don*, Collins, London 1949

—— *Brown and Company*, Collins, London 1951

—— *Cricket Crisis*, Cassell, Melbourne 1946

—— *Fingleton on Cricket*, Collins, London 1972

—— *Four Chukkas to Australia,* William Heinemann, London 1960

—— *The Ashes Crown the Year*, Collins, Sydney 1954

—— *The Greatest Test of All*, Collins, London 1961

—— *The Immortal Victor Trumper*, Collins, London 1978

—— *Masters of Cricket*, Pavilion Books, London 1990

Foot, David, *Beyond Bat and Ball*, Aurum, London 1993

Frindall, Bill, *England Test Cricketers*, Collins Willow, London 1989

Frith, David, *Archie Jackson: The Keats of cricket*, Pavilion, London 1987

—— *Bodyline Autopsy*, ABC Books, Sydney 2002

—— *Caught England Bowled Australia*, Eva Press, London 1997

Geddes, Margaret, *Remembering Bradman*, Viking, Melbourne 2003

Griffen-Foley, Bridget, *The House of Packer*, Allen & Unwin, Sydney, 1999

Growden, Greg, *A Wayward Genius: The Fleetwood-Smith story*, ABC Books, Sydney 1991

Haigh, Gideon, *The Summer Game: Cricket and Australia in the 1950s and 1960s*, ABC Books, Sydney 2006

Haigh, Gideon and David Frith, *Inside Story: Unlocking Australian cricket's archives*, News Custom Publishing, Melbourne 2007

Hutchins, Brett, *Don Bradman: Challenging the myth*, Cambridge University Press, Cambridge 2002

Jardine, D.R., *In Quest of the Ashes*, Methuen, London 2005

Larwood, Harold with Kevin Perkins, *The Larwood Story*, Bonpara, Sydney 1982

Leckey, John Alexander, *Records are Made to be Broken: The real story of Bill Ponsford*, Arcadia, Melbourne 2006

McHarg, Jack, *Stan McCabe*, Collins, Sydney 1987

—— *Bill O'Reilly: A cricketing life*, Millennium, Sydney 1990

McKay, Claude, *This is the Life*, Angus & Robertson, Sydney 1961

Mallett, Ashley, *Bradman's Band*, University of Queensland Press, Brisbane 2000

Mallett, Ashley with Ian Chappell, *Chappelli Speaks Out*, Allen & Unwin, Sydney, 2005

Mant, Gilbert, *A Cuckoo in the Bodyline Nest*, Kangaroo Press, NSW 1992

Miller, Keith and R.S. Whitington, *Bumper*, Latimer House, London 1954

—— *Catch*, Latimer House, London 1951

—— *Cricket Caravan*, Latimer House, London 1950

—— *Straight Hit*, Latimer House, London 1952

Morris, Barry, *Bradman: What they said about him*, ABC Books, Sydney 1994

The Observer on Cricket, Unwin Hyman, London 1987

O'Reilly, Bill, *Tiger*, Collins, Sydney 1985

The Oxford Companion to Australian Cricket, Oxford University Press, Melbourne 1996

Page, Michael, *Bradman: The illustrated biography*, Macmillan, Melbourne 1983

Parkinson, Michael, *The Best of Parkinson*, Thomas Nelson, Melbourne 1983

Perry, Roland, *Miller's Luck*, Random House, Sydney 2005

—— *The Don*, Pan Macmillan, Sydney 1995

Pollard, Jack, *Australian Cricket: The game and the players*, Angus & Robertson, Sydney 1988

Richardson, V.Y., *The Vic Richardson Story*, Rigby, Adelaide 1967

Robinson, Ray, *Between Wickets*, Collins, London 1948

—— *From the Boundary*, Collins, London 1951

—— *On Top Down Under*, Collins, Sydney 1975

Rosenwater, Irving, *Sir Donald Bradman*, Batsford, London 1978

Sekuless, Peter, *Jessie Street*, University of Queensland Press, Brisbane 1980

Smith, Sir Joynton, *My Life Story*, Cornstalk, Sydney 1927

Smith, Rick, *Cricket's Enigma: The Sid Barnes story*, ABC Books, Sydney 1999

Walker, R.B., *Yesterday's News*, Sydney University Press, Sydney 1980

Wallace, Christine, *The Private Don*, Allen & Unwin, Sydney, 2004

Warner, Sir Pelham, *Cricket between Two Wars*, Sporting Handbooks, London 1942

Webster, Ray and Allan Miller, *First Class Cricket in Australia*, Vol. 1: 1850–51 to 1941–42, Ray Webster, Victoria 1991

Whitington, R.S., *Australians Abroad*, Five Mile Press, Melbourne 1983

—— *The Datsun Book of Australian Test Cricket 1877–1981*, Five Mile Press, Melbourne 1981

Williams, Charles, *Bradman*, Little Brown & Company, London 1996

Wilmot, R.W.E., *Defending the Ashes 1932–33*, Robertson & Mullens, Melbourne 1933

Interviews
Bill Brown
Rob Chalmers
Ian Chappell
Mike Coward
Philip Derriman
Grey Fingleton
Jacqui Fingleton
Jim Fingleton
Larry Fingleton
Wally Fingleton
David Frith
Belinda Gemmell
Mal Gemmell
Neil Marks
Keith Miller
Leo O'Brien
Bill O'Reilly
Alan Ramsey
Ian Wooldridge

Newspapers and periodicals
The Age (Melbourne)
Australian Cricketer
The Courier Mail (Brisbane)
The Daily Telegraph (Sydney)
The News (Adelaide)
The Observer (UK)
The Referee
Smith's Weekly
The Sun (Sydney)

The Sunday Times (UK)
The Sydney Mail
The Sydney Morning Herald
The Times (UK)

References
The prime reference was the Jack Fingleton Collection, housed in the Mitchell Library in Sydney. This vast collection includes correspondence with a variety of identities, including John Arlott, Keith Miller, Sir Donald Bradman, Alec Bedser, Neville Cardus, Richie Benaud, Bill Brown, George Duckworth, R.C. Robertson-Glasgow, Bill O'Reilly, Michael Parkinson, Pelham Warner, Ian Wooldridge, Learie Constantine, Clarrie Grimmett, Tom Goodman, Les Haylen, Sir Robert Menzies, Lindsay Hassett, Brian Johnston, Bill Jeanes, Harold Larwood, Ian Peebles, Graham Perkin, Rohan Rivett, Ray Robinson, E.W. Swanton, John Woodcock and Bill Woodfull. The collection also includes Fingleton's scrapbooks, note-books, contact books, photographs, and diaries.

Sir Robert Menzies Collection in the National Library, Canberra.
The Chappie Dwyer–Don Bradman letters in the State Library of NSW.

Index